Terror by the Oppressors:

"PHILIPPINES' TORTURE–A political prisoner subjected to the "San Juanico bridge" is forced to lie with his naked body suspended between two beds and is beaten and kicked in the stomach and thighs whenever he sags or falls. . . . Stripping, sexual abuse, electric shock, and the use of "truth-serum" drugs are other standard procedures. . . . The extent and severity of torture in the Philippine detention centers came as a shock to Amnesty International investigating team that visited Luzon at the end of 1975."

Jeri Laber, Amnesty International
The New York Times, Oct. 30, 1976

Terror by the Oppressed:

"TERROR IN THE PHILIPPINES–. . . later, a bomb blast roared through the glittering conference hall on the edge of Manila Bay. Just twenty rows from where [Philippine President Ferdinand] Marcos sat, eighteen people lay bloodied in the wreckage, eleven of them foreigners. . . . That was a triumph for the country's shadowy urban guerrillas–and a deep embarrassment to the Marcos martial law regime."

Newsweek, November 3, 1980

"S.F. MAN ACCUSED AFTER MANILA TERROR BOMBING. Manila–President Ferdinand Marcos ordered the arrests of nine opposition members, a U.S. businessman and 20 other people today in the wake of a flood of terrorist bombings . . . . Listed in the arrest order were American businessman Steve Psinakis of San Francisco."

Associated Press, Oct. 20, 1980

"The biggest terrorist is Mr. Marcos. For eight years he terrorized the people –and now they are reacting. The more oppression, the bigger the explosives. And then the blood will really flow."

Senator Benigno S. Aquino, Jr., Nov. 3, 1980

"LIKE THE SHAH, PRESIDENT MARCOS . . . Like the Shah, Marcos and his consort pursue an ostentatiously luxurious style of life, as do their families and friends–while an estimated 40 percent of their people live in extreme poverty, some approaching the starvation level . . . . Like the Shah, Marcos must take responsibility for gross violations of human rights, subversion of the electoral process, and the spectacular enrichment through favoritism, graft and corruption of his and his wife's coterie of family and friends . . . ."

Like the Shah, Marcos has to contend with rising opposition among middle-class intellectuals, business and professional men and women, plus a number of Catholic priests and, at the very least, a dozen bishops . . . . Like the Shah, Marcos relies on American-supplied arms to maintain himself in power . . . . "

John B. Oakes
The New York Times, July 6, 1980

"A STATISTIC OF HUNGER. Official malnutrition figures show that slow starvation is more prevalent in the Philippines than in Bangladesh, India, or Pakistan."

United Press International, October 7, 1976

"Since President Marcos imposed martial law in 1972, his relatives and cronies, as well as those of his glamorous wife Imelda, have been amassing huge fortunes. Their blatant influence peddling has prompted one amazed diplomat in Manila to observe: 'It's incredible what they've taken over.'

Time, January 23, 1978

"Injustice reigns when within the same society some groups hold most of the wealth and power while large strata of the population cannot decently provide for the livelihoods of their families even through long hours of back-breaking labor in factories or in the fields."

Pope John Paul II in the Philippines
February 20, 1981

"WHO ARE THE BOMBERS? They are unlikely terrorists. For the most part, they are well-educated members of the middle class. . . . They are becoming effective bomb-makers who have resorted to violence out of frustration and a determination to change the Manila government."

Newsweek, November 3, 1980

Two "Terrorists" Meet

Steve Psinakis

Alchemy Books
San Francisco, California

Published by Alchemy Books, 681 Market Street, San Francisco, CA 94105.

Library of Congress Cataloging.

ISBN: 0-931290-61-9

First Edition

Cover Design: Floy Gunner

Printed in the United States of America

10 9 8 7 6 5 4 3 2 1

To the Tanadas, Olaguers, Aquinos, Rodrigos, Dioknos,
Salongases, Macapagals, Manglapuses, Avilas, Alvarezes,
and the thousands of nameless and faceless Filipinos
dedicated to the liberation of their country from tyranny,
but, most of all, to my wife, Presy,
whose principles and courage have been an inspiration

Contents

Preface xi

Introduction xv

Part I: The Meeting 1

The Appointment 3

The Motive 9

Ninoy Meets Imelda 25

The Letter 31

The Death Warrant 43

The Bad Omens 60

The Test 73

Part II: The Dialogue 91

The Tape Recording 93

Let's Stop the Violence 96

The First Signs of Revolution 113

Two of Ours for Two of Yours 128

You Are Always Welcome 144

Fifteen Years Is Long Enough 168

Sincerity Is the Key 177

Can We Have a Moratorium? 206

Imelda's Day in Court 212

Yes! We'll Give It a Try 232

The First Signs Were Encouraging 245

The Hardliners Prevailed 276

You Tell Reagan . . . 294

Epilogue 303

Appendix 305

About the Author 345

Preface

Oppression has been the root cause of revolution since ancient times. *Terrorism* has been the term used by all oppressors to condemn the initial stages of the revolution by the oppressed. Revolutionary movements spring up when all avenues to obtain justice seem closed off. It is the tenacity of those in power more than the fervor of the dissidents that gives impetus to such movements. The boiler explodes only when the hand in control shuts off the safety valve that allows the excess steam to escape safely. But power-hungry and corrupt men and women never learn this lesson despite innumerable examples throughout history.

Interestingly, successful revolutionary movements are rarely the work of radicals and extremists. Radicals and extremists do not have the popular support of the masses to generate a successful revolution. It is only when the moderates are forced to resort to violence—because all other means have failed—that revolutions succeed. The radicals and extremists play an important role in all revolutions, but they are not the *cause* of the revolutions. Inevitably, the cause is the authority which removes all rights (civil, political, and human) from the people. What happens, as shown in case after case, is that the moderates are supplanted by radicals; these extremists then use the repression as proof that justice can be obtained only by revolutionary acts.

Some historians believe that even the American Revolution would not have taken place if the mad and arrogant British ruler, King George, had recognized that the moderates, the Ben Franklins, were asking not for independence but for fair treatment and for respectful consideration of their views and their human rights. When the modest demands of the Ben Franklins were denied, then the revolutionaries, the Sam Adamses, found the field wide open for revolution. Thus, the moderates who desired a peaceful reconciliation with Britain were left with no other choice but violent revolt.

The lessons of history go unnoticed by the despotic and corrupt politicans. Dictators like to believe that they will be the exception to the rule. They like to believe that they will remain in power indefinitely through absolute control of their people. But they very seldom, if ever, maintain control.

Recently, one more corrupt and oppressive dictator, the Shah of Iran, became another statistic of history. Days before his fall, like all other naive dictators, he claimed to enjoy the overwhelming support of the Iranian people. The revolutionary activities in Iran, which had been evident for some time and represented the true feelings of the majority of people, were attributed by the government-controlled press to "the few extremists trying to undermine the legitimate and constitutional government of the Shah." But it is now obvious that this was not the case.

Anastasio Somoza of Nicaragua added one more number to the same statistic. Similarly, the dictators of Chile, South Korea, the Philippines, and many other countries also claim to enjoy the overwhelming support of the people—until they, too, are overthrown. They all attribute the revolutionary activities of the moderates to a "few extremists trying to undermine the legitimate and constitutional government." Perhaps they all share the same speech writer, or they all copy each other's speeches. Eventually, however, they become victims of their own illusions.

The subject of this book is the "Conjugal Dictatorship" of Ferdinand and Imelda Marcos of the Philippines. Since 1972, when Marcos declared martial law and established his dictatorial regime, he has ruled the Philippines through the usual means employed by all despots: force, repression, torture, and terrorism. Although Marcos was viewed as an "astute politician," he has committed and continues to commit almost all of the errors of his fellow dictators—past and present. The revolution by the moderate democratic forces of the Philippines has started. The "first signs of revolution" are all much too clear. The question is now whether Mr. Marcos and his partner in life and government, Imelda Romualdez Marcos, will be an exception to the rule or one more addition to the same statistic.

Introduction

Eduardo Olaguer is a 44-year-old successful Filipino businessman with a master's degree from Harvard Business School. He is today (January 10, 1981) a political prisoner, held in one of the military detention camps in Manila.

Olaguer was arrested by agents of Marcos' dreaded Presidential Security Command on Christmas Eve of 1979. Along with some 20 other urban guerrillas arrested about the same time, he is under the custody of a certain Colonel Rolando Abadilla. Abadilla is a notorious torturer of political prisoners. All of the respected international human rights organizations, such as Amnesty International and International Commission of Jurists, have confirmed Abadilla's acts of torture and terrorism when they sent fact-finding missions to the Philippines.

Marcos has treated Olaguer and his group as "terrorists" and "common criminals." The group has been formally charged before the military tribunals of the martial law regime and is presently being tried for terrorism and subversion. I am included in the group as one of its "key leaders," and I am also being tried in absentia. On August 14, 1980, Olaguer was brought before the military tribunal to formally submit his plea but when he started to read his three-page prepared statement, the military "judges" stopped him. His statement was not read, but it was later circulated by the underground throughout the Philippines. Excerpts from his 3-page statement are quoted below:

August 14, 1980

Gentlemen of this Tribunal:

Allow me to present my plea.

Before God, and to you and all our countrymen, humbly and almost with joy, I solemnly declare:

That I, EDUARDO OLAGUER, have taken up arms against the corrupt and illegal dictatorship of Ferdinand Marcos. I have done so, moved by a sense of Christian duty, by a sense of honor of an outraged Filipino, and I assure you out of love for this country–love for its past glories and our forebears and heroes, for its present generation of freedom-fighters and ordinary citizens such as they are. Yes, such as some of you have become, under the oppressive influence of martial law and the corrupting example of our illegitimate rulers . . . .

I have committed no crime! For there can be no crime when a citizen acts in self-defense to lance off a cancer. The crime is elsewhere. The crime is this present regime.

The crime is the subversion of fundamental laws and historic precepts of liberty and government, born out of a conspiracy to satisfy *one man's* diseased ambitions and to gratify that same man's insatiable greed for wealth and the power necessary to maintain himself as dictator beyond the endurance of the minds and hearts of 47 million Filipinos by incessant lies and insidious propaganda.

Surely, it is no crime to rise up in arms against such a legal, moral and political monstrosity. No, not a crime, but a fulfillment and a consummation—the fulfillment of a sacred duty, and the consummation of one's love for his country . . . .

But not all have been asleep in this dark night of our generation. I dare say a true and proud record is being written by the very lives of those who are awake and vigilant in order to defend and conserve the truth, which alas, is being twisted daily by Marcos and by denizens of the dark beholden to Mr. Marcos . . . .

Some facts are clear enough for all to see, provided we are willing to see them. It is clear enough to see that the martial law government is patently illegal, that it is hopelessly corrupt, that it has no intention of relinquishing power back to the people. It is equally clear that in order to remain in control, Mr. Marcos has repeatedly ignored, even flouted the people's will, and worse, repressed it by fraud, deceit, intimidation, force, and the misuse of public funds. To top it all, Mr. Marcos continues to do so and I am convinced that he intends to continue doing so . . . .

Yes, gentlemen, I have taken up arms—but certainly without the aid and support of any foreign power—purposely to overthrow the real subversive, the real enemy of the people, the corrupt and unconstitutional regime of Ferdinand E. Marcos. And in this resolve, in this enterprise, I know I AM NOT ALONE!

Gentlemen of this Tribunal—I therefore definitely plead NOT GUILTY. So help me God!

The following brief news item on the Olaguer trial proceedings appeared in the *New York Times* on August 15, 1980:

THE NEW YORK TIMES, FRIDAY, AUGUST 15, 1980

Around the World

Filipino Accused as a Rebel Calls Marcos 'Subversive'

MANILA, Aug. 14 (UPI) — A Harvard-educated Philippine engineer told a military court today that he had taken up arms to overthrow President Ferdinand E. Marcos, who he said was the "real subversive" for keeping the Philippines under martial law.

The defendant, Eduardo B. Olaguer, submitted the statement, which he was not allowed to read, in pleading not guilty to rebellion charges. In it, he said he did not think it was a crime to rise in arms against a regime that was illegal.

Mr. Olauger, a 44-year-old geodetic engineer who holds a master's degree in business administration from Harvard Business School, is accused with 16 others of conspiring to assassinate President Marcos and his wife, Imelda.

What follows in this book is essentially a chronicle of the events that transpired prior to the author's December 19, 1980 meeting with Imelda Marcos, the powerful partner in the Filipino "Conjugal Dictatorship" and an accurate account of the dialogue that took place during the five-and-a-half-hour meeting. It is also a chronicle of the important events that transpired after the meeting through March 23, 1981, the date this book was completed.

The cover of this book illustrates the perception the two "terrorists" have of each other. The contents of the book allow the reader to reach his own conclusions.

Steve Psinakis
San Francisco

PART I

The Meeting

CHAPTER 1

The Appointment

It was 2:08 p.m. of December 19, 1980 when I entered hurriedly the small but elegant lobby of the Waldorf Towers Hotel in New York. It was already 8 minutes past the deadline which I myself had set for confirmation of "the appointment" with Imelda Romualdez Marcos, the beautiful "First Lady" of the Philippines.

As I entered the lobby, I literally bumped into an old acquaintance, Ramon Jacinto, the son of Fernando Jacinto, a well known Filipino industrialist. It was evident that Ramon was there to see "Her Majesty the Queen" as many refer to the controversial Imelda Marcos. Whenever Imelda is at the Waldorf Towers, any well dressed Filipino in sight is either with "Her Majesty" or waiting to see her—mostly the latter.

After exchanging a few quick pleasantries with Ramon, I did confirm that he was there for an appointment with Imelda for 2:30 p.m. "Good" I thought to myself with relief "if my meeting with Imelda goes through, she doesn't expect it to be long." My doubtful appointment had been scheduled for 2:00 p.m. and she had already scheduled another appointment with Ramon for 2:30.

My own appointment was indeed very doubtful. I felt that there was only one chance in ten that the meeting, which Imelda herself had requested, would go through after she read my letter which was handcarried to her just twenty minutes earlier by Heherson "Sonny" Alvarez. Frankly, I was hoping my letter would outrage her to the point where she would no longer want to see me, even though her insistent requests to former Philippine Senator Benigno "Ninoy" Aquino, Jr. during the previous four days, betrayed her anxiety to meet with me.

Four days earlier, during the evening of December 15th, Senator Aquino had called me from Boston at my house in San Francisco to tell me that the "Queen" had granted him an appointment for 5 p.m. the following day. A few days before that, Ninoy Aquino had requested an appointment with Imelda through Philippine Ambassador to Washington, Eduardo Romualdez, Imelda's uncle.

Senator "Ninoy" Aquino is not the average Filipino one is likely to bump into in the streets of Manila. Ninoy had been a prisoner of Marcos for seven years and seven months. He was—and is—the one political figure Marcos always feared the most.

On the day Marcos imposed martial law, September 21, 1972, several thousand opponents and "potential enemies" of Marcos had been picked up by the special military intelligence units. Aquino was one of the first to be arrested. For seven years and seven months Aquino had been kept in solitary confinement at the Fort Bonifacio military detention center. Suddenly, on May 8, 1980, the military escorted Ninoy to the airport and put him on a Philippine Air Lines flight bound for San Francisco.

Speculations run high as to why Ninoy was "released." Did he make a deal with Marcos? Did his long solitary confinement break his spirit? Did he sell out?

The speculations ended soon after his arrival. Ninoy was in need of an urgent heart by-pass operation. He had refused to permit the inexperienced Philippine military doctors to conduct the delicate surgery and had asked Marcos to allow him to go to the United States. Imelda Marcos reviewed the medical reports of her military doctors and went to see Ninoy at the hospital.

The medical reports and her personal meeting with Aquino at the military hospital convinced Imelda that his days were numbered. "What will the people think if I die in the hands of your doctors?" Ninoy had asked Imelda.

Imelda discussed Ninoy's condition with her husband and with a few of their confidants. "This is a rare opportunity, Mr. President, to be magnanimous" one of the confidants reportedly told Marcos. "You can release Aquino for 'humanitarian reasons' without risking anything. Even if Aquino survives the heart operation, he will be in no condition to continue with his aggressive stand against your leadership."

Marcos was convinced. Aquino was taken to the airport the same afternoon and boarded the PAL flight to San Francisco. The following morning all Philippine dailies headlined Aquino's "temporary release" by the President for "humanitarian reasons" to undergo an urgent heart operation.

After his arrival in the U.S. on May 8, 1980, Ninoy and I became good friends. His "release" from prison was considered one of the most important events which occurred after the imposition of martial law. Ninoy had always been acknowledged as the arch political rival of Ferdinand Marcos and as the man who would have been President of the Philippines, had Marcos not imposed martial law and cancelled the presidential elections which were scheduled for late 1973. Most importantly, Ninoy was viewed as the only politician capable of uniting the fragmented opposition.

Talking to me now on the telephone from his home in Boston,

Ninoy sounded happy about his forthcoming meeting with Imelda. "Good for you, buddy" I said. "It ought to be an interesting meeting."

"You haven't heard all of it yet," Ninoy went on with a nervous laughter. "The 'Queen' is inviting you to join me. She told me she wants to see you."

I assumed he was joking. "You must be kidding. You can have her all to yourself."

Ninoy insisted "No! I am serious Greek. She wants to see you and, it seems, very badly. But, God! I don't want you with me when I see her. I don't trust your temper. You'll blow things up" he said with a laughter which betrayed real concern.

I began to believe that Ninoy was serious but I still had my doubts. "Are you really serious? She wants to see me? How is that possible?" I asked with disbelief.

During the previous twelve months–since December 1979 to be exact–all the newspapers in the Philippines as well as the radio and TV stations had been featuring many news stories about the "terrorists" operating in the Philippines. In practically all of these news stories, my name had been prominently mentioned as a leading member of at least two "terrorist" groups. The "crimes" attributed to me ranged from "supplying arms and explosives to the terrorists"; to "training Filipino terrorists in the U.S."; to "plotting to overthrow the Marcos regime"; to "plotting to assassinate Mr. Marcos, Mrs. Marcos, their son Bong-Bong and other Philippine Government officials"; to "plotting to kidnap Marcos' daughter"; etc.

I had even been formally charged by the Philippine Government with several of these crimes and was being tried in absentia in Manila before the military tribunals of the martial law regime.

Also, during the past six years, my syndicated column, published regularly by the two largest Filipino community papers in the U.S., had been attacking the Marcos martial law regime for its oppression; its inhuman tortures of political prisoners; its murders of young activists and its violations of human rights. Worse than that, I had been exposing to the press and the U.S. Congress the personal corruption of Mr. and Mrs. Marcos, their relatives and friends.

How was it possible for this woman to be asking to see me, I thought. "Are you really serious?" I repeated to Ninoy.

"Yes, Greek. How many times do I have to tell you?"

Oh Jesus, I said to myself. What the hell could she want? "What do you think Ninoy?"

"I think you should see her, but not together with me."

We talked things over for a while and decided that Ninoy should go alone to the December 16, 5 p.m. meeting. Depending on how things went, we would decide whether I should agree to see her.

When I placed the phone back on its receiver, I knew that the invitation was not a hoax. I leaned back in the desk chair of my study and took a sip of the cold Greek coffee from a demitasse which Presy had brought me an hour earlier.

Why does Imelda really want to see me, I asked myself. To threaten me? No! Marcos' goons had already tried it several times unsuccessfully. To bribe me? No! They've tried that too with no success. To abduct me or kill me? No! That's stupid; they wouldn't do it at the Waldorf Towers. To charm me into her camp? Well!!! That was possible. Imelda is reputed to have such an inflated opinion of her own charm that it wouldn't be entirely impossible. But no, I decided, she wouldn't be that stupid. I lit a cigarette, got up and walked to the bedroom where Presy was busy clipping out some of the aritcles from the previous week's Daily Express—one of Marcos' newspapers published in Manila.

"I have some news, darling. Guess what?"

"Good or bad?" she asked jokingly.

"Good."

"Marcos dropped dead?" she laughed.

"No, seriously."

"What? If you want to play games with me, come to bed. If you want to talk, talk."

"O.K! You win. Ninoy is seeing Imelda tomorrow and she wants to see me too."

"What on earth is good about that? Is it a joke?"

"No! I am serious. She wants to see me."

Presy seemed disturbed. "You're not considering seeing that woman, are you? What's the point?"

We discussed that matter at length. Presy was right, I thought. There was nothing to be gained by seeing Imelda. On the contrary, a meeting with her could be used against us. Imelda could, as she had done with others so many times in the past, use the meeting for her propaganda. I could just imagine our picture together in her newspapers with a headline "Terrorist pleads for forgiveness from the First Lady."

Yes; Presy was right. There was no point in seeing Imelda.

"Tell you what we'll do" I told Presy. "Let's give this some thought. Anyway, it's time for dinner. Let's take a break."

CHAPTER 2

The Motive

I was getting up from the dinner table when the doorbell rang. It was Charlie Avila.

Charlie is a Filipino in his mid-thirties whose opposition to Marcos goes back to pre-martial law days. The imposition of martial law by Marcos in 1972 had only deepened his convictions for the need of social justice for his people.

"Grab some coffee Charlie, and come up to the study. I've got some interesting news for you."

Charlie is a dear friend. We'd met less than two years earlier but both Presy and I consider him as part of the family. He is an accomplished man, according to our standards, and a man whose vision for a just Philippine society makes his eyes sparkle. We'd spent a great deal of time together during the previous fourteen months and both Presy and I developed a lot of respect for his capacity to analyze events methodically, to use his intelligence effectively and to react to crises soberly.

I briefed him on my call with Ninoy and watched for his reaction. Imelda's invitation to see me clearly pleased him.

"This, more than anything else, confirms what you and I had been saying all along. Marcos and Imelda are finally running scared," Charlie said.

During the past twelve months, the "Conjugal Dictators," as many refer to Ferdinand and Imelda Marcos, had seen the emergence of a new form of opposition to their 8-year martial law regime—urban guerrilla warfare. During the three month period of August to October 1980, at least thirty buildings in Manila had been bombed, causing the death of an American and injuries to at least sixty persons.

"In the eyes of the Marcoses," Charlie continued "you are seen as the military strategist of the guerrilla warfare and as the main supplier of the explosives; even the supplier of the funds."

"Yeh! That may be so. But isn't it obvious to them that by asking to see me, they're betraying their weakness?" I asked.

"Obviously; but if they feel you are the brains behind the guerrilla military operations, they'll have to size you up better and try every possible way they can think of to neutralize you."

"How can they have such a distorted impression? Can't they understand that it's illogical for anyone, especially a foreigner, to be directing guerrilla operations from ten thousand miles away?"

"The fact is," Charlie argued "that every article in Marcos' papers pictures you as the guerrilla trainer, the explosives supplier, the . . ., the . . . etc."

"Yes, but that doesn't mean they believe what they say in their own papers for propaganda purposes."

"Well," said Charlie in a very matter-of-fact tone "we can debate about the various reasons until we're blue in the face, but one thing I'm sure we won't argue about: they're really scared of the destabilization plan of the urban guerrillas, particularly after they screwed-up and let Ninoy out of jail."

Charlie and I had spent countless hours analyzing the effects of the destabilization plan which became known publicly when the "Light-a-Fire Movement"surfaced in the summer of 1979.

During the summer and fall of 1979, a number of government and commercial buildings in Manila were put to the torch, including the "floating casino" which was reputed to be one more of the many illegitimate income sources of Imelda's family. A revolutionary group calling itself the "Light-a-Fire Movement" claimed credit for the fires.

In December of 1979, the Marcos-controlled news media announced that Philippine intelligence operatives had arrested an American citizen, Ben Z. Lim, at the Manila International Airport. Lim was charged with attempting to smuggle explosives into the Philippines. His arrest led to the arrest of fifteen other "terrorists," reportedly all members of the Light-a-Fire Movement, headed by a well known Harvard-educated Filipino business executive, Eduardo Olaguer.

Olaguer admitted during his military trial proceedings that he "has taken up arms against the corrupt and illegal dictatorship of Ferdinand Marcos" because Marcos is "the real subversive." According to one of the thousands of decrees issued by Marcos during his eight years of martial rule, the crime of using force to overthrow the regime carries a death penalty.

Ben Lim died on May 16, 1980, five months after his arrest, in a military hospital while still under detention by the military.

According to the many published reports in the Manila papers and the official statements issued by the Philippine Government, Lim had signed "confessions" admitting that he was smuggling in explosives for the Light-a-Fire Movement—a movement he allegedly was part of. The explosives, according to his alleged confession, were supplied to him by me in San Francisco. Also he allegedly confessed that he, along with other members of the Light-a-Fire Movement, were trained by me somewhere in the Arizona desert on the use of explosives and on techniques of urban guerrilla warfare.

During the previous five years, Marcos had been trying to manufacture credible evidence of "crimes" which could be attributed to me. The Marcos paranoia to collect such "evidence" against me was confirmed by the wife of one of the arrested leaders of the Light-a-Fire Movement. She personally confided to me that all those arrested with her husband were told by their captors that they could go free if they signed "confessions" admitting that I was guilty of the crimes which the military told them I was supposed to have committed. Some of those who did not accept this "generous offer" were tortured until they signed similar "confessions." The case of Ben Lim is a classic example.

Lim was a man in his early sixties. He was a Filipino engineer who had come to the U.S. in the fifties and was given employment by Boeing Aircraft in Seattle, Washington. Like most of his countrymen, Lim had found it difficult to earn a decent living in the Philippines to support his large family. He had applied for U.S. citizenship and had become an American citizen but his love for his native land had not diminished.

I was introduced to him in San Francisco by Eddie Olaguer in 1978. Eddie had told me that Ben Lim was one of his best friends even though Ben was old enough to be his father. Eddie had met him in the sixties when the Lim family had gone to Manila for an extended vacation. The two had met during a cursillo—a religious retreat—and "during those few days" Eddie had told me he "became very close to Ben. You know, the atmosphere of the cursillo is conducive to forming close relationships."

Ben had spoken to Eddie of his dreams for his native country. "I hope I can come back some day and contribute something to my land," Ben had told him. "I've been away too long. I hope to come back and live here after I retire."

The Olaguer-Lim friendship became very strong and although the Lim family returned to the States, Eddie and Ben maintained contact through correspondence and occasional visits when Eddie travelled to the United States on business. During his 1978 visit to San Francisco, Eddie had invited Ben to join him for a "week-end in California." It was then that I was introduced to Ben.

Ben Lim was a sick man. He had suffered several heart attacks and had been retired early by Boeing on "disability pay." He was also suffering from a severe case of asthma. The medical kit which he always carried with him, contained a great assortment of pills which he would swallow in batches several times a day.

"I am living on borrowed time," Lim had told me. "I had a good life in America but I haven't done much for my suffering countrymen. I guess the good Lord didn't let me die without granting my wish. I always prayed that I be given a chance to help my people. That's why the Lord didn't let me die and that's why I am here."

Lim had explained to me his heart ailment in great detail and had told me that without his pills, he'd be dead within 2-3 days.

On May 21, 1980, the Philippine newspapers carried the brief news item shown below.

PHILLIPINES DAILY EXPRESS **Wednesday, May 21, 1980**

'Light-A-Fire' suspect dies in military hospital

A Filipino naturalized American who had been detained with 14 others by the military for an alleged plot to terrorize Metro Manila died last Friday in a military hospital from a heart ailment, the defense ministry said yesterday.

The deceased was Ben Z. Lim, 62, a Filipino who resided in Seattle, Washington. Lim was arrested last December at the Manila International Airport when government agents discovered explosives in his luggage.

The military said that the explosives found formed part of a plan by the subversives to smuggle arms and other materials.

Deputy Defense Minister Carmelo Z. Barbero said that he had already informed the U.S. Embassy of the case, Lim being an American national.

Doctors at the AFP Medical Center (formerly V. Luna Hospital) in Quezon City where Lim was being treated said he died due to coronary arteriosclerosis.

Military agents said Lim was a member of the so-called "Light a Fire" movement, some of whose leaders are in custody. The military said it was an arson operation of subversives in Metro Manila.

That was how the Marcos newspapers in Manila reported Lim's death but the true circumstances of his death were narrated to me one month later by the wife of one of his co-detainees.

Lim had been arrested on the morning of December 14, 1979 when he had gone to Manila International Airport to claim his missing piece of luggage. He had arrived in Manila two days earlier and one of his three pieces of luggage could not be located. "Come back in a couple of days to claim your luggage" the airline supervisor had told Lim "it will probably arrive with our next flight tomorrow."

My contact narrated: "When Lim returned for his luggage Saturday morning, he was picked up by the military and locked up at some safehouse all alone. He was left there until the next day without food, water and, of course, without his pills. The following morning he was taken to the interrogation room where several men in civilian clothes and only one man in uniform, a colonel, were present. By that time, Lim was already in bad shape. His anxiety for what they would do to him had caused a severe attack of asthma. Without his pills for 24 hours, his chest had started to ache. He was already gasping for air when his interrogators confronted him. Lim immediately explained his health condition to the colonel and asked for his pills.

"We are very lucky" one of the men in civilian clothes had told Lim. "In your case, we don't have to torture you. We'll just watch you die from natural causes if you don't tell us what we want to hear. Your goddamn Embassy people will not see any of our marks on you. With your heart condition, what could be more natural than for you to suffer a fatal heart attack? That fuckin' Jimmy Carter has been sticking his nose in our business but he won't be able to do much for you. Yes sir, we're real lucky with you."

It didn't take long to break Lim and to make him "confess" to whatever his interrogators wanted. In addition to naming his contacts in the Philippines, Lim had told them about his introduction to me in San Francisco.

"That's another son of a bitch of a foreigner who has been sticking his nose in our business" the colonel had told Lim. "We'll take care of that bastard Psinakis one of these days. Meantime the confession you will sign will state that Psinakis supplied you with the explosives and was your training officer in the United States."

"One more thing," the colonel said, "we'll let your Embassy people see you, but if you complain to them, you are a dead man. Don't forget; you are in our custody and so are your heart pills," the colonel concluded as he handed Lim his medical kit.

All this happened on December 15, 1979. During the next few days the military quietly rounded up most of those named by Lim. Few received word in time and were able to escape arrest. Eddie Olaguer, the head of the group, was arrested on December 24. By the end of December the military had not only arrested the "suspects" named by Lim but had also arrested more than 200 other men and women considered by the Marcos intelligence forces as "potential sources of information."

On December 30, 1979, Marcos decided to break the "big news" to the public. All of the newspapers reported in banner headlines the same "news story."

The Daily Express, which carried front-page photographs of Lim, Olaguer, and myself, headlined the news story:

PHILIPPINES SUNDAY EXPRESS **December 30, 1979**

---

15 Suspects Arrested

by Alex D. Allan

The military arrested during the week 15 members of a group which, the military said, was responsible for several big fires in Metro Manila and the attempted liquidation of a number of Cabinet ministers with the use of sophisticated, gift-packaged bombs this year.

The intelligence coup, scored by the PC Metrocom with the assistance of agents of the Presidential Security Command, also resulted in the seizure of a fearsome amount of explosives and incendiary devices, the latest batch of which had been brought in by a "balikbayan" from San Francisco.

The balikbayan, Ben Z. Lim, who was arrested at the Manila International Airport, identified the supplier of the explosives as Steve Psinakis, a brother-in-law of Eugenio Lopez, Jr., one of the harshest critics of President Marcos.

Psinakis was among those instrumental in the escape in October 1977 of Lopez, Jr. and Sergio Osmena III from a detention center here to the United States. The two were among 24, including several foreigners, charged in connection with a plot to assassinate President Marcos.

A progress report on the intelligence operation submitted yesterday to Defense Minister Juan Ponce Enrile, by Brig. Gen. Prospero A. Olivas, PC Metrocom chief, identified the arson suspects arrested as:

Lim, a Filipino turned US citizen residing in Seattle, Washington who brought in explosives, blasting caps, and incendiary devices aboard a Philippine Airlines plane last Dec. 12.

Eduardo Olaguer, president of the Business Day Information System and Services, part-time professor of the Asian Institute of Management, and chief executive of the Pantranco North Express;

Othoniel Jimenez, administrative manager of the Pacific Memorial Plan and residing at No. 1028 Aurora Blvd., Quezon City.

Mrs. Esther P. Jimenez.

Reynaldo Maclang, the EOD or explosives, ordnance and demolition expert of the group who was picked up at his residence at No. 9 Salalila St., Quezon City.

Magdalena de los Santos Maclang.

Carlos M. Lazaro, who resided at the "safehouse" Olaguer was renting at No. 113 V. Luna Road Extension in Sikatuna Village, Quezon City, and who admitted having delivered incendiary bombs to target establishments.

Gertrudes V. Dingal, also of No. 113 V. Luna Road Extension.

Miguel Panuringan, who resided with the Jimenezes.

Sergio Martinez, also of 1028 Aurora Blvd.

Rene Marciano, of No. 31 Champaca St., Roxas District, Q. C.

Marie Marciano.

Danny Ocampo, who gave his address as c/o Business Day, West Avenue, Quezon City.

Deogracias Arellano, of barrio Manggahan, Montalban, Rizal.

Illuminada Arellano, also of barrio Manggahan.

The identity of the 15th man was withheld by investigators on his claim that he was merely a boarder at one of the suspects' residences.

During the raid on the Olaguer safehouse, Captain Lacson recovered a piece of paper which the business executive attempted to tear up and flush down the toilet. Recomposed later, the paper revealed that the subversive arson group planned to explode incendiary bombs on New Year's Eve at the offices of the **Times Journal**, the **Daily Express**, the Kanlaon Broadcasting System, and the Herdis Company.

Major Berroya, the Metrocom's explosives expert, told General Olivas that an attache case bomb which was intended for the target offices contained eight pounds of Composition 4 explosives which would have leveled the entire block on which the **Times Journal** bldg., in Port Area, is situated.

In addition to explosives, incendiaries, and timing and detonating devices, the military agents also confiscated from the suspects numerous manuals on sabotage and terrorism.

Some of the manuals carried the following titles on the covers: "CIA Explosives for Sabotage Manual," "CIA Field Expedient Incendiary Manual," "CIA Field Expedient Methods for Explosives Preparations," "OSS Sabotage and Demolition Manual," and the "Manual of the Urban Guerilla" by Carlos Marighella.

From the amount and nature of the explosives and incendiaries confiscated, Olivas assessed the group as having an "utter disregard of human rights."

"The burning of the Sulo Hotel and similar attempts made on other places of public assembly where many innocent people would have been killed or maimed exemplify the little value placed by these irresponsible persons on human life," Olivas said.

He added that the fact that many of the explosives had already been rigged for immediate use "clearly shows that they were ready to operate anytime and commit urban guerilla warfare and terrorism."

The December 1979 arrests of the Light-a-Fire Movement operatives were reported for several days by the Manila news media. Marcos bragged about the efficiency and alertness of his intelligence forces and informed the public that the small band of "amateurish terrorists" had been crushed and all its members had either been arrested or fled the country. "There is no cause for concern" Marcos assured the people.

Manila was very quiet during the next seven months. It appeared that the arrests of the Light-a-Fire Movement leaders and their operatives had put an end to what Marcos had referred to as their "wild dreams" of destabilizing the Marcos regime and causing its collapse. Unknown to Marcos however, several urban guerrilla groups had been training and preparing for their "BIG BANG" which would take place on August 22, 1980.

Meantime, Ben Lim had outlived his usefulness to the Marcos agents. The last thing Marcos wanted to do was to put Lim through a military trial and risk any statements in the presence of foreign correspondents of how Lim's "confessions" were extracted. Soon after Lim signed his confession, his pills kept "disappearing" and on May 16, 1980, his agony was over. His heart finally gave up.

Between the December 1979 arrests of the Light-a-Fire Movement and the first "BIG BANG" of the urban guerrillas in August of 1980, Ninoy Aquino had arrived in the United States. Prior to his departure from Manila, he was virtually forced to sign "an agreement" promising to (a) return to the Philippines after his operation and (b) refrain from any statements on the political situation in his country.

His triple heart by-pass operation at the Baylor Medical Center in Dallas was a total success and his recovery was phenomenal.

Long before Ninoy's doctor felt that he had recovered enough from his operation to engage in any kind of normal life, Ninoy was globe-trotting all over the United States and abroad, meeting with many people and developing a somewhat different perspective of the Philippine situation than the one he had developed during his seven and-a-half years of solitary confinement.

For the first three months after his arrival, Ninoy held to his agreement with Marcos to refrain from any public political statements. However, after tremendous pressures from representatives of all sectors of Philippine society, Ninoy became gradually convinced that the call from his people overrode the agreement with Marcos—an agreement which he had to accept in order to literally save his life.

It became clear to him that his duty to his people was far more important than his agreement with Marcos. "A pact with the devil is no pact at all" Ninoy finally declared and on August 4, 1980, he decided to break his silence.

In a stinging speech which caused headlines in the Philippines and in other countries, Ninoy warned Marcos of the "gathering storm." He told his audience that he had talked to the leaders of several "young idealistic groups of Filipinos" who have been preparing for "massive urban guerrilla warfare." The guerillas,

Aquino said, had revealed to him their "destabilization plan" which included "bombings, assassinations and kidnappings of public officials and military officers . . . in order to bring the Marcos regime to its knees." Ninoy warned that unless Marcos moved quickly and sincerely toward normalization, the urban guerrillas will start implementing their destabilization plan.

The Marcos reaction was predictable. His controlled media in the Philippines quoted Ninoy out of context and pictured him as a crazy terrorist with wild ideas. On August 8, 1980, Marcos delivered a speech castigating Aquino: "Today, the media is full of lurid tales about somebody who is supposed to be mounting a rebellion against the Philippines. Such a fantastic tale is so stupid, is so ridiculous that I cannot dignify it by any comment" Marcos told his audience. "He (Aquino) claims it is their intention to kill and assassinate hundreds of public officials, military men and businessmen, kidnap their children and raise money by robbery, ransom, kidnapping and arson. We should instead not only ask them (the doctors) to cure his heart but cure his mind as well."

Less than three weeks after Ninoy's speech, on August 22, 1980, all hell broke loose. On that date, a coordinated bombing operation was carried out by a revolutionary group calling itself the April 6th Liberation Movement (A6LM). Bombs exploded simultaneously in nine buildings after the occupants had been warned to evacuate. No one was hurt and, although the bombs were small, the successful operation attracted the attention of the international press.

The A6LM took credit for the bombings and issued its first "MANIFESTO." Excerpts from the two-page manifesto read as follows:

MANIFESTO OF THE APRIL 6 LIBERATION MOVEMENT

We, the April 6 Liberation Movement and one of its urban guerrilla units, the April 6 SANDIGAN, proudly proclaim to the Filipino people and to the whole world our determination to bring about the speedy overthrow of the Marcos dictatorship. Today, several bombs have exploded in various parts of Metro Manila.

THIS IS ONLY THE BEGINNING!

Last April 6, 1978, we heard the true voice of the people as expressed through their "noise barrage" which has no parallel in Philippine history. The people have clearly expressed their desire to see the end of martial rule and the Marcos dictatorship. This is the reason for our name. . . .

We have decided to stand up for our rights. We have decided to FIGHT for our freedom and dignity. We have decided to use force as our ultimate weapon against a repressive regime that has refused to listen to reason. . . .

Today, bombs have exploded in the business establishments owned by known Marcos cronies and allies. This is symbolic of the people's resistance to the dictator's conscious plan to control the economy. The dictator has promised to destroy the oligarchy. But after eight years, he managed to simply cripple the old oligarchy in order to replace it with a new one—an oligarchy which he heads and which is dominated by his Octopus gang. After scandalously enriching themselves, these new oligarchs are now systematically bringing out the wealth of this country for safekeeping abroad. Let our ACTION serve as a clear warning to these avaricious specimen of the Filipino race.

YOU CANNOT BLEED OUR COUNTRY DRY. YOU WILL PAY DEARLY FOR YOUR GREED. The destruction of your buildings is only a symbolic act. You are our next targets.

Today, selected government buildings have been bombed. This is symbolic of the people's anger against the dictator's use of the governmental machinery to sow fear among the populace and to control the people . . .

TOMORROW, we shall strike again. We shall not stop until the Filipino people shall have liberated themselves from the tentacles of the Marcos dictatorship. . . .

This is our perspective and it is with this consciousness that we have launched our armed struggle, our share in a gigantic task. Thus, we call on all the democratic forces in this country to unite. This is the unity that will liberate our people, the unity that will lead to VICTORY!!!

PANAHON NA!!! MAGKAISA AT KUMILOS!!!
(It is time!!!) (Join together and act!!!)

Since August 22, the A6LM has carried out and claimed credit for similar bombing operations which resulted in the death of one American woman and injuries to scores of others. The most dramatic bombing operation, which caused headlines in many U.S. cities and in other foreign countries, took place on October 19, 1980.

On that date, a bomb explosion rocked the grand opening of the American Society of Travel Agents (ASTA) Conference just five minutes after Marcos delivered his welcome address. The conference, attended by some 4,000 delegates from the U.S. and other countries, was being held at the ultra-modern Philippine International Convention Center (PICC), one of the many extravagant multimillion dollar projects of Imelda.

The bomb exploded a few feet behind where Marcos was seated causing chaos in the grand hall full of guests and causing the cancellation of the scheduled week-long conference. News stories around the world reported that the ASTA bombing was by far the most embarrassing incident for Marcos since the imposition of martial law in 1972.

Three weeks before the Conference, the A6LM had sent letters warning delegates not to go to Manila for the conference, lest they "get caught in the crossfire." Letters were also sent to the members of the ASTA Organizing Committee asking the cancellation of the conference. The A6LM September 25 letter to the ASTA Chairman, Curtis Nabors, read:

September 25, 1980

RE: ASTA Convention in Manila

As you may have discerned from recent newspaper coverage (clippings enclosed for your perusal), the Filipino people have begun their revolution—a revolution against the Marcos dictatorship.

We are fighting for our democratic rights and our freedoms. We are fighting to bring about a new social order that is equitable and just. We are fighting in order to realize the dreams of our forebears for an independent and proud Philippines.

In this fight we have resorted to violence as the only means by which we can bring about the downfall of a dictator who has refused to listen to reason.

Thus we ask you to sympathize with our cause. We ask you to cancel your forthcoming ASTA Conference in Manila. Tourists coming to the Philippines now do so at their own risk. We ask you *not* to visit the Philippines in these times of great uncertainty and unrest. We do not want you to get caught in the crossfire.

Please heed this warning—or you will be responsible for lives lost during a time of upheaval in our nation.

When the people shall have finally succeeded in bringing down the dictator, then we shall again invite you to visit our beautiful country.

Regretting the inconvenience we might be causing you at this time, we want to express, nonetheless, our sincerest thanks for the cooperation we hope that you won't deny us.

Yours sincerely,

THE EXECUTIVE COUNCIL
APRIL 6TH LIBERATION MOVEMENT
PHILIPPINES

During the welcoming address, Marcos had attempted to ridicule the A6LM warnings and present his government as the ideal example of order and stability. "You come to the Philippines, perhaps for the first time, and you are warned that the Philippines is under martial law, raising fear and apprehension that you come to visit a country where bloodshed is rife, kidnapping, arson, murder, pillage and destruction is commonplace" Marcos told the 4,000 delegates. "But this is a nighmare which is past and gone . . . by your coming you certainly do away with these speculations and rumors by men whose only dream is to take over power and political authority. Let them dream. They live in a world of fantasy."

Just minutes later the bomb exploded fifty feet from where he was seated, making him look like the world's greatest "dreamer" and the ruler who was really living "in a world of fantasy."

Most of the news reports throughout the world treated the ASTA bombing as another "terrorist" incident. However, the more well informed reporters recognized the political significance of the event and commented on its implication. The prestigious *Washington Post* devoted its October 23, 1980 Editorial to this subject.

The *Post* editorial commented on the bomb explosions in Manila and of "the utter familiarity and predictability of it all." It mentioned Aquino's warning "that violence would be the sure result of the continuance of martial law." It also mentioned ASTA's disregard for the warning by the revolutionaries to cancel the Manila convention. The editorial took a clear stand on the corrupt one-man rule of Marcos: "For years, while President Marcos was consolidating a personal dictatorship that has made his one of the richest families in the world, it has been plain that he would eventually have to cope with the challenge of terror." Although the *Post* editorial did not condone the bomb explosions, it made it clear that the erupting violence was the result of Marcos' refusal to heed the advice of his "political rivals and some officials and citizens of the United States. . . . to return to the country's traditional democratic ways."

The editorial concluded by stating that "Mr. Marcos could do himself and his American friends a world of good by deciding himself to end personal rule."

Since the summer of 1979 when the urban guerrilla activities first emerged, Charlie and I had sat together for hours at a time analyzing the developments and evaluating the effects of each major operation.

We both felt very strongly that the "stability" of the Marcos regime hung on a few thin threads and that a well-organized urban guerrilla plan could easily snap the threads and cause the collapse of the Conjugal Dictatorship.

We always analyzed the statements of Marcos and his officials and studied the propaganda in the controlled media in the Philippines.

It was becoming more and more evident to Charlie and me that the modest successes of the urban guerrilla groups, particularly the A6LM, were causing more damage to Marcos than most observers realized. "Unfortunately," I had told Charlie, "only Marcos and his few confidants know the extent of their own insecurity and their fear of the DESTABILIZATION PLAN of the urban guerrillas."

Now Imelda wanted to see me. Ninoy's call that night informing me of Imelda's invitation, kept Presy, Charlie and I awake until the wee hours of the morning. We reviewed again the main events of the past few months and speculated on the motive behind Imelda's invitation. We all agreed that "FEAR" for the destabilization plan of the urban guerrillas was "the motive."

CHAPTER 3

Ninoy Meets Imelda

About 6 p.m. the following day, December 16, I was in my study when the phone rang. It was Senator Aquino.

"Hi Steve! This is Ninoy."

"Hello Ninoy! How was the meeting with Imelda?"

Ninoy's meeting was scheduled for 5 p.m. New York time and it was now 9 p.m. in New York. Ninoy had said he would call me after his meeting was over and give me his impressions. It was now four hours past his appointment time and I assumed that his meeting with Imelda had been over long ago. In fact, I was wondering why he hadn't called me yet.

"Fine," said Ninoy. "I met with the First Lady for four hours. In fact, I am still here with her in her suite."

"You mean you've been with her all this time?"

"Yes! We had a long friendly meeting. I believe it was quite useful. Look Steve," Ninoy said with some emphasis. "Mrs. Marcos really wants to see you and Presy. She is leaving tomorrow for the Middle East and will return to New York Friday morning of the 19th. She wants to meet you and Presy after she freshens up a bit, at 2 p.m. on Friday."

Realizing that Ninoy was still in Imelda's suite and that the call might be monitored, I decided to make my point clear to Imelda rather than to Ninoy. "What is this all about Ninoy? Why does she want to see us?"

"Well, believe me it's important that you see her. Please say you will."

"Yes! But I want to know what for. If you wish, I'll ask her myself. Why don't you put her on the phone? I'll talk to her."

"You know, your name has come up in connection with these rumors about plots to kill Bong-Bong. Also about the bombings and other related matters in Manila. I guess the First Lady would like to hear first-hand your comments," Ninoy said in a tone which betrayed a little impatience with me.

"I really have nothing to discuss with her on these subjects, Ninoy. What's the point? I'd rather not go through the expense, trouble and time to fly all the way to New York. How about Imelda? Isn't she passing through San Francisco, as usual, on the way home? Maybe we can meet briefly here, if you insist."

"No, Mrs. Marcos is rushing back home. She is arriving in New York on Friday and flying back to Manila the next day via the polar route. Please, confirm the appointment; I think it's important," Ninoy said in a tone of unquestionable exasperation.

It became clear to me that Ninoy was not sure whether I was talking for the benefit of the monitor or whether I was serious.

"OK, but we'll talk more about it later when you're out of there."

By that time, Presy had walked into the study and was listening to the conversation. I put the phone down and started to laugh. "Poor Ninoy! He thought I was giving him a hard time. He evidently did not realize that I was talking for the benefit of Imelda."

Presy smiled, "I can tell, however, from what I heard that she is still asking to see us. I don't know if you want to play politics with her but I can't. If you decide you should see her, count me out," she said quite emphatically.

"Look, I don't want to see that woman any more than you. But we both have one priority and one priority only—our commitment to the Filipino people. If, after talking things over with Ninoy later, when he is free to tell us what happened, it appears that seeing her could somehow help the country, we must see her. Anyway," I added with gusto, "what is this? I thought I was supposed to be the hardheaded and inflexible one; not you."

Presy knew exactly what I was trying to do—to soften her up.

"That's the wrong perception," she snapped back at me. "It's your intimidating personality which gives that impression. But you and I know, I am more of a hardliner than you, especially when it comes to dealing with people like Imelda who are responsible for so much suffering of my countrymen," she said in her customary soft gentle tone which conceals the steel determination of her character.

"You're right, and that's why I love you so. Anyway, I don't think I'll see that shameless hussy myself but, if I have to, you don't need to see her also."

"Great! Now hurry and get dressed. We'll be late for the children's Christmas mass at the Cathedral."

"Yes, Mammmm," I said obediently and rushed to the shower.

When we returned home at about 10 p.m., the phone was ringing. I rushed to pick it up. It was Alex Esclamado. Alex is the publisher of the *Philippine News,* the largest Filipino community newspaper in the United States. He is an outspoken critic of Marcos' dictatorial regime, and his paper's editorials have launched the most vitriolic attacks against the Conjugal Dictators.

"Hello," I said.

"This is Alex. I'll pick you up in five minutes to go out to a safe phone. Our friend is waiting for your call."

"Fine."

Alex was very disturbed. On the way to the public phone booth, he explained that Ninoy briefed him on his private meeting with Imelda and told him of her insistence to see Presy and me.

"Ninoy is in his hotel room in New York City expecting your call but before you call him, I want to talk to you." Alex is quite excitable and often somewhat impulsive.

"I'm listening."

"I don't think you should see Imelda," he voiced with all the emphasis he could muster. "We have nothing to gain by seeing her and everything to lose. You know how she can twist things in her controlled press. She'll make it look like you were trying to strike a deal for yourself. You and Presy are a symbol of the few who have not succumbed to any of their threats or bribe attempts. Your stand has been an inspiration to our people. If you give Imelda a chance to destroy this image by seeing her, our people will be demoralized."

Alex went on for some time along this line. He was genuinely concerned and seemed upset at Ninoy for recommending that I see Imelda. I told him not to worry. "I'll weigh the pros and cons very carefully before I decide whether I will see her," I assured Alex.

"Why don't you snub her or at most, just write her a letter giving her a piece of your mind?" he said angrily.

"Those are two good options. Let's see what Ninoy has to say about his meeting." I took out a dime and placed the call to Ninoy at his Manhattan hotel.

It was about 2 a.m. New York time but when Ninoy answered the phone, it was obvious he was wide awake.

"Hello."

"Yeh! This is Steve."

"OK," he said. "Number One: it was a good friendly meeting.

Number Two: She did almost all the talking for more than four hours. I just let her talk. I didn't want to argue at this point. Number Three: She tried to appear confident and impress me with her contacts with Reagan. I understand Reagan and Bush were also staying at the Waldorf and she met with them. She told me they spent more time with her than with West German Chancellor Helmut Schmidt. Number Four: You won't believe this but she gave a dinner for Nixon in her suite last Sunday and she videotaped the whole affair. She showed me the program. Nixon couldn't praise her enough. He referred to Imelda as "the Angel from Asia" who came to him when he was down and out. Nixon said there's nothing he wouldn't do to support the Marcos government. Imelda claimed that Nixon is back in the Reagan camp with lots of influence. Lots of bigshots at her party; bankers, oil people, etc. Number Five: She told me that you and I have sent assassination teams to Manila to knock off some of her people. She said if we do, they'll do the same to us and no one will come out ahead. She told me we should put a stop to that. Number Six: She sounded confident that the Reagan administration will go after us here, especially you. They have evidence, she says, on your activities. That's it in a nutshell," Ninoy concluded.

This was very typical of Ninoy. No fanfare, no flowery analysis, no long-flowing sentences. I laughed. "What do you make of it?" he asked.

"She is scared," I said without any hesitation. "Offense is the best defense. That's the strategy she is using. She's scared and is trying to see if she can scare you instead."

"Hmmmm, Hmmmm," sounded Ninoy.

"Did you get back at her?" I asked.

"No!" he said. "I just let her do the talking."

"I see," I said with some disappointment.

Ninoy changed the subject. "She wants to see you badly, man."

"Now we can talk," I said. "What do you really think, especially after your meeting?"

"I think you should see her. I prepared the ground. I told her you're no English gentleman. You're a Greek, a tough, hard character who will tell her what's on your mind, and she won't like it. She told me she knows, and she can take it. She still asked me to try to convince you to see her. You *should* see her."

"Okay! This is serious. We don't want to screw things up. We ought to think things out carefully. How about this?" I asked. "Suppose I come to Boston tomorrow to talk things over. Let's look at all the options and examine the pros and cons. Then we'll decide. I'll abide by your decision, whatever it is, but let me think and play the devil's advocate first. Then you decide."

"Fine, I'll see you tomorrow then. Call me when you know your schedule."

When I concluded the conversation, Alex was waiting nervously outside the phone booth. "What's the verdict?" he asked.

"No verdict. We agreed to think things out. I'll fly there tomorrow to talk about it before we decide."

Alex persisted in his views: I should not see her; I should snub her; at worst I should write her a letter.

"The more I think about it, the more I like your idea of writing her a letter. Let me work on it, and I'll call you tomorrow."

Alex then dropped me off at my house and went home.

CHAPTER 4

The Letter

I woke up about seven the next morning feeling rested and in good spirits. It is said that when you sleep with a problem, your subconscious keeps working, and by morning the problem is solved. I don't know if that's true, but I know that when I woke up the morning of December 17, I had already decided what I wanted to do. I had a hearty breakfast, joked with Presy and the kids, and withdrew to my study.

I had decided to write Imelda a tough letter explaining where we stood. Instead of going to my appointment with her, I would send the letter by messenger so that it would arrive at exactly 2 p.m. on the 19th, the time of my appointment.

I called TWA and made a reservation for New York on an overnight flight leaving San Francisco at 8:45 p.m. I then called Heherson "Sonny" Alvarez and asked him if he would meet me at Kennedy Airport the next morning at six and come with me to Boston to discuss our final strategy with Ninoy. He agreed to come. Then I called Ninoy in Boston and told him Sonny and I would be there late in the morning. I asked Ninoy for more details about his meeting with Imelda and informed him that I had come up with a plan I thought he'd like. I did reiterate, however, that in the end, I would abide by his decision.

I took my pad and was about to start drafting my letter. My thoughts drifted for a second to Sonny Alvarez. 'There's another man,' I thought, 'who gives me hope about the Philippines.' With people like Sonny, Charlie, Eddie Olaguer, the "Grand Old Man" Tanada, and many others like them whose faces flashed through my mind, it's cruel for anyone to feel that the Filipino people are not worthy of freedom.

Sonny is a man in his late thirties. In his younger days he was a student activist and flirted with the extreme left. The communist reforms attracted his idealist heart, but the evils of the totalitarian system had not clearly registered in his innocent mind. He matured quickly and came to realize that social justice for the poor masses can be attained without sacrificing the dignity and freedom of the human spirit and soul. He now sympathizes with the sincere aspirations of his former communist colleagues for the emancipation of the poor, but there is no question in his mind that the answer to his country's future is an honest, free, democratic form of government.

Sonny and Senator Raul Manglapus were the first two outspoken critics of the martial law regime. By chance Raul found himself in the United States after Marcos declared martial law. He had been in Tokyo and was on the way to California for a speaking engagement. Marcos' soldiers went to Raul's house in Manila to arrest him along with the thousands of others, but, of course, they found him gone.

Sonny Alvarez was informed of the massive wave of arrests before the soldiers got to him. He went into hiding and was able to sneak safely out of the country.

As early as 1973, when many people applauded the imposition of martial law, Raul and Sonny had already started to expose its evils and the evils of the man who imposed it solely for the purpose of perpetuating his power. Sonny's parents and brother in the Philippines had been warned by General Fabian Ver's dreaded secret agents that if Sonny didn't stop his anti-Marcos activities abroad, "he would be sorry."

Sonny did not stop, and General Ver's men were right. Sonny *was* sorry. On June 26, 1974, the military picked up Sonny's brother, Marsman Alvarez, at his house. The following day his mutilated body was found in the town square. Marsman's eyes had been gouged out; his nose, ears, and tongue had been cut off; most of his teeth were missing; his head was bashed, and many of his bones were broken. A few weeks later Sonny's father died of a "heart attack." But friends knew it was from a "broken heart."

Yes! Ver's men were right. Sonny was sorry. But Marcos was wrong. Sonny did not waver from his chosen course.

These were some of the thoughts flashing through my mind as I started to draft my letter to Imelda:

San Francisco, California
December 17, 1980

Mrs. Imelda Marcos
Waldorf Astoria Towers
New York City

Mrs. Marcos:

Senator Aquino called me on the evening of December 15 to inform me that you had agreed to meet with him at your Waldorf suite at 5 p.m. the following day and that you were also inviting me to participate in the meeting. I asked the Sentator if he knew the reason for your invitation to me. I explained that I would consider meeting with you if such a meeting would cover a mutually agreed-upon agenda.

As you know, my wife's and my views on the martial law regime in the Philippines and its leaders are public knowledge. Equally of public knowledge are your views about my wife and me. The attached piece published yesterday in the *San Francisco Examiner* accurately summarizes the status of our past and present relationship.

Under the circumstances we feel that a meeting without any pre-arranged agenda could be counterproductive. Therefore, we respectfully requested Senator Aquino to convey to you my willingness to accept your invitation, provided the specific substantive points of discussion are known in advance.

Yesterday at about six in the evening, San Francisco time, Senator Aquino called me from your suite after meeting with you for approximately four hours. He reiterated very emphatically your wish to see me together with my wife. He conveyed your suggestion to meet at your hotel suite on Friday, December 19, at 2 p.m. Again I inquired on the proposed agenda, but it became clear that Senator Aquino felt restrained to discuss the matter further while in your hotel room. I therefore expressed to him our willingness to meet with you, subject to further clarifications by the Senator.

Later that evening, we contacted Senator Aquino who explained to us that, from what he could gather from the discussions during your meeting, there were two important matters you wished to discuss with us, namely:

1. You and my wife were good friends for many years, and you knew of nothing that had transpired to damage this friendship. Consequently, you were surprised at our activities during the past five to six years and wished to know "why we hated you and why we were committed to your destruction."

2. You alleged to know that Senator Aquino and/or I had sent "assassination squads" to the Philippines to murder some of your people and that, if any of your people were killed, you would have to respond with similar actions against us.

Your two points are quite specific and clear. Presy and I have decided that it is best to answer those two points in writing with equal specificity and clarity and without a personal meeting.

1. It is quite true that in the 1960s my wife considered you a very good friend and also looked upon Mr. Marcos with great admiration, not only for his competence and intelligence, but mostly for his proclaimed idealistic vision for the future of the Philippines. As you know, in 1964, my wife worked very hard with you for the election of Mr. Marcos.

   Soon after your husband was elected President, it became quite clear to my wife that she had misjudged you both. You used her genuine "friendship" to extract economic and political favors from her family. The "competence and intelligence" of Mr. Marcos were being used very effectively to satisfy his and your greed for power and wealth.

   As these disturbing facts became clearer with the passage of time, my wife gradually withdrew from your company and blamed no one except herself for her error in judgment. She felt that, unfortunately, most Filipinos were deceived by your charm and by your husband's intelligence, resulting in his election to the Presidency. However, my wife found consolation in the belief that the democratic process stipulated in the Philippine Constitution would rectify her and her people's error by the end of 1973 when your husband's maximum legitimate term of office would have expired.

As the world now knows, a small group of conspirators headed by your husband, decided to usurp power by subverting the Constitution. A Palace coup was organized and, on September 21, 1972, the corrupt and oppressive "Conjugal Dictatorship" was established. Since then, the injustices committed, not against my wife or her family, but against the Filipino people are blatant and well known.

The foregoing is our response to your question of what "transpired to damage this friendship." As to the second part of your question, neither my wife not I feel any hatred toward you, nor are we committed to your destruction. Perhaps, it is very difficult for you and Mr. Marcos to accept that our differences with you are on matters of fundamental principles, not on personal considerations.

My wife and I are strong believers in truth, freedom, justice, and human rights. We are committed to assisting in promoting the truth and restoring freedom, justice, and human rights to the Filipino people whom we also love.

2. We know, as we believe you know, that we have not sent assassination squads to the Philippines to murder any of your people. On the other hand, your statement that you are prepared to retaliate against us is clear, although not new. Your emissaries and those of your husband, including your brother Kokoy, have made such threats several times in the past. Your record indicates that you are quite capable of carrying out your threats. Many Filipinos and at least one American, Mr. Ben Lim, have died at the hands of your henchmen. We are obviously concerned about your threats but we have managed to resist the sort of fear that you have so effectively utilized on others to dehumanize them and force them to trade dignity for a safe existence.

We were told by Senator Aquino that he cautioned you against asking me such questions because he felt that my replies would be very candid and undiplomatic. I believe he was correct on both counts.

We were also told by the Senator that you asked his own opinoin as to what he thought "we wanted in order to stop our unfair and vicious campaign against you and your husband." Presy and I expected this.

This question suggests that we would be willing to bargain for a "deal" for our personal benefit! If this is the question's intent, the answer is simply: *No deal.*

What do we really want?

As Senator Aquino has so eloquently expressed in his recent speeches, we want a sincere "agreement in principle" by Mr. Marcos to implement the following:

a) Lift martial law.
b) Release all political prisoners.

c) Hold free and honest elections.
d) Address the Moslem grievances and end the senseless killings in the South.

If we saw any concrete signs toward the sincere implementation of these four reasonable steps, you and your husband would hear nothing from us but praise. Unfortunately, your recent moves toward lifting martial law and holding elections, again, are clearly what Filipinos call "lutong Macoy." These are endless manipulations and deceptions, all intended to indefinitely extend your absolute power at the expense of the Filipino people. Unless you show good faith in giving back the inalienable rights of the Filipino people who are now striving to regain them, we will continue on our present course, undaunted.

In closing, Mrs. Marcos, we wish to assure you that we denounce the use of violence, and we abhor terrorism. These are the methods used by the present martial law regime in the Philippines and the main reason for which we condemn it.

We hope you do not mind our candor. Senator Aquino cautioned you about our directness, but you stated that you know us quite well and were prepared to receive our views as honestly as we cared to express them.

We wish to reiterate our willingness to meet with you, at your convenience, if, notwithstanding the foregoing, you still feel that such a meeting would help promote the human rights of the Filipino people—the fundamental issue that vastly divides us.

Sincerely,

Steve E. Psinakis

The article attached to the letter was published the day before, December 16, in the *San Francisco Examiner.* It read:

S.F. EXAMINER Tuesday, December 16, 1980

Terrorism in the Philippines

EDITOR'S NOTE: Steve Psinakis, a San Francisco businessman, is a son-in-law of the late Filipino industrial tycoon Eugenio Lopez, Sr., a political foe of President Ferdinand Marcos.

By Steve Psinakis

During the past few months, the front pages of all controlled newspapers in the Philippines (including radio and TV stations) have been featuring "news stories" on the so-called "terrorists" responsible for a series of bombings in Manila which started last August.

President Marcos himself has repeatedly appeared on nationwide TV, sometimes side-by-side with allegedly "confessed terrorists," pointing the finger at an ever increasing number of people who, according to Marcos, are "terrorists."

Several news stories on this subject have appeared in the major newspapers in the United States. The Marcos list, which has now come to be known as the "honor list," includes respected personalities like Sen. Jovito Salonga, a known advocate of peace and himself a victim of an as yet unsolved terrorist bombing which, many believe, was the handiwork of Marcos' own group of terrorists.

It includes Jesuit priests like Fr. Romeo Integan and Fr. Antonio Olaguer.

It includes several Filipinos and Americans residing in the U.S. who admit being guilty of what Marcos considers a "crime"—criticizing the martial law regime for its oppression, corruption and gross violations of human rights.

It includes the son and granddaughter of the most prominent Filipino elder statesman, Sen. Lorenzo Tanada.

It includes Sen. Raul Manglapus who, since the imposition of martial law in 1972, has been working relentlessly for the peaceful restoration of civil, political and human rights to his people.

Finally it includes Marcos' arch-political rival, the man Marcos vengefully kept in solitary confinement for eight years, Sen. Benigno Aquino. Aquino, after his providential arrival in the U.S. last May, pleaded with Marcos to dismantle his martial law regime peacefully and warned that, if he did not, violence would break out. Similar warnings have been given by many others including the head of the Catholic Church, Jaime Cardinal Sin.

The "honor list" also includes me. This is the nth time Marcos has accused me of some sort of crime ranging from plots to assassinate him, kidnap his daughter Imee, murder his son Bong-Bong, supply arms and explosives to his opponents, etc. It all started in late 1974 when my wife and I stood up for the cause of the oppressed Filipino people. Since then, we have been privileged to be placed near the top of Marcos' 'most wanted' list.

Why should we deserve such an honor? Simply because we have been relatively successful in documenting and presenting to the U.S. Congress and the international press several cases of Marcos' criminal activities, not only in the Philippines, but also in the United States.

In December of 1974 and January of 1975, my wife and I were instrumental in documenting and publicizing the theft of the Lopez properties by the Marcos-Romualdez families through sheer extortion and terrorism. This was the first well documented case of the Marcoses' corruption; its publicity in the U.S. press caused Marcos great embarrassment.

In June and July of 1975, we were instrumental in documenting and publicizing Marcos attempt to bribe Primitivo Mijares in order to dissuade him from testifying against the Marcos regime before a U.S. congressional committee. The bribe did not work and Mijares did testify. A few months later, Mijares disappeared and is believed to have been murdered by Marcos' agents. The Mijares incident received extensive publicity, not only in the U.S. but throughout the world.

In July of 1975, furious with the success of our exposés, Marcos released to the press a voluminous report accusing my wife and I of hideous crimes, such as plotting to assassinate him and to kidnap his daughter Imee. His aim was clear: to vilify us and damage our credibility.

The Marcos strategy failed. We responded to these malicious fabricated accusations by filing a libel suit against Marcos in the U.S. federal court. Instead of attempting to substantiate the false accusations before the U.S. courts, Marcos retreated and hid behind his official status. He applied for "diplomatic immunity" and, with Henry Kissinger's favorable recommendation, the federal court granted Marcos diplomatic immunity.

In September 1975, we were instrumental in documenting the theft of MFP (Movement for Free Philippines) documents by Marcos' agents during the MFP Convention in Los Angeles.

In April 1977, we participated in the preparation of the legal defense of Napoleon Lechoco, Sr. Lechoco was being tried in Washington, D.C. as a "terrorist" for having held the Philippine ambassador to the United States hostage at gunpoint demanding that Marcos allow Lechoco's teenage son to leave the Philippines. The senior Lechoco had been a vitriolic critic of the Marcos regime and Marcos was, in effect, holding Lechoco's son "hostage" in Manila, hoping to force the senior Lechoco to end his criticism. When the jury in Washington heard the methods used by Marcos to silence his critics, it acquitted Lechoco, thus confirming that Marcos was the terrorist rather than the other way around.

In September 1977, we were instrumental in engineering the successful escape of two more of Marcos' personal hostages, Eugenio Lopez, Jr., and Sergio Osmena, III. Lopez and Osmena had been held in prison by Marcos for five years.

In the spring of 1978, with Lopez, Jr., now free in the United States, we were instrumental in convincing the Lopez family to consider filing a suit in the U.S. courts against the Marcos-Romualdez families. U.S. lawyers were hired to study the available evidence. A thorough and costly investigation convinced the U.S. lawyers that a case for extortion filed in the U.S. federal court against the Marcos clan could indeed prosper. When information on the preparation for filing the suit reached Malacanang, Marcos looked for a way to stop it. He ordered his frontment to immediately start payments to the Lopez family in order to give some degree of legitimacy to the "extorted contracts." Since then, Marcos painfully watched the Lopez family receive some 30 million pesos. The suit was not filed and to date the Lopez family continues to receive the semi-annual "contractual" payments.

Meantime, during these past six years, Marcos has attempted to neutralize us with all the means available to dictators like Marcos, i.e., intimidation and harassment; extortion; bribe; and finally threats on our lives. The most recent vulgar threat by the Marcoses took place only last month, when the mother and brother of my wife (Mrs. Pacita Lopez and Manual Lopez) were brought to Malacanang Palace in Manila and told by no less than Imelda Marcos herself that I, among others, was planning to murder her son Bong-Bong, and that "two can play the same game."

Having failed to neutralize us through all his unscrupulous schemes it is no surprise that Marcos is again trying so desperately to discredit us by picturing us as "terrorists." But the facts are clear and the truth is known. The criminal and terrorist is unquestionably Marcos.

It is this confirmed notorious terrorist who now points his finger at others and asks the U.S. government "to assist in extraditing to the Philippines" innocent people to be tried and convicted by Marcos' kangaroo military tribunals.

It would indeed be a dark day in the history of American justice if the U.S. authorities were to act on "evidence" fabricated by a confirmed notorious terrorist and criminal like Ferdinand Marcos and/or "evidence" contained in "confessions" obtained through extortion and torture.

Any action by the U.S. government against Marcos' critics and opponents in the U.S. would only serve the unscrupulous political goals of the corrupt and oppressive "Conjugal Dictatorship" of Ferdinand and Imelda Marcos.

When Charlie returned to the house around 10:30 a.m. the following day, I offered him some coffee and invited him into the study to look over my letter. As usual, Charlie went directly to the bathroom, proceeded to the kitchen to make himself a cup of instant coffee, and then sat down to talk. This routine has become almost a ritual with Charlie.

I gave him the four-page letter, and he read it without comment or interruption. He handed it back to me, and with a mischievous smile, uttered his favorite word, "Approved."

"Okay then, buddy," I said. "We'll see what Ninoy has to say."

Early in the afternoon, I called Alex Esclamado and told him I had taken his advice and had written Imelda a letter in lieu of keeping the appointment. Alex was thrilled. I asked him to come over and give me his views on my draft letter.

"I'll be there in five minutes," he said with excitement.

Alex liked the letter. He read it a second time and made some changes. Then Presy typed the final draft, and I was ready for my trip to the East Coast.

I thought of calling Raul Manglapus in Washington, D.C., to ask his advice on my plans, but I changed my mind. I decided it would be better if the two top Filipino opposition leaders here in the United States (Raul and Ninoy) discussed the matter together. I didn't want to take the chance of confusing the issue by dealing with each one individually. Besides, the initiative for the meeting with Imelda came from Ninoy.

I also knew that Raul was against any private meetings with Imelda—a view generally shared by both Presy and me. Raul had had opportunities to meet with Imelda during the past five years, but had refused to do so under the conditions dictated by her. She had sent feelers insisting that their meeting would be kept secret and private. Raul had rejected the stipulation of secrecy. "If Imelda wants to talk to me," Raul had said, "I will see her only under open conditions where the meeting cannot be twisted by her controlled media."

Raul Manglapus—a former Senator and former Foreign Minister—has been by far the most consistent and most effective opposition leader operating outside of the Philippines. As early as 1973, Raul organized the Movement for a Free Philippines (MFP), an organization dedicated to the peaceful restoration of democracy in his country. From a small organization of a few courageous Filipinos, the MFP grew into a prestigious international organization with chapters in many U.S. cities as well as in several foreign countries. The prestige and growth of the MFP is due primarily to the relentless effort of Senator Manglapus.

The impact of the MFP on congressional leaders in Washington and on the American press has been significant. The MFP has had a primary role in alerting the U.S. Congress to the violation of human rights by the Marcos regime. The MFP also urged the U.S. Department of State to pressure Marcos for meaningful reforms toward normalization. Furthermore, it was Raul Manglapus and the MFP who fed U.S. newsmen with factual, documented information on the repressive measures of the martial law regime and the corruption of the Marcos-Romualdez families.

Sadly, the hard work and successes of Raul and his widespread organization have not been given due recognition by the Filipino people because of a news blackout imposed by the controlled media in the Philippines. Sonny Alvarez, Secretary General of the MFP, has also been one of its main supporters since its organization in 1973.

Presy and I joined the MFP in 1974. During the past six years, I have worked very closely with Raul and developed a great respect for his idealism, consistency, and honesty, and for his dedication to his people and country. I have always consulted with him and asked his advice on all important decisions. In regard to the meeting with Imelda, however, I thought it more appropriate for the two prominent leaders to discuss it between themselves.

CHAPTER 5

The Death Warrant

I landed at Kennedy Airport at 5:30 a.m., December 18, a half hour ahead of schedule. The airport was a mess. Holiday travelers were stepping all over each other. It took an hour and a half to find my suitcase among the piles stacked up on the carousels.

Manoling Maravilla, the loyal, hard-working, New York chapter chairman of the MFP, was waiting for me.

"Welcome to New York," Manoling greeted me. "Sonny didn't come because he was up half the night; he asked me to pick you up. We'll drive into the city, pick him up and then go out to La Guardia to get the shuttle for Boston. Anyway, the first shuttle does not leave until 8 o'clock."

"Fine," I answered. "Thanks for picking me up again at this ungodly hour." Manoling had picked me up at the same time only a few days earlier.

Sonny and I got to Boston's Logan Airport at 10 a.m. and walked into Ninoy's office at the Harvard Center for International Affairs at 10:30 a.m. Ninoy looked odd with a cast on his left leg all the way up to his hip. The previous week he had had a freak accident. When he stepped out of a van into a shallow hole, he had felt a sharp pain. He later learned he had torn his Achilles' heel tendon and had to undergo surgery. The doctor decided to give him a full cast up to his hip.

"Well, that cast ought to keep you at home and out of mischief for a while," I said. We all laughed, and then Ninoy suggested we get down to work.

"I have a plan I'd like to try on you. The idea is to deliver this letter to Imelda instead of showing up for the appointment," I said as I handed Ninoy my letter. He read it carefully. His reaction was hard to gauge from his face. He raised up his head and said in a tone that revealed concern, "Well, if you send this letter to Imelda, you'll probably be signing your own death warrant."

Sonny and I were taken aback. We didn't expect this kind of reaction. We thought Ninoy would like the plan, although we expected he would suggest some modifications. Sonny kept quiet.

"Well, what do you suggest, Ninoy?"

"As I see it, we have three options. Number one: You just go to the appointment. Number two: You snub her and don't show up. Number three: You send your letter. But I don't like the last one. We don't want to lose you, Greek. Not yet, anyway . . ." he said, trying to break the tension.

"In that case, we'll have to go back to the drawing board," I said. "I didn't expect your reaction. We have to rethink all our options. One thing I must tell you honestly. If you want me just to show up for the appointment, I'll do it; I told you I will abide by your decision, but I think you should be more afraid of that option than of my letter. Without my letter preceding the meeting, she'll probably have the wrong idea about why I agreed to see her, and I'll be forced to tell her face-to-face what I was explaining in the letter. This may be harder for Imelda to take and much more dangerous for all of us. At least with the letter, she'll have the option of tearing it up in a rage and throwing it in the fireplace. I'd hate to have her goons do that to me instead of to my letter," I said, laughing.

We discussed the pros and cons of Ninoy's three options without reaching any conclusion. I tried to emphasize what I thought were the merits of sending my letter, hoping to convince Ninoy to change his mind.

"I don't know," said Ninoy, "it's pretty hard to take something like this right in the face. I'm afraid it may slam all doors shut, not just for you, but for all of us. Don't ever forget our objective," Ninoy said emphatically. "We're not here to teach Imelda a lesson or get even. We're here to give the peaceful process one more chance. We want our country back in one piece, not torn up by revolution with half a million Filipinos dead. Besides, I am really concerned for you, Steve. You don't realize what can happen. Someone might kill you, if not right away, when the time is right. I lost one good friend this week. Look at poor Joe Lingad."

Joe Lingad was indeed a good old friend of Senator Aquino. Two days earlier the press had reported, "Joe Lingad, an outspoken leader of the opposition to the Marcos regime was shot dead at close range by an unidentified gunman. Lingad sustained two gunshot wounds from point blank range—one near the left eye and another in the chest. He died on the spot."

There was silence in the room for a few seconds. "I have no evidence proving that Marcos or Imelda ordered Joe killed, but, believe me, it can happen." Ninoy sensed our depressing thoughts. "Let's not get too morbid. It's time for lunch. I'll show you guys our cafeteria." We helped Ninoy get up on his crutches, and he struggled clumsily to the cafeteria in Harvard's Coolidge Hall.

As we made our way to the cafeteria, everyone greeted Ninoy

with friendship and respect. There was no question that this "fellow"–and that's what Ninoy is at Harvard, a "fellow"–is popular and quite a celebrity. It's not every day that Harvard can boast that one of its "fellows" is a notorious "terrorist," at least as far as the Marcos newspapers are concerned. After lunch, Ninoy's daughter picked us up and drove us to his house.

The afternoon was hectic. Ninoy had to rush off a report to his colleagues at home on his meeting with Imelda. There was danger that Imelda would leak some news about her meeting with Ninoy that could cause confusion and consternation among the opposition leaders at home. What the Marcos press writes, and what the truth really is, are unrelated. It was therefore important for Ninoy to transmit a factual report about his meeting to his friends in Manila, and to do it as soon as possible. Fortunately, a trusted friend was flying straight to Manila the next morning and would hand-carry Ninoy's report to the right people within minutes after his arrival. That was a relief to me.

Ninoy pulled up his typewriter and with his two fingers, reporter-style, started to bang away. His report, he had decided, would be in the form of a letter to Marcos summarizing the key points of his discussion with Imelda and offering his comments and recommendations. At the same time, he would also write a memo to his colleagues, informing them of his meeting with Imelda and again offering his recommendations–although this time the recommendations would be made directly to his friends. He would then send copies of both the letter to Marcos and the memo to both parties. 'Very clever,' I thought to myself, 'sort of killing two birds with one stone.'

I watched him type without hesitation, and I had to admire his talent. Here he was, writing an important document to the "President" of the Philippines and to the opposition leaders, and he needed less time to think about what he was writing than I would need to write a Christmas card to my folks. I first became aware of Ninoy's talent in August of 1980. Ninoy had decided to break his three-month silence and deliver his first political speech since his arrival in the United States.

August 3 was a Sunday, and Ninoy's small New York apartment was like Grand Central Station. I couldn't help feeling sorry for his wife, Cory, and for his children. Besides having lost their peace and privacy, they could hardly keep up with serving coffee, snacks, lunch, and dinner to all kinds of welcome, but unexpected, guests.

In this atmosphere, Ninoy was writing one of the most important speeches he would ever deliver. I knew that, on Monday, he would be busy with important appointments right up until the time of his speech before the New York Asia House. Consequently, his speech had to be drafted, discussed with some of his friends, and finalized before he went to bed Sunday night.

It was already late afternoon, and he hadn't even gotten close to his typewriter. I was really getting concerned, until I realized that, being an experienced politician, Ninoy knew what he was doing. I was just curious to see how he did it. Throughout the day, Ninoy exchanged views on his forthcoming speech with several of his guests, including Sonny and me. I knew Ninoy valued Sonny's judgment, as he should; I didn't know how he felt about mine.

The last guest left at 8 p.m., and I thought Ninoy could not possibly prepare a written speech that night. I assumed he would just jot down a few notes and speak extemporaneously. I was disappointed because I was anxious to learn how he would handle his first speech. Many of us believed that this was a crucial turning point in the struggle for the return to democracy in the Philippines.

"Why don't you go next door and get some rest," Ninoy urged me, "and I'll call you in a couple of hours to look over my speech and give me some of your views." I wanted to answer,

"You must be kidding! You'll never finish any kind of speech in two hours, least of all write one that can be read for comments. You'll be lucky to get some organized notes down on paper," but I didn't say anything. I had only met Ninoy three months earlier. I didn't feel I had the right to get cute or fresh. I only said "Okay" and walked next door to my sister's apartment.

It was exactly 9:48 p.m. when the phone rang. "Come on over. The speech is ready." I didn't say anything. I remember just laughing. "Come on over, you Greek," Ninoy said as he hung up. I walked back to his apartment wondering what he really wanted. I was certain he wasn't calling because the speech was ready. However, the speech *was* ready. I read it and shook my head in disbelief. No changes were needed, nor were any suggested by those who read it before it was delivered the following day. "It's good, Ninoy," I commented at the time, concealing my amazement.

Ninoy was now typing quickly his December 18th letter to Marcos, much the same as he must have typed his August 4 speech. As he finished typing each page of his letter, he passed it on to Sonny and me. The finished letter was four pages long and read:

December 18, 1980

President Ferdinand E. Marcos
Malacanang

Dear Mr. President:

I would like to reiterate what I told the First Lady during our meeting at her Waldorf Towers suite last Tuesday evening, December 16, 1980.

1. I shall return to the Philippines sometime after June 30, 1981 at the end of my present fellowship at the Center of International Affairs of Harvard University. You will recall I accepted the fellowship only

after the international press reported that my "stay in America has been extended indefinitely." I was given the same message by General Ver when he contacted me in Dallas, Texas last May.

2. I shall consider myself freed from my political contract with our people who elected me to the Senate the day martial rule is dismantled and the full freedoms of our people restored. Till then, I shall continue to contribute my efforts in hastening the end of martial rule and the speedy restoration of our normal political process.

I am presently working on a manuscript I started in prison, which is a conceptual model for a transition government from dictatorship to democracy. The work attempts to answer the many nagging questions being asked: how can the military be returned to the barracks after tasting political power; what would be the macro and micro economic strategies; what form of government; what to do with ethnic minority problems; how to keep the electoral process tolerably cheap to prevent corruption in high office, etc. I expect to submit my draft not later than March 15 and the final draft not later than May 15, 1981.

The First Lady informed me during our conversations that you intend to lift martial law soon. This is the best news I have heard in years. I hope this time, it will be for real and there won't be any great letdowns. For example, if you lift martial law in name only, and substitute in its place emergency measures which would in effect keep all the martial law restraints in place, then it would be the same mad dog with a different collar.

I pray that when you start dismantling martial rule you will go all the way unmindful of the advice of some of your so-called friends who by their greed have done you a great disservice. There will be many who have been fattened by presidential patronage who will raise the voice of prudence and will caution you to go very slowly in restoring the freedoms of our people. These advisors have the most to lose and therefore their advice must be weighed against their motives.

Last November 20, 1980, I was given the honor of delivering the Eleanor Roosevelt Memorial Lecture at Brandeis University. At the end of my lecture I said:

The best thing that can happen to the Filipino people is for Mr. Marcos to return the freedoms he suspended in 1972.

Free press, free elections, free assembly, right of labor to strike, right of students to form their own student governments and publish their journals, the right of civilians to be tried by civilian courts and the privilege of the writ of Habeas Corpus among others.

Once these freedoms are restored, peace would not be far behind.

If Mr. Marcos agrees to return our freedoms, I for one, would use all my moral influence to convince our fellow oppositionists who are inclined to the use of force to give peaceful negotiations a chance.

More specifically, I shall immediately contact all anti-Marcos elements in the United States to agree to a truce and to designate and send representatives to Manila and join the bulk of the opposition leaders in the Philippines in a national dialogue for peace.

I shall then immediately return home—should my presence be needed—by way of the Middle East, so I can contact the leaders of the Muslim secessionist movements in Libya and Saudi Arabia and try to convince them to join the Manila peace talks.

I have time and again said: I am not interested in any GOVERNMENT POSITION during or after martial rule. I believe, my contract with the Filipino people who sent me to the Senate ends once our freedoms are restored.

If I have continued this lonely struggle when I had the chance to enjoy my new-found freedom in peace and quiet, it is because I believe the foundation of democracy is the sense of spiritual independence which nerves the individual to stand against the powers of the world.

I stand by these words.

This morning I received a long distance call from former Congressman

Raschid Lucman and his wife Tarhata, the former governor of Lanao del Sur who are both presently residing in Riyadh, Saudi Arabia. They told me they will visit with me here in Boston before the end of the year to discuss common strategy in the anti-martial rule struggle.

In a letter to former Congressman Pendatun, dated October 26, 1980, Raschid disauthorized him "from involving me in your dealings with President Marcos." (I am enclosing a photo-copy of the letter which is self-explanatory.) My point: I am afraid you are collecting Muslim DEALERS and not the true LEADERS.

I gathered from my conversations with the First Lady that 14 out of the 15 founding leaders of the Moro National Liberation Front have already joined up with the government and that Nur Misuari is the last hold out. That the situation in the southern Philippines is now very much under control and the government can live with the "banditry" of Nur's MNLF holdouts.

Mr. President, I met and talked with Nur Misuari. He is not only an able leader, he impressed me as a sincere and a dedicated Muslim, one who can never be bought with favors nor money. You may have won over the 14 out of the 15 founding leaders of the MNLF, but Nur like the fabled Sir Galahad "has the strength of ten because his heart is pure." In the current struggle it is not quantity but the quality of men that counts.

By now, Mr. President, you are fully aware of my plans and my intentions which I never kept secret. I have spoken out very openly and candidly fully aware of the consequences of my acts.

I have endured almost eight years of solitary confinement for my convictions and to prove to you my good faith, I shall return and suffer more years of imprisonment rather than compromise my stand against martial rule and the suspension of the freedoms of our people. While I do not expect you to love me for my obstinacy, at least, I think I deserve your respect for my consistency.

Attached is a memo I have written to the leaders of the opposition urging them to dialogue with you because I dread the consequences of a protracted struggle. Violence has inevitably been resorted to by desperate men and a sincere dialogue should hold back reasonable men from desperation.

It is true, you have an efficient police apparatus. But you have been a guerrilla in your own youth and you know that the might of the Japanese Imperial Army could not crush the dedication of a handful of idealistic men and women. The Philippines we both love has not changed since then. There will always be dedicated men and women imbued with idealism who would not hesitate to give up their lives for justice and freedom.

You were a guerrilla leader in your youth and you know from hard experience that to destabilize a regime, you do not need an army of thousands but only a handful of dedicated fighters. You do not need an army of operatives to create an unhealthy climate for tourists in our metropolis. All you need is a handful of dedicated freedom fighters with a good propaganda arm to dry up the tourist flow.

Mr. President, it is within your power to decide the fate of our people. You have been in office for well over fourteen years and you have had your days of glory. Martial rule may have been justified during the first six months, but surely, there is no reason for martial rule to be maintained for more than eight years. A few hours of general anesthesia is imperative during a major surgery, but to put a patient under anesthesia for months and years on end would be folly.

I have stopped questioning your motives. I shall leave to the Muse of History to render the verdict for all our acts. I now only question the duration of martial law and the continued suspension of the basic freedoms of our people.

I agree with you, our nation is in crisis. We can overcome this crisis only if we are united and even if we are united, it would require the herculean efforts of all our people who must willingly accept hard sacrifices. Divided we can only fall.

In my speeches in the various universities here in America, I have catalogued not only the grave failings of martial rule but its achievements.

And I always ended my lectures with the observation that the present crisis presents you with both an opportunity and a danger. You can either end your public service in a BLAZE OF GLORY or in a BLAZE. It would indeed be a great human tragedy should you miss the right turn at the fork and your rendezvous with history.

Mr. President: We are fraternity brothers and I have always looked up to you as my elder. I gave the First Lady a copy of the Boston Magazine where an article written by Arnold Zeitlin—who has had a distinguished journalistic career in our country—appeared. Please read it because Arnold is one of the few writers who have really articulated what I sincerely feel. Please believe me when I said, it would be my greatest pleasure to share a room with you here at the Center for International Affairs and enjoy the books of Widener Library. Maybe here at the Center away from the pressure of day to day administration and ghost writers you can craft the real political guidebook for the Filipino people with your unmatched experiences.

Please accept my advance Christmas greetings, I am

Fraternally yours,

BENIGNO S. AQUINO, JR.

Ninoy took a short break from his typing and asked Sonny's and my opinion on his letter. We both thought it was good and told him so.

"The problem, I think, is how to explain accurately the substance of your meeting to your colleagues," I interjected. "Marcos has no problem because he'll have Imelda to explain the details of your discussion. But our friends, who are obviously very suspicious of Imelda's motives, will have no one to explain the details to them. It's very tough to put everything down on paper."

"We have no other choice right now," Ninoy said. "If any serious problem develops, we can always ask someone to come here for clarifications."

After talking for a while about the important points that should be conveyed to the opposition leaders in the Philippines, Ninoy returned to his two-finger typing. In a few minutes, he had finished his memo to Tanada et al. The memo read:

MEMO TO: Senators Tanada, Rodrigo, Salonga, Roxas, Kalaw, Laurel, Mitra and Diokno.

RE: Conversations of BSA, Jr. with Mrs. Imelda R. Marcos at her Waldorf Towers suite between 1700 hours and 2130 hrs., Tuesday, December 16, 1980.

1. Two weeks ago, when I learned that Mrs. Marcos was coming to America, I sought the good offices of Ambassador Eduardo Romualdez to request an audience with her. My purpose was to personally disabuse her mind of a reported "assassination/kidnap plot by my men" on BONG BONG.

2. Unfortunately, last December 6, 1980 on my way to address the student body of the OHIO STATE UNIVERSITY in Columbus, Ohio, I ruptured (tore) my Achilles tendon while debarking from a van. Because of previous commitments (a speaking engagement before the New York Council of Foreign Relations on December 8, 1980 and another speaking engagement at the Secretary's Forum at the U.S. State Department on December 10), I had to postpone the recommended operation to reconnect my ruptured tendon, which was finally done last Thursday afternoon—December 11—in Washington. I returned to Boston last Monday, December 15. That same evening I was contacted by former Senator Maceda who told me that the First Lady was ready to receive me at her Waldorf Towers suite at 5 p.m., Tuesday, December 16. Maceda added that Mrs. Marcos was scheduled to fly to Rabat, Morocco, on Wednesday, December 17.

3. I was promptly received at 5:05 p.m. accompanied by Senator Maceda and Dr. Rolando Solis, my personal cardiologist who flew in from Texas to check my post-operative condition. With a cast up to my left thigh and in crutches, I called on Mrs. Marcos.

4. The First Lady informed me that the President is planning to lift martial law soon. That the Batasan is presently studying the possibility of amending the 1973 Constitution to allow for a direct presidential election. That the newly elected President would serve the remaining three years up to 1984 when the elections are held for the regular national assembly members.

5. The First Lady assured me that the President was sincere in his call for a dialogue with the leaders of the opposition but that the opposition leaders in Manila snubbed his call. I explained to her that the President's invitation was relayed only through the press without any personal follow ups which is the usual custom. Hence, opposition leaders were reluctant to respond because they were not sure who the President intended to dialogue with. If the President really wants to meet with the leaders of the opposition, he should call them directly since he knows all of them personally. The First Lady observed that it would be embarrassing if the President were turned down even in the remote possibility. I then suggested that maybe, the President use Deputy Minister Barbero to contact the leaders of the opposition and make the preliminary contacts.

   I also suggested that maybe, it would be useful if the President could itemize or spell out the agenda. And because of the reluctance of some opposition leaders to go to Malacanang, maybe a neutral site be chosen, i.e. VILLA SAN MIGUEL, the official residence of Cardinal Sin.

6. For any presidential election to be credible, the United Opposition must be convinced to join the contest by fielding a respected and credible Opposition standard bearer. Otherwise, the entire exercise would be a costly farce. It is estimated that some P150 to P200 million would be spent for the Constitutional amendment plebiscite and for the presidential election. And if only President Marcos would run, the President would not only look funny but such an effort would be a criminal waste of precious public funds.

7. The legitimate opposition has been deprived of a forum to air its ideas and/or alternative proposals. The media has almost totally ignored the opposition views. This terrible situation could be corrected if the

President decides to meet with the Opposition leaders with full media coverage.

8. One of the common observations here and even in the Philippines is that there is no visible opposition leadership and that the political opposition is badly fragmented. This may be true before the formation of the National Covenant for Freedom. However, there is now an umbrella organization for the United Opposition which can speak for the majority of the political opposition.

RECOMMENDATIONS:

1. After consultation with opposition leaders here in America, it is recommended that the UNIDO select a panel that would meet with the President to discuss a specific agenda which should include the following points among others:
   1.1 Mechanics and timetable for the lifting of martial rule;
   1.2 Rules governing the proposed plebiscite and the subsequent Presidential elections;
   1.3 Definition of the powers of the interim President, i.e. what happens if an Opposition President gets elected and the Batasan is controlled by the KBL?;
   1.4 Possible revamp of the COMMISSION ON ELECTIONS; and
   1.5 Possible amnesty of political prisoners.
   1.6 Placing the government under the Supreme Court for the duration of the presidential campaigns; and
   1.7 Enactment of a law providing for equal time and space in the national media.

Finally, Ninoy typed a very brief letter of transmittal to Mrs. Marcos thanking her for their meeting and enclosing the letter to the "President" with a copy of his memo to Tanada et al. Sonny was to handcarry these letters to Mrs. Marcos the following day. With this done, Ninoy turned to me and said, "Now Greek! What do we do with your problem?"

"Well, I have nothing much to add to what I said this morning," I replied. "Now it's your decision."

"You really don't want to just go to your appointment and play it by ear?"

"No! Not really; but I'll do it if that's what you decide."

Ninoy did not respond directly to my comment. "And I don't want you to send that letter. That leaves us only with the third choice: no show."

"I guess so," I responded.

"Okay, then. That's it. Let's get some sleep."

When I woke up the next morning, Ninoy was again banging away at his typewriter.

"I am rushing off a private letter to our friends in Manila," he said as I entered the room, "explaining a few more details about my four and a half hour meeting with Imelda. They'll want more facts than those I supplied in the letter to Marcos and in my memo to them."

Sonny was sitting next to Ninoy sipping some coffee. Cory asked me about breakfast, but I only wanted orange juice and coffee. We sat there silently while Ninoy finished his letter to Tanada and company. For the first time since I met Ninoy, I felt uncomfortable. The atmosphere was charged. I could feel it, but I chose to keep quiet. Ninoy seemed tense.

"I couldn't sleep last night," he said finally. "I was thinking about your letter, and I agree with some of its merits. I just think it's dangerous and I'm worried, but I do see its good points. If you want to go through with it, I wouldn't want to stop you. It's up to you."

There was silence for a few seconds. All three of us felt tense. No one seemed particularly eager to resume the discussion of the previous day. We had reached a decision that was no one's favorite, but we were resigned to it. Now, Ninoy re-opened the discussion.

Sonny was the first to talk. "Suppose we go through with Steve's plan and send the letter but a bit toned down. Suppose it's just a brief letter transmitting the *Examiner* article. After all, the article speaks for itself. The letter doesn't have to restate the same things."

Sonny hit the right chord. "That's it," Ninoy jumped at the idea. "That's it. The article says it all, but it avoids the personal confrontation. It's sort of impersonal. Great idea. What do you think, Steve?"

I agreed it sounded reasonable.

"Great! That's it then," Ninoy concurred. Write a brief transmittal letter to Imelda, and I'll type it while you pack your things. We're cutting it close. It's already 9:10."

Sonny confessed, "I wasn't really happy with last night's decision. I hated to lose the opportunity of learning some more about what's really on Imelda's mind. I'll deliver Steve's letter together with yours and have Steve wait at Rufo's office in case Imelda still wants to see him."

I took some white paper and started to scribble hurriedly:

Mrs. Marcos:

Presy and I thank you for the invitation to meet with you and discuss matters of mutual concern regarding events in the Philippines.

Senator Aquino informed me of the possible subject matters you may want to take up. My wife's and my views on the subject matter to be discussed as outlined by Senator Aquino are of public record. The attached S.F. Examiner article of December 16 reflects our views. We believe that our differences are not in any way personal but rather a matter of principle. It is therefore our humble opinion that a private, personal meeting may prove of little value.

If, however, after reading my article you still would like to talk to me, I shall await your pleasure and I shall be waiting at this number: (212) 335-7275 to 76. I will hold myself available till 2 p.m. If I do not get a call by then, I shall return to San Francisco.

> Let me assure you that my activities in opposing the martial law regime have not and will not include anything which may result in any physical harm to your son.
>
> Sincerely,

I gave the sheet to Ninoy and rushed upstairs to pack my things. When I came down with my suitcase, Ninoy showed me the final letter he had typed. He had placed "Dear" in front of my "Mrs. Marcos" and had added a closing paragraph which read:

> In closing, Mrs. Marcos, we wish to assure you that we denounce the use of violence and we abhor terrorism in the struggle for freedom and human rights. We are opposed to terrorism from any source and in whatever form. My wife and I are strong believers in truth, freedom, justice and human rights. We are simply committed to assisting and promoting the truth and restoring freedom, justice and human rights to the Filipino people whom we also love.

I didn't particularly like either the "Dear" or the last paragraph but we had discussed the matter enough. Besides, there was no time for further discussion. It was now 10 a.m., and Ninoy had asked his daughter to call a cab.

CHAPTER 6

The Bad Omens

The taxi arrived at 10:15 and although we were cutting it a little close, we expected to get to the airport in time to catch the 11 a.m. shuttle for LaGuardia. The plan was for Sonny to go straight to the Waldorf Towers and hand-deliver the two letters by about 12:30. That would have given Imelda time to read my letter before the deadline of 2 o'clock. I was to get to the office of Sonny's friend by 1 o'clock and wait there for her call until 2, in case Imelda decided she still wanted to go through with the meeting.

Omen No. 1: On the way to the Boston airport, *the taxi blew a tire.* This was the first time in my life when my taxi had a flat.

Omen No. 2: We reached the airport at 11 o'clock sharp, exactly one minute after they had closed the gate. *We missed the 11 o'clock plane.*

Omen No. 3: We took the 12 o'clock shuttle which got us to La Guardia at 1:05 p.m. Sonny rushed straight to the Waldorf to deliver the letters and I stayed behind for the luggage. *My luggage was lost.*

Omen No. 4: After waiting twenty mintues for my luggage, I gave up. It was now 1:25 p.m. I grabbed a cab for New York City. I told the driver to please rush to 9 West 57th Street. "Rush?" asked the driver. "The traffic is backed up. *The cable of the bridge into Manhattan snapped.*"

Anyone who believes in "omens" or is the least bit superstitious would have taken the first plane back home to San Francisco. I did not.

When we reached 57th Street, it was exactly 2 p.m. "Forget it," I said to the driver. "Let's go straight to the Waldorf Towers Hotel." We got there at exactly 2:07 p.m. By 2:08 I was in the lobby talking to Ramon Jacinto. While Ramon was still talking to me, I picked up the phone and asked for Imelda's suite, extension 3724. A stern male voice answered "Hello."

"May I speak to Ms. Fe Jimenez?" I asked.

"Who's calling please?" queried the same stern voice.

"This is Steve Psinakis," I responded.

"Oh! Oh! Yes, sir. Just one minute, please, sir," said the voice with evident excitement. It was much less than "one minute" when an equally excited female voice said, "Mr. Psinakis, we have been trying to reach you at the number you indicated in your letter; the First Lady wants to see you in spite of your letter."

Oh hell, I thought to myself. How can she possibly still want to see me?

"I am sorry Ms. Jimenez," I said. "I had some trouble getting here from LaGuardia. I was late and came directly to the hotel instead of going to the office where I had asked you to call me. That's why you couldn't reach me there."

"Fine, fine," responded the courteous Jimenez, Imelda's girl-Friday for many years. "Would you please come up, Mr. Psinakis? The First Lady is waiting for you."

While I had been waiting for my bag at LaGuardia, Sonny had been picked up by Manoling Maravilla. They had arrived at the Waldorf Towers at 1:30 p.m. and, realizing that time was getting really short, Sonny decided to deliver only my letter at first and hold Ninoy's letter for delivery after 2 p.m.

Manoling had gone to the 37th floor and had delivered my letter to Fe Jimenez. Sonny had called Rufo's office to alert them about the possible call from Imelda. Fe had called Rufo's office and was told that I was late but on the way.

As I walked into the Towers elevator, two Filipinos in dark suits, overcoats and short hair walked in with me. Oh, no, I thought to myself.

"37th floor, please," I told the lady operator. There was no word from the two Filipinos . . . they were also going to the 37th floor, or . . . Oh, no! I thought again, if Marcos had plans to knock me off, this was not a bad time and place to do it. They could pull out a gun with a silencer, take care of the elevator operator along with me, get off at the second or third floor, walk down to the huge main lobby of Waldorf Astoria–adjacent to the small Towers lobby–and disappear into the crowd. Next day's *New York Times* would read, "Known oppositionist to Philippine President Marcos' martial law regime, Steve Psinakis, was shot dead in the Waldorf Towers elevator on his way to see Philippine's First Lady Imelda Marcos. The elevator operator was also shot dead. The unidentified gunman or gunmen fled undetected. Philippine opposition leaders are accusing the Marcos regime for the Psinakis murder. A spokesman for Mrs. Marcos issued a brief official statement expressing her 'regrets' for the murder. 'It must have been some fanatic,' Mrs. Marcos was heard telling her assistant."

As it turned out, nothing like this happened. The elevator stopped at the 37th floor, and I saw several people, Filipinos and Caucasians, crowding the hotel corridor leading to Imelda's suite.

Among the dozen or so people, I saw Sonny and I also recognized former Philippine senator, Ernesto Meceda. He was the first to greet me. "How are you, Steve? Ready for your appointment? Ah! Here is Ms. Fe Jimenez." A short petite Filipina in her forties approached. "Mr. Psinakis, thank you for coming. The First Lady will be right with you. How is Mrs. Psinakis?" Fe knew my wife quite well. When Presy helped the Marcoses during the 1964 campaign, she used to spend a great deal of time with Imelda. Fe was always around to attend to Imelda's needs. "Fine," I replied, "just fine."

In the meantime, a husky, bearded Caucasian in his early thirties approached and flashed an identification badge. "My name is so-and-so," he said, although I don't remember his name now, "and I am from the U.S. State Department. U.S. security regulations require that we search all visitors. Would you mind terribly, sir, coming with me to our security room for a few seconds?" the man asked politely.

"I do, but you have to do it; so let's get to it." I didn't like the idea of being searched, and I would have refused to be searched by Imelda's personal security guards, but this poor fellow was just a U.S. official doing his job. I felt like asking him if he had searched Imelda. After all, it was Imelda who had threatened several times to kill me, not the other way around.

As I came out of the security room, Fe Jimenez guided me toward the suite, and, on the way, she also asked Ramon Jacinto, who was waiting in the hallway, to join her. I was a little surprised. I wondered why Ramon would be seeing Imelda at the same time I was. I have had nothing to do with Ramon and have not seen him in years, I thought to myself. He is only a businessman; I am viewed as a revolutionary. Nevertheless, we were both shown into the suite by Fe Jimenez and were told that the First Lady would be with us in a minute. We were then asked to have a seat. Jimenez then turned around and walked out.

The living room of the suite was huge and luxurious. On the left side of the main entrance there was a grand piano and an organ. On the right, where Fe Jimenez had asked us to be seated, there were three huge sofas arranged in the shape of the Greek letter π, a fireplace, a wet bar and several combinations of coffee tables and lounge chairs elegantly grouped. The suite was full of beautiful flower arrangements and the pleasing fragrance of the red roses, which were in abundance, permeated the air. I had no idea how many other rooms surrounded the living area, but I assumed at least six or seven: several bedrooms, a main dining room, servants' quarters, a complete kitchen, and who knows what else.

It occurred to me that the daily rate for the suite alone must be at least $2,000, maybe closer to $3,000. I quickly calculated that with a daily pay for the average Filipino farm hand or factory worker of less than two dollars, the rental of the suite alone was more than the daily earnings of one thousand Filipinos.

I sat in the left corner of the center sofa while Ramon sat in the middle of the sofa to my right. I was ready for the entrance of the "Empress." I felt very much at ease and was a little surprised that I did. I thought I would have, or should have been, somewhat nervous. I looked at Ramon. He, too, must have been wondering why he was there with me. My presence clearly made him nervous.

Why am I here with this notorious "terrorist?" Ramon must have been asking himself. The thought made me smile. I recalled the discussion I had with Presy the day Ninoy told me of Imelda's invitation.

"Imagine!" Presy had said angrily, "Imelda wants to lecture you on terrorism, and it is *she* and *her husband* who have institutionalized terrorism in my country. What gall!"

"Maybe she wants to tell me how I can improve my terroristic techniques," I said laughing, "after all, look at all the experience they've had."

"I don't see how you can sit there and laugh. It's not funny," Presy had answered.

"Well, maybe not but I expect to have some fun talking to her about terrorism. I wonder what she'd have to say, for instance, about Nap's acquittal after he held her uncle hostage at gunpoint in Washington."

Earlier in the day, Presy and I recalled the events that transpired in November of 1974 when Nap Lechoco took Ambassador Romualdez, Imelda's uncle, hostage at gunpoint, asking Marcos to exchange him for Lechoco's son.

Napoleon ("Nap") Lechoco is a Filipino lawyer now living in Washington, D.C. with his wife and seven children. Prior to the imposition of martial law, Nap had criticized publicly the "unprecedented corruption" of the Marcos-Romualdez families and their "small clique of bandits." Nap had become well known in the Philippines as the legal counsel of the Anti-Graft League of the Philippines.

In December, 1970, Lechoco had filed, on behalf of the League, the "White Paper on Graft," citing 25 specific cases of corruption pending before the Philippine courts. The Paper traced the blame for the corruption to Marcos. All of the accused were relatives, close friends and/or cronies of the Marcos-Romualdez families. One of those accused was Eduardo Z. Romualdez, who, ironically, was later appointed Philippine Ambassador to the United States. This was the same Romualdez whom Lechoco took hostage in 1974.

All of the Lechoco family, except for the eldest son, Napoleon, Jr., fled to the United States after the declaration of martial law. The 16 year-old boy was not able to leave. For two years the Lechocos exhausted every possible legal avenue to have their son join them in Washington. Marcos always blocked his departure.

"Why don't you put it through your head," one of Nap's

friends told him, "the only way that bastard Marcos can keep you quiet here is to hold your son hostage in Manila. He'll never let him leave the Philippines."

At 3:30 p.m. on November 18, 1974, Nap Lechoco was in the Washington office of Ambassador Romualdez. A few days earlier he had managed to arrange an appointment on the pretext of discussing an important cultural event to be held by the Filipino community in Washington, D.C. Suddenly, Nap pulled out a gun and placed it on the temple of Imelda's uncle. "You son of a bitch! For two years you have been holding my boy hostage to keep me quiet. Now, you either get him on the first flight to the States or you'll never live another day to spend the millions you have been stealing from my people."

The incident drew newspaper coverage; headlines in Washington read: "Terrorist Holding Philippine Ambassador Hostage." Other newspapers had equally inflammatory headlines.

The drama went on for ten hours. Negotiations were conducted with the special anti-terrorist squads, and by 2 a.m., November 19, Nap received assurances from the U.S. authorities that his son was aboard a flight from Manila. Nap threw his pistol from a second floor window and surrendered. The Ambassador was unharmed.

Lechoco was charged with kidnapping, and his trial was set for early 1975. His friends told him not to worry. Alex Esclamado, the publisher of the *Philippine News* and a friend of the Lechoco family, assured him by saying, "There are many of us here in the United States who are victims of Marcos' terrorist tactics. Raul Manglapus, Sonny Alvarez, Steve and Presy Psinakis, Raul Daza, and myself." When the jury hears how Marcos terrorizes the people, not only in the Philippines, but even here in the States, they'll understand that Marcos is the real terrorist, not you."

I also tried to comfort Lechoco. I told him we would all testify at his trial. Furthermore, I mentioned that, "We have lots of evidence. You know, the mutilation of Sonny's brother by Marcos' soldiers is a well-documented case. It was in all the papers just last week. The most credible man in the Philippines, Archbishop Sin of Manila, protested to Marcos about the inhuman torture and murder of Alvarez."

By coincidence, on November 23, 1974, the *Washington Post* had published a news story on the Archbishop's attack against the martial law regime. Archbishop Sin had cited the case of Sonny's brother, Marsman Alvarez, and the *Washington Post* had quoted Sin as saying that Marsman's body was "found mangled beyond recognition and bearing marks of diabolical torture."

I told Nap that Presy and I would be happy to testify on our first-hand knowledge of Marcos' terroristic tactics. "Please let me know when your lawyer wants to see us and we'll fly to D.C.," I promised.

During the next few months, Nap did not contact any of the key people who had volunteered to testify on his behalf. Thus, we were surprised when we suddenly learned that the Lechoco trial had started. We contacted Nap's wife and were told that their lawyer had convinced them not to invite us as witnesses "due to the political implications" of the case. The trial ended quickly. Lechoco was found guilty of kidnapping and terrorism. He was sentenced to 10 years in jail.

Nap later confessed, "I was very naive. I didn't believe that in this country of freedom and justice I could be railroaded into prison so the U.S. government would not embarrass a criminal like Marcos." Nap explained that his lawyer had advised him against having anti-Marcos witnesses testify at his trial. "I didn't realize then," Nap told me, "that the Department of State had gotten to my lawyer. Marcos was Kissinger's friend, and Kissinger was the Secretary of State. It has now become clear that the Department didn't want the American people to know what kind of criminal dictators their government supports."

Nap spent fifteen months in jail. He appealed his case, and the U.S. Court of Appeals ordered a retrial, ruling that, "certain witnesses had been barred from testifying on Lechoco's behalf." The retrial was set for April, 1977. This time Lechoco was ready. Senator Raul Manglapus and his wife, Pacing, former Philippine Congressman, Raul Daza, and Presy and I were all listed as Lechoco's witnesses.

During the initial stages of the trial, the prosecutor from the U.S. Attorney's office again attempted to bar testimony on the conditions in the Philippines under martial law. But this time, Lechoco's new lawyer, Stewart Stiller, was not willing to exchange justice for political expediency. He easily convinced Judge Howard Corcoran that his client's case would be prejudiced if testimony on the prevailing conditions in the Philippines was not presented. Stiller told me, "this is clearly a case where the defendant should be the accuser, not the accused. Don't be concerned. The truth will be told this time."

Indeed, the truth was told. Raul Manglapus was the first to testify. He explained to the jury the general situation in the Philippines and then cited his own family's case using impressive documentation. He told the jury how he found himself in America by coincidence on the very day Marcos declared martial law and how the soldiers had gone to his house in the Philippines to arrest him. Manglapus presented evidence on how Marcos had virtually held his family hostage in the Philippines to prevent him from speaking out against the ruthless Marcos dictatorship. He presented letters from U.S. Senators, including Ted Kennedy and Hubert Humphrey, asking Marcos to allow Raul's wife and children to leave the Philippines. He presented copies of the Marcos government's responses that denied his family permission to leave. Finally Raul explained how his wife, children, and his 8-month-old granddaughter had escaped at great risk to their lives.

Raul Daza was the next witness for Lechoco. An experienced

trial lawyer and a former Philippine Congressman, Daza gave the jury a graphic description of the conditions in his country after the declaration of martial law. His province of Samar is one of the strongholds of resistance to the Marcos regime. The atrocities committed by the military in Samar—rapes, tortures, killings, etc. —have been frequently reported in the American press.

By the time the two Rauls had ended their testimonies, tears appeared in the eyes of at least two members of the jury. The defense lawyer decided that Presy's testimony and my testimony were no longer necessary. "I knew," Stiller told me later, "that the trial was over. There was no need for more witnesses."

The jury withdrew to deliberate and in less than 45 minutes it rendered its unanimous decision. Lechoco was now a free man. As Presy and I stood chatting outside the courtroom with Nap, his wife and children, the Manglapuses, Raul Daza, and other friends, we happily celebrated our victory. I noticed one of the jurors walking in our direction and looking at our group with a sympathetic smile. I greeted her and thanked her. "We are very appreciative for your just verdict, mam. Thank you very much," I said.

"This was a very clear case, sir," the lady responded, "there is no question in our minds that President Marcos is the terrorist, not Mr. Lechoco. It is hard to believe that such things are happening today. We are ashamed that poor Mr. Lechoco had been convicted and spent fifteen months in jail. We don't understand what happened during his first trial."

"The jury was not allowed to hear evidence on the current situation in the Philippines," I explained.

"That was a crime," she commented.

"You are *absolutely* right," I agreed.

Earlier that afternoon, Presy and I were outside the courtroom waiting for our turn to testify. The Prosecutor's legal adviser from the State Department came out of the courtroom to smoke and I decided to talk to him.

"I wonder if you would be willing to answer me one question?" I asked. He agreed, so I continued:

"We are Americans. We are, or are supposed to be, the beacon of freedom and justice for the whole world. We are the hope to the oppressed people in countries such as the Philippines. Tell me, how do you feel knowing that you're trying to send an innocent man to jail by hiding the truth from the jury just to *avoid embarrassing* your friend Marcos?"

"Mr. Psinakis, you must understand that a lawyer's duty is to win his case," he responded.

"Even at the expense of truth and justice?" I asked as I turned my back and walked away without waiting for his answer.

Two years after the trial, Lechoco was able to obtain a few "confidential" government documents about his case. He had applied for release of the documents under the Freedom of Information Act. The official communications confirm the "efforts" of the State Department to "bar" any testimony on the "conditions in the Philippines."

One of the released documents is a telex from Secretary of State Cyrus Vance to the U.S. Ambassador in Manila. The telex is dated April 26, 1977 and reads in part as follows:

> WITNESSES LISTED FOR TESTIMONY BY LECHOCO'S LAWYER INCLUDE RAUL MANGLAPUS AND WIFE. STEVE PSINAKIS AND WIFE. FORMER CONGRESSMAN RAUL DAZA AND OTHER MEMBERS OF MOVEMENT FOR A FREE PHILIPPINES. WHILE *PROSECUTOR FROM U.S. ATTORNEY'S* OFFICE *WILL MAKE EFFORT HAVE TESTIMONY* ON ALLEGED *CONDITIONS IN PHILIPPINES BARRED,* HE HAS ADVISED DEPARTMENT IT MAY NOT BE POSSIBLE PREVENT AT LEAST PRELIMINARY HEARING OF TESTIMONY OUT OF JURY'S HEARING BUT IN THE PRESENCE OF PRESS. IT POSSIBLE, THEREFORE, THAT TESTIMONY OF MANGLAPUS, PSINAKIS AND OTHERS MAY BE CARRIED BY MEDIA IN NEXT FEW DAYS.
>
> (CYRUS) VANCE

Note: Complete telex appears on the following page.

GROSS MARGARET A
77 STATE 93944

LIMITED OFFICIAL USE

LIMITED OFFICIAL USE
PAGE Ø1 STATE Ø93944
ORIGIN EA-Ø9
INFO OCT-Ø1 ISO-ØØ L-Ø3 JUSE-ØØ CIAE-ØØ DODE-ØØ INR-Ø7
NSAE-ØØ PA-Ø1 USIA-Ø6 PRS-Ø1 SP-Ø2 /Ø3Ø R
DRAFTED BY EA/PHL:DPSULLIVAN:PAW
APPROVED BY EA/PHL:BAFLECK
L SFP:LFIELDS (INFO COPY)
------------------2711177 ØØ3251 /23-11
R 26221ØZ APR 77
FM SECSTATE WASHDC
TO AMEMBASSY MANILA
LIMITED OFFICIAL USE STATE Ø93944
E.O. 11652: N/A
TAGS: PFOR, RP, US
SUBJECT: LECHOCO TRIAL
REF: STATE 45275 FEB 76

1. REHEARING OF COMPETENCY PORTION OF TRIAL OF NAPOLEON LECHOCO BEGAN IN U.S. DISTRICT COURT FOR DISTRICT OF COLUMBIA APRIL 25. TRIAL IS RESULT OF APPELLATE COURT RULING IN SEPTEMBER 1976 THAT TRIAL JUDGE ERRONEOUSLY EXCLUDED TESTIMONY BEARING ON LECHOCO'S REPUTATION AND HONESTY DURING ORIGINAL COMPETENCY TRIAL.

2. WITNESSES LISTED FOR TESTIMONY BY LECHOCO'S LAWYER INCLUDE RAUL MANGLAPUS AND WIFE, STEVE PSINAKIS AND WIFE, FORMER CONGRESSMAN RAUL DAZA AND OTHER MEMBERS OF MOVE-MENT FOR A FREE PHILIPPINES. WHILE PROSECUTOR FROM U.S. ATTORNEY'S OFFICE WILL MAKE EFFORT HAVE TESTIMONY ON ALLEGED CONDITIONS IN PHILIPPINES BARRED, HE HAS ADVISED DEPARTMENT THAT IT MAY NOT BE POSSIBLE PREVENT AT LEAST PRELIMINARY HEARING OF TESTIMONY OUT OF JURY'S HEARING BUT IN PRESENCE OF PRESS. IT POSSIBLE, THEREFORE, THAT TESTIMONY OF MANGLAPUS, PSINAKIS AND OTHERS MAY BE CARRIED BY MEDIA IN NEXT FEW DAYS.

VANCE

LIMITED OFFICIAL USE

Copy of actual April 26, 1977, telex from Secretary of State Cyrus Vance to the U.S. Embassy in Manila. Document was declassified and released to Mr. Lechoco on August 21, 1978, under the Freedom of Information Act.

When I showed this telex to a reporter interviewing me, he appeared surprised and asked, "isn't this a case of an attempt to obstruct justice?"

"I am not a lawyer," I responded, " but it sure looks that way to me. However, I can show you evidence on other cases involving illegal activities of Marcos' agents in the United States that is more convincing than the Lechoco case. There is no question in my mind that Kissinger conspired to cover up Marcos' illegal activities in the Philippines and, sadly, even in the United States."

Here I was then, three years after the Lechoco retrial, in the fabulous Waldorf suite, waiting for Imelda's lecture on terrorism. 'This should be interesting,' I thought.

I was about to make some insignificant comment to Ramon when he looked to his left and abruptly stood up. I turned around and saw Imelda walking straight toward me. She was followed by a middle-aged, average size but stern-looking man. He had a military air about him, only he was dressed in a plain, grey suit.

CHAPTER 7

The Test

As Imelda approached on my left, she extended her hand and greeted me with a hesitant smile and a formal but courteous tone. "Hello, Steve, how are you? Nice to see you again."

I gave her my hand and smiled back. "Fine, thank you, Mrs. Marcos."

She greeted Ramon in the same manner and sat down in the corner of the sofa to my left, fairly close to me. The man who followed her positioned himself a few feet behind her and stood expressionless, almost at attention. He was to remain in that position for the next five and a half hours.

For a second, I studied Imelda carefully. She was wearing a simple but very elegant suit with a silk blouse and a green silk scarf around her neck. Her jewelry was equally simply and elegant: small earrings, a brooch, and ring. Her sitting position was definitely studied. She sat erect, with her hands clasped together on her lap and her legs carefully crossed.

I don't like being presumptuous, but I couldn't help thinking that her simple and elegant appearance had been arranged for my benefit. Imelda is known for her extravagance, as well as her eagerness to display her fabulous jewelry collection, which is reputed to be second to none in the world. In several of my syndicated columns, I had attacked Imelda's "vulgar display of jewelry" and had criticized the corruption in and around the palace that was the source of her astronomical wealth.

As I studied Imelda now, I said to myself, "Yes, her simple and elegant appearance is for my benefit."

Imelda is a beautiful woman. I had seen her, talked to her, sat next to her, and danced with her several times during the past 15 years but I had never really studied her face before. Individually, her features were attractive: her eyes, her nose, her cheeks, her lips, her chin, her neck. As a combination, they fell into place like a puzzle and formed a beautiful picture. For a woman in her fifties, I thought, she could really be a trophy for any man.

Her expression, as she looked straight at me, betrayed some tension but not any undue nervousness. Facing her, I found myself feeling more comfortable than I had before she entered. "Time for the test," I told myself. "The tone and direction of the meeting will be decided during the first three to four minutes."

"How is Presy, Steve?" she asked warmly.

Bingo! That was the opening question I had expected; I had prepared an answer to test Imelda and set the direction of the meeting—one way or the other. It was not hard to anticipate her question. Presy had been one of Imelda's closest friends, and, as far as Imelda was concerned, Presy was supposed to come to New York with me. Obviously, Imelda *had* to ask me how and where she was.

"Fine," I answered, "more beautiful than ever and looking ten years younger than when you last saw her."

"Where is she? Didn't Presy come with you?"

"I am afraid not, Mrs. Marcos. I believe you have been warned by Senator Aquino that I would be very candid and direct with you. This is a good way to start our discussion, *if* we'd like to have a constructive discussion," I said firmly but without anger or arrogance. "Presy does not wish to see you." As I deliberately dropped the bomb, I studied her face. The reaction was immediate; her beautiful lips thinned into a line, her cheek muscles tightened, her clasped hands squeezed each other, and she twisted uncomfortably in her seat. She managed a timid, "but why?"

"Presy felt that you would not be able to understand what she wanted to discuss with you. She felt it would be a waste of her time and yours."

The effects of the bomb were now very clear. Her reaction seemed to be more of a retreat than readiness to counter-attack. In the corner of my eye, I caught a quick glimpse of Ramon. He looked like he was praying that the sofa would swallow him and make him disappear. He made a motion to get up as he mumbled. "Mam, would you . . ."

Imelda ignored him as if he was not there. "Why would Presy feel that way? We were such close friends," she insisted.

"I think she has good reasons, Mrs. Marcos. Actually, I feel exactly the same way. I did not want to see you, either. I felt our meeting would be a waste of time. I am only here because of my respect for Senator Aquino. He asked me to see you before his meeting with you, and, he asked me again, more insistently, after he met you. That's why I am here."

By now, Ramon had had enough. The last thing he wanted to do was to get caught in the crossfire. He managed to say, "Perhaps, mam, you would prefer to be alone with Mr. Psinakis." He anticipated the reply and had already stood up. "Yes, Ramon, I will talk to you a little later."

The relief in Ramon's face was evident. He sort of tip-toed away as if he didn't want to be heard leaving. Imelda's "little later" amounted to the five-and-a-half-hour duration of our meeting, perhaps longer. In fact, I don't know if she actually saw Ramon that day.

I thought "the test" was successful. Imelda was retreating. She had no cause to retreat unless she was really afraid of the *Destabilization Plan* and believed that my role in the Plan was important.

Right or wrong, I reached the conclusion then and there that our evaluation of the situation was accurate. Ninoy, Sonny, Charlie and I were correct. The Marcoses understood the crisis and were very concerned.

For seven years since the imposition of martial law in 1972, Marcos had ruled the Philippines with an iron grip, confident in his ability to control the country and its people. The only period of insecurity occurred briefly in the first month following the imposition of martial law. This was the period of consolidating power. Marcos was not sure of the people's reaction and must have anticipated (and prepared for) greater opposition than he encountered. In fact, there was hardly any opposition. All "dangerous" political leaders–starting with Ninoy Aquino and most of the known "enemies," all the way to the young student activists and labor leaders–had been rounded up and safely tucked away in military detention centers. The "private armies" of the powerful politicians disappeared when their "patrons" were locked up in jail. The feared old man Lopez–vacationing in the United States at the time–refrained from any public or private statement challenging Marcos for his bold step. And in general, the Filipino people seemed to welcome the declaration of martial law. Nixon and Kissinger certainly welcomed it and the U.S. press treated it as "a necessary step for the restoration of peace and order," suppressing the actually non-existent but allegedly "mounting communist threat."

Indeed, the whole exercise must have seemed simple and easy to Marcos. By the time opposition began to surface, Marcos was well entrenched and in absolute control of all aspects of Philippine life.

While maintaining firm control of the situation, Marcos had to contend with three forms of opposition: 1) The Muslim war in the Southern Philippines, 2) The New People's Army (NPA)—the Maoist communist rebels scattered throughout several rural areas, particularly in the island of Samar, and 3) The few courageous moderate political opposition leaders headed by the "Grand Old Man," the widely respected Filipino statesman, Senator Lorenzo M. Tanada.

None of the three opposition groups was considered to be a serious threat to the stability of the martial law regime. On the contrary, many political observers believed that the Muslim conflict and the NPAs provided a reason, or an excuse, for the continuation of martial law.

Things went well for Marcos during the first four years of martial law. Even the economy turned upward in 1973, primarily due to an unprecedented price increase in most Philippine export commodities, sugar, copra, copper and lumber, but also due to the astronomical increase in foreign borrowing.

In 1976 and 1977 things started to change. The economy took a turn for the worse. Prices of export commodities had dropped sharply; the foreign debt, which had increased from about one to close to eight billion dollars, required more than one billion dollars of foreign exchange a year just to service its interest charges. The corruption of the Marcos-Romualdez families and their associates, combined with the mismanagement of public funds had absorbed most of the billions that had poured into the Philippine economy in 1973 to 1975, leaving few, if any, benefits for the great majority of the impoverished Filipino people. The election of Jimmy Carter and his human rights policy added a new and unexpected problem to the Marcos one-man rule.

All these problems were becoming more and more acute

throughout 1977 and 1978, but Marcos, the astute politician, was still able to manuever well enough to maintain firm control over the country.

The events surrounding the April 7, 1978, "election" jolted Marcos' confidence, and the jolt was followed by the emergence of a militant force from the ranks of the moderates. Political observers believe the events that followed in 1979 and 1980 gradually convinced Marcos that, for the first time since 1972, his regime was faced with a real threat of being overthrown.

Faced with serious problems at home, and with mounting pressure from the Carter administration and the U.S. Congress to improve his dismal human rights record, Marcos decided to stage the April 7, 1978, elections for a so-called "Interim National Assembly." To add prestige to the elections and present it as a mandate, not only for his regime but also for his family's rule, Marcos decided to make Imelda the leading candidate of his New Society Party, the KBL. Adding insult to injury, Marcos allowed his political arch-rival, Senator Aquino, to participate in the elections as the leading candidate of the LABAN opposition party–LABAN is an acronym for Lakas ng Bayan–and, in the Filipino language, LABAN means FIGHT.

Aquino was still in solitary confinement, convicted of murder and possession of firearms and sentenced to death by the military courts. His conviction and death sentence were in a state of confusion when Marcos, succumbing to international pressure, ordered the Aquino trial reopened.

"But this is a comedy," one of the many U.S. Congressmen I visited at the time told me, "what kind of an election is this? An alleged convicted murderer running from his solitary confinement cell against Imelda Marcos? What is Marcos trying to prove? Is he taking us all for fools?"

"I am afraid he is, Mr. Congressman," I responded, "millions of hard-earned American dollars are being given to this man with the approval of your Congress. I guess he must be taking you for fools. Congressman Clement Zablocki, the Chairman of the Committee on Asian Affairs praised Mr. Marcos for this so-called election, calling it "a real step toward the restoration of full democratic processes in the Philippines." It was Zablocki who urged the Committee members to vote for an increase in U.S. economic and military aid to Marcos. I think I must conclude that Marcos is deceiving you. It is also possible that he believes you don't give a damn. All you may need is an excuse to approve his millions of U.S. aid. So he is holding a farcical election to provide you with that excuse."

The April 7th elections took place. Initially, the opposition had planned to boycott the futile exercise, but Senators Tanada, Aquino, and some of their colleagues decided to use the elections as a forum to reach the people. They had no illusions of being allowed to become the victors over Imelda. Aquino campaigned from his cell through letters to his colleagues. The twenty other opposition candidates in Manila campaigned without press coverage or TV and radio time. Despite the insurmountable obstacles, the opposition candidates attracted tremendous crowds.

On March 2, 1978, the *New York Times* devoted an editorial to the Philippine elections. Entitled "Handcuffed in the Philippines," the *Times* editorial condemned Marcos for keeping Aquino in jail and denying him freedom to campaign. The editorial stated in part:

> The opposition Liberal Party, despite misgivings over some of the ground rules, has entered a slate of candidates headed by former Senator Benigno S. Aquino, long Mr. Marcos' most formidable rival. But he remains in detention, facing charges of subversion and murder that have dragged on unconvincingly for years. Mr. Aquino petitioned for temporary release in order to campaign, even offering to wear handcuffs and leg irons if need be. But that request has now been denied on the ground that it would endanger national security.

The *Times* editorial concluded: "If Mr. Marcos believes his own claims, he should have nothing to fear from letting Mr. Aquino campaign."

Ridiculed by the foreign press for what the *San Francisco Examiner* in its April 5, 1978, editorial branded "The Stacked Philippine Election," Marcos responded by allowing Aquino to make one nationally-televised TV appearance from his prison cell. The streets had never been so quiet and empty in the raucous city of Manila as they were on the evening of March 10, 1978, when Ninoy Aquino appeared on TV. Every TV set in the city was plugged in, and the extension cords were visible outside every home with a TV. Every Manila eye was glued to the TV screen while Ninoy was being interviewed by antagonistic Marcos "news reporters." This event sent the first wave of fear through the Marcos camp. This was the only public appearance Ninoy was allowed to make throughout the entire campaign.

Then, on April 6, 1978, the eve of the "election," Manila burst into a "noise inferno." The now-famous noise demonstration was the first concrete expression of the people's pent-up hatred for Marcos and respect for the opposition LABAN candidates. The unprecedented and spontaneous noise barrage sent a second and more unnerving wave of fear through Marcos and Imelda.* Perhaps responding in panic, Marcos made the April 7th election the most blatantly fraudalent one in the annals of Philippine history.

The free world press, particularly the U.S. press, condemned the farcical election and ridiculed Marcos for announcing "the election results" of a clean sweep by his 21 party candidates—only hours after the polls were closed and before any of the votes had been counted and reported even in Marcos' controlled media.

---

*It is this April 6th event that one of the urban guerilla groups later adopted as its name.

THE WASHINGTON POST April 12, 1978

"INGRATES! YOU LET THEM VOTE AND THE NEXT THING, THEY WANT THEIR BALLOTS COUNTED"

Cartoon on the April 7, 1978, Philippine election from the editorial page of the *Washington Post.*

The *Washington Post* editorial of April 11, appropriately titled "Thrillah in Manila," read in part as follows:

> Not since Muhammad Ali took on Joe Fraser has there been a "thrillah in Manila" to match the elections that the Philippines' strongman president Ferdinand Marcos, ran the other day. The very last thing Mr. Marcos had in mind was to give his opposition a fair crack at power. But he did wish to sweeten up the Carter administration and, specifically, to put Congress in the mood to pay the Philippines heavy compensation for the military bases whose continued use the State Department is currently negotiating. His purpose was, in brief, to run a phony election that looked good. So he allowed competition for seats to a legislature—that he can overrule. He let his chief rival, Benigno Aquino, whom he jailed in 1972, on television—once. The opposition did campaign strenously in Manila—but the president's chief political aide, his wife, Imelda, unleashed extra dollops of her formidable patronage and charm.
>
> Mr. Marcos won, big, but the evidence is, nonetheless, that he badly miscalculated. The opposition, though restricted, drew more support than he had bargained for. The foreign press, which he had invited in to validate his good faith, instead became witness first to his political embarassment and then—when he cracked down hard on the opposition as soon as the votes had been counted (or miscounted)—to his revenge.

Similar editorials appeared in practically all the U.S. papers including the *New York Times*, the *Los Angeles Times*, the *Washington Star*, the *Chicago Tribune*, and even the conservative *Christian Science Monitor*. I was surprised to see in the *Monitor's* editorial the clearest condemnation of the fraudelent election. "The elections might have been construed as a meaningful initial step toward the establishment of a democracy, had the voting not been rigged in the government's favor and not marred by what all accounts were flagrant abuses and fraudulent ballot counts," the *Monitor's* editorial said. In addition to the stinging editorials, many papers included appropriate cartoons. Two typical cartoons are shown on pages 81 and 83.

S.F. EXAMINER Tuesday, April 11, 1978

'I have discovered the key to efficient Philippine government . . . or more accurately, the keys'

Cartoon on the April 7, 1978, Philippine election from the editorial page of the *San Francisco Examiner.*

I devoted two of my own "It's NOT all Greek to me" columns to the April 7th "elections"–one, on a few confirmed incidents that were as tragic as they were comic and the other, on the more serious subject of its long-term effects. I predicted then that Marcos' fraudulent election had closed the door to the peaceful process and had "left the Filipino people with only ONE solution: FORCE." Less than a year after my prediction, the use of force erupted.

Philippine News (AE) WEEK OF APRIL 22-28, 1978

A LITTLE HUMOR AND A LOT OF TRAGEDY

DURING one of the campaign rallies, Imelda told her audience that "not a **single** Laban candidate must be allowed to win a seat in the IBP because it may lead to a bloody revolution." She didn't explain WHO would cause the "bloody revolution"; Imelda with her husband or the **single** Laban candidate! ! ! Anyway, not a **single** Laban candidate was allowed to win. Who can blame Imelda for **cheating a little** in order to prevent a bloody revolution?

***

Marcos announced the clean sweep of his party (KBL) on **April 8th.** When the foreign correspondents asked how he knew the results of the election so soon when only a few thousand votes had been tabulated, he accused the correspondents of being "insulting." I fully agree with Mr. Marcos. How can anyone insult him by questioning whether he knew the results before they were tabulated? Of course **he knew**! ! !

***

Marcos' favorite mouthpiece Doroy Valencia is reportedly in the doghouse. His April 7 column reads as follows:

"The counting will definitely be honest. So will the voting. There is no need to cheat. What for did President Marcos campaign so hard and so methodical if he had

intentions to cheat at the polls? He **could have cheated if he wanted to** *but he's testing the strength of the New Society under the condition he himself set."*

Poor Doroy got carried away and contradicted his boss when he stated that "Marcos could have cheated if he wanted to." Marcos had repeatedly stated during the campaign that the election rules were so fool-proof that it was virtually impossible for the "people in power" to cheat. Of course, Marcos never said that the election rules would not permit the opposition to cheat; so it was quite humorous when Marcos, after the election was over, accused the opposition of "cheating." Did they cheat themselves to lose?

***

The "election" is now over but some of its humorous and tragic events will affect the future of the Philippines. The victory clearly belongs to the Filipino people and whether Ninoy's leadership and the Laban's courageous campaign is a clear manifestation of this victory, is NOT all Greek to me.

Philippine News (AE) WEEK OF APRIL 15-21, 1978

MARCOSES LEAVE FILIPINOS WITH ONLY ONE SOLUTION

THOSE WHO HAVE been hoping against hope that the Marcoses would allow a return to "normalcy" voluntarily without violence and without bloodshed received their answer last April 7.

Those who know the Marcoses well and have been insisting that the only way to liberate the Philippines from its oppressive Conjugal Dictators is through force, are now saying "I told you so."

The April 7 election has made it clear to everyone that the Marcoses have left the Filipino people with only ONE solution: FORCE.

There is a great feeling of disappointment among the group who were working towards and hoping for a peaceful solution. They are now convinced that the door to a peaceful restoration of freedom, civil and human rights and constitutional democracy has been permanently SHUT.

At the same time, there is a feeling of relief among the group who knew that a man like Marcos who started his political ascent to power with the Court's conviction for the murder of Marcos' opponent, Nalundasan, significantly on **September 21**, 1935 and who, many believe, continued his murderous career by attempting to exterminate all of his opposition during the Plaza Miranda bombing, signifantly on August **21**, 1971 and who persisted with his murderous methods by, this time, murdering the country's democracy itself, significantly on September **21**, 1972 (always the **21**st) would never give up his power to the people peacefully. Murderers like the Marcoses, this group insists, have no respect for human life and are not concerned with how many innocent Filipinos may have to die. Their only concern is to hold on to their absolute power at any cost.

This writer belonged to the group of those who were "hoping against hope" for the peaceful solution, not because I did not know Marcos and Imelda well, but because the alternative to a peaceful position is so dreadful that a decent person forces himself to hope that there is a chance even for the worst type of criminal to reform. But a time comes when reality sets in and the false well-intended hopes disappear.

Just two weeks ago, citing the campaign statements of Marcos and Imelda, I had predicted in this column that "the Marcoses would resort to their usual gross election fraud" and would proclaim a clean sweep victory. In the same column I reiterated my "hope against hope" attitude by stating that I hope my evaluation and prediction would be wrong. Unfortunately, it was not.

One of two major accomplishments of the April 7 so-called election was to convince even the most moderate thinking Filipino and every political observer at home and abroad that freedom in the Philippines can only be regained, as in the past, through bloodshed. The only reasonable hope one can hold on to, is that the bloodshed will not be extensive.

Those who in the past were working for a peaceful solution (consisting of the great majority of the oppositionists to the one-man rule) will now join that minority which was advocating the overthrow of the illegal martial law regime through force. This fact comes as a sad realization to all peaceful-minded Filipinos but they are somewhat consoled by the lessons of history that the price for freedom, justice, and human rights has almost always been very high. The Filipino people will have to pay for it again as their history and heritage prove they paid it in the past.

The second major accomplishment of the election was to prove that the fire in the hearts of the great majority of Filipinos for their freedom, their dignity and their human rights is burning. Those who believed or claimed that the Filipinos are apathetic, or cowards, or unappreciative of the values of freedom and self-respect, or unwilling to take risks for their rights, have been proven wrong.

Considering that martial law was in force during and AFTER the election, that the controlled news media was used primarily to discredit, malign and weaken the small symbolic opposition, that the Marcoses spent fantastic sums of money to buy votes, and that the powers of the military were used to intimidate the populace, the enthusiastic support for the opposition and the willingness of the people to openly express this support, has astonished not only the Marcoses but even those of us who knew that most Filipinos were against the oppressive and corrupt martial law regime. All that was needed to fuel the burning fire was an opportunity and the "spark" of leadership which was provided mainly by Ninoy Aquino even though Marcos held him in in prison cell.

The significance of the two major accomplishments of the so-called election IS OBVIOUS.

Whether LABAN (FIGHT) was defeated or strenghtened by the April 7 election is NOT all Greek to me.

The events surrounding the April 7th "election" marked the beginning of the crisis. While Marcos initially appeared to be recovering from the aftermath of the elections, a sector of the moderate opposition was approaching an important decision. They were beginning to acknowledge that *force* was the only road to freedom. Until 1978, the moderates had agreed to pursue only peaceful approaches to the solution of the country's problems. They believed that the ballot would prevail over the bullet. The April 7th exercise of the ballot had changed the minds of many a moderate. They now had come to the conclusion that the bullet was necessary for the liberation of the Filipino people from their "Conjugal Dictators."

By the summer of 1979, the first effects of the decision to use force became evident. A small group of urban guerrillas, calling itself the "Light-a-Fire Movement," had surfaced. Using crude incendiary devices–gasoline containers with Katol igniters–it burned several government buildings and hotels, including the luxurious "floating Casino," a lucrative gambling operation controlled by the Marcoses through Imelda's brother.

The controlled media blamed the fires on arsonists, extortionists, criminal elements, disgruntled employees, and other non-political elements. But Marcos knew that it was the work of an independent group of moderates who were initiating urban guerrilla tactics. That is what Marcos really feared. He knew that his defenses were limited against a well-organized Destabilization Plan, implemented through urban guerrilla warfare.

The "Light-a-Fire Movement" was broken up in December, 1979, and many of its operatives arrested, including its alleged leader, a Harvard-educated, successful business executive. But months later, what Marcos really feared actually happened. The April 6th Liberation Movement, an urban guerrilla group, better organized, better trained, better financed, and better equipped, emerged with literally a "BIG BANG." The success of its August 22 coordinated bombing operation could not be covered up. The Marcos media condemned the bombings as "a hideous crime of terrorists," but they could not conceal the political significance.

Marcos now realized that the Destablization Plan, a written account of which was discovered by the military in December,

1979, when they raided the safehouses of the "Light-a-Fire Movement," was not just a "wild dream" of a small group of radicals, but a well-studied, long-term, and complete Plan for the overthrow of his martial law regime. Marcos knew that such a Plan, supported by a significant sector of the moderate opposition, presented the first real threat to his regime.

The mission, which I now believe Marcos had assigned to Imelda, was to meet with Ninoy, Sonny Alvarez, and me and try to learn as much as possible about the Plan: Who is really behind it?; How well is it funded?; how badly was the A6LM hurt by the recent wave of arrests?; Were there more "cells" besides the A6LM ready for operation?; Is the second step of the Plan ready for implementation? [In his August 4th speech, Ninoy had explained that the first step of the urban guerrillas was bombing and the second step was assassination of people symbolizing the oppression and corruption of the regime.] Can Ninoy and/or the rest of us here in the United States be persuaded—either by rewards or by threats—to change sides? Were we confident and irrevocably committed to the complete Plan, or was it only a "maneuver" aimed at getting concessions?; were we united and supportive of the opposition leaders in the Philippines, or could we (as other opposition leaders had previously been) be lured into intrigue and divided? Finally, what concession, if any, would assuage us and lead us to abandon the Plan?

Marcos' decision to send Imelda on this mission was not necessarily a bad decision. Sure, he would betray his vulnerability by confirming his fear of the urban guerrillas and the Plan. However, Marcos had much to gain by such a tactic. Imelda might succeed in persuading Ninoy and/or some of the others to switch to the Marcos side or at least to abandon the Plan. Or, she might discover we could be satisfied with concessions that Marcos could readily grant without significantly weakening his position. Furthermore, she might learn that the A6LM was dealt such a deadly blow that the guerrillas were ready to settle for just "forgiveness and amnesty."

There is no doubt that Imelda's participation in this mission had the potential to bring the Marcoses handsome dividends. In fact, it is quite possible that Marcos considered Imelda's meetings with Ninoy, Sonny, and myself a success. Although Imelda did not succeed in neutralizing the opposition, she definitely succeeded in: (1) obtaining a clear idea of our views on the Plan and our confidence in it; (2) more accurately evaluating the strengths and weaknesses of Ninoy and his associates in the United States, and, most importantly, (3) learning what it would take to prevent the implementation of the Destabilization Plan. Even though she was unable to achieve Marcos' initial objective, Imelda did gather some valuable information.

By the end of our five-and-a-half-hour meeting, I felt guardedly optimistic that Imelda clearly understood two key points. Firstly, the only way for Marcos to prevent the implementation of the Plan was to dismantle his martial law regime and agree to the establishment of a freely-elected constitutional government. Secondly, Marcos' defense against a well-organized and well-executed Destabilization Plan was limited, and, consequently, the Plan would ultimately succeed; it was only a question of time before it did.

PART II

The Dialogue

CHAPTER 8

The "Tape Recording"

The dialogue of a five-and-a-half-hour meeting cannot possibly be recalled in its entirety. However, in this meeting the key issues were so clearly defined in my mind that it was not particularly difficult for me to recall the conversation accurately.

When the meeting was over, I wondered whether Imelda had recorded our conversation for analysis by her Intelligence staff. I really wished she had. The meeting, I thought, would be much more constructive if Marcos or some of his Intelligence Service people were to evaluate the dialogue. On the other hand, it occurred to me that the man standing behind Imelda throughout the meeting may have been the Intelligence operative with the qualifications required to succintly evaluate the main points of the discussion.

The dialogue started tensely—as a test or even as a challenge to confrontation—but it ended very amicably. Imelda must have felt partly satisfied that her charm was not totally wasted, even though her fear of the Plan had obviously been exposed.

The first two to two-and-a-half hours of the dialogue covered the substantive points of the meeting. Ninoy had cautioned that it might be difficult for me to say much because, "Imelda really likes to talk rather than to listen." I assured him that I would make time to say what I thought had to be said. I was prepared to be rude, if necessary, and ask Imelda to listen. In fact, I was prepared to tell her, "I didn't come here for a lecture. If you want a monologue, write it down and mail it to me. If, on the other hand, you want a dialogue, then you'll have to listen to me as much as I listen to you."

As it turned out, bluntness was not necessary. Partly because of Ninoy's comments to Imelda about me, partly because she knew I would probably walk out if she attempted just to lecture, and mostly, I believe, because my opening remarks established the tone of the meeting, I found myself being listened to more than talked to. Imelda was really very gracious. She rarely interrupted me, and, during the first two hours or so, when the substantive issues were being discussed, she listened carefully.

The last three hours constituted "Imelda's day in court." During this period, Imelda attempted—mostly through monologue—to describe the benefits of martial law and the achievements of the new society. Understandably, she talked a great deal about her own pet projects.

The dialogue presented in the next few chapters as direct quotations is *not* intended to be an exact duplication of the actual conversation. Only a transcript of a tape recording could achieve this. However, it is as close to the conversation as I can recall. Although the actual words were somewhat different, the general gist of the conversation *is* entirely faithful.

It is my hope that a tape recording of our conversation will, someday, be found in the files of Marcos' intelligence vaults.

When I returned home a few days after the meeting and told Presy the highlights of my conversation with Imelda, she commented, "Too bad you couldn't tape record your conversation. Of all the hundreds of recordings you have collected with your 'mania' for recording all your phone conversations and all your secret meetings, this one is the most interesting and most historic."

"You're right," I answered knowingly, "but how could I sneak in my '007' tape recorder? I knew I would be searched."

CHAPTER 9

Let's Stop the Violence

"You know, Steve," Imelda began, hesitantly, "What you people are doing is not the answer to our country's problems. Bombings, killings, and other terroristic activities will not get you what you want. Such activities will only make it harder for the President to move toward normalization. You know, the President is a kind and understanding man, but he is also a strong man. He will never act when he is pressured to act. He will only act when he can do things voluntarily. Let me confide to you, Steve. Last summer the President had decided to lift martial law. He was planning to make the announcement on his birthday, September 11. Instead of celebrating the 8th anniversary of martial law on September 21, we were planning to celebrate the lifting of martial law. But look what happened. You people started blowing up Manila. How could the President lift martial law under such conditions? He can only do it without these kinds of pressures. Believe me, Steve, now he has decided to act. Martial law will be lifted next month. Let's not ruin it again. Let's stop the violence." Imelda was slowly recovering from her initial nervousness; however, she was still talking cautiously—as if she were reading from a prepared text. When she paused at this point, I interjected:

"Mrs. Marcos, you covered quite a bit of ground with your opening statement. First, we should try to avoid use of the word "terrorist" because our definition, evidently, is quite different. You find my activities terroristic and accuse me of being a terrorist. I, on the other hand, find the activities of the martial law regime terroristic and accuse you of being the terrorist. You and I will not agree on this point, and it really does not matter. What the people decide in the future is what counts.

"Secondly, let me clarify that when you say 'you people,' I take it you mean the Filipino patriots in your country. I would be personally proud to be included with them, but I do not deserve it. You must understand that the revolutionary activities in your country are the work of Filipino freedom fighters *in the Philippines*—not people like me here in the United States. I will explain a little more about this later.

"Thirdly, let me assure you that you will find no one who would agree with you more that violence is the worst route to normalization. I am certain that every respectable Filipino on both sides of the fence and, for that matter, every interested foreigner, realizes that if the country is freed through violence, the destruction and loss of lives will be great. No one I know in the opposition , whether political leaders or young activists, wants to bring destruction to the country. However, for eight years, your husband has methodically closed every door and even every window to the peaceful process. The Filipinos want freedom and dignity, and," I said with emphasis, "*they will soon get it.* They want it peacefully but they are now ready to break the closed doors with violence, if that is the only choice Mr. Marcos leaves them. You see, Mrs. Marcos, the choice of reaching normalization through

Imelda Marcos: According to Psinakis, a "terrorist."

Steve Psinakis: According to Marcos, a "terrorist."

peaceful or violent means is *yours*—not the revolutionaries.

"Fourthly, regarding your revelation that Mr. Marcos was planning to lift martial law on his last birthday, but was forced to change his mind because of the bombings, I find it difficult to comment without appearing rude. But the fact is your credibility is zero. You will be surprised, I am sure, if I were to show you, from clippings of your own newspapers, how many times your husband has announced his intention to lift martial law—but something always supposedly happened to prevent him. I think we'll make more progress if we do not discuss what Mr. Marcos had *planned to do* and *didn't do,* but rather what he *has to do* to prevent violence. I'm certainly on your side all the way when you say, 'let's stop the violence.' "

"Steve, the President has decided to lift martial law next month. He is very sincere about it, and he has already made an announcement. You know, last week I met with President-elect Reagan and Mr. Bush; they both expressed their friendship and support for the Philippines and for the President. They realize what an important ally we are to the U.S. and how important our country is to the security of the U.S. interests in the region. Reagan is quite different from Carter. I told Reagan—please, Steve, keep this to yourself—that the President plans to lift martial law next month and he told me not to act hastily. He said the stability and security of our country is vital to the U.S., and we should not rush into any changes which might affect the stability of the Philippines. He practically told me not to lift martial law yet, but the President has made up his mind. He will do it next month."

Imelda's remark about Reagan had a clear purpose. I had anticipated it because Imelda had told Ninoy the same thing, and Ninoy had mentioned it to me the previous day. I decided to face the issue squarely and honestly.

"There is no doubt, Mrs. Marcos, that the Reagan administration will be much more supportive of a regime like yours than President Carter was. Naturally, we were hoping that President Carter would be re-elected because he is much more sensitive to the cause of human rights throughout the world. We were quite disappointed with the election results . . . " Imelda sensed a weakness and cut in before I could continue. I let her.

"America swung to the right," she explained. "The people here realized that the liberals were the cause of the problems with the U.S. economy and with America's allies. Carter liked to lecture us and interfere with our internal affairs. Not so with Reagan. American people now understand the need for a strong U.S. President. Reagan will support his true allies, not lecture them."

"Yes, I quite agree that Reagan will give more support to your regime than Carter. Now, this presents your husband with a golden opportunity. You said he doesn't like to act because of pressure. In the past he repeatedly criticized the pressure of the Carter administration. Now, he has an opportunity to prove his sincerity. He can take the proper steps, and no one can say it was due to pressure, at least not pressure from the U.S."

"Precisely," she cut in triumphantly. "The President is going to lift martial law next month in spite of Reagan's comments."

I did not doubt Imelda was telling me the truth about Reagan's comments on martial law. Reagan had made it clear during the campaign that he would support any tin-horn dictator who would claim to be pro-American and anti-communist. Whether the dictator was in power illegally or whether he was staying in power by terrorizing his people and violating their human rights, would not be reason enough for Reagan to put some distance between such a dictator and the U.S. government. This sort of amoral foreign policy, which characterized the Nixon-Kissinger years, was clearly the policy Reagan advocated during his campaign.

After his victory, Reagan confirmed his views on foreign policy by choosing Alexander Haig as his Secretary of State. Even before Reagan took office, his advisors criticized Ambassador Robert White for expressing concern over the human rights violations of the oppressive regime in El Salvador. It was, therefore, no surprise that soon after Haig was confirmed by the Senate as the new Secretary of State, he not only recalled Ambassador White from El Salvador, but he actually fired him from the Foreign Service.

White's protests to the Reagan administration over the murders of the three American nuns and one Catholic laywoman by the El Salvadoran regime fell on deaf ears. When Ambassador White later testified before the House Foreign Affairs Committee, he said: "Last week, this administration informed me that I must leave the Foreign Service. I regard it as an honor to join a small group of officers who have gone out of the service because they refused to betray their principles. To have gone along with the department's misleading statement would not only have been morally wrong, it would have placed the life of every American missionary in El Salvador—Protestant or Catholic—in jeopardy from oppressive security forces. If the price of keeping a job is to participate in the continuing coverup of those responsible for this barbaric act, the price is too high for me to pay."

When I read White's testimony, I said to myself: 'I also regard it as an honor that Ambassador White joined the small group of those who refuse to betray their principles.' White also condemned the State Department's "cover-up of those responsible for this barbaric act" (the murders of the four American women). At that point, I also said to myself, 'Now, Ambassador White has joined an even smaller group. I wonder if the FBI will be ordered to go after him.'

Presy and I did not like Reagan's campaign statements. We had worked very hard for Carter's election in 1980, as we had for his election in 1976. We were as delighted with his 1976 victory as we were disappointed with his 1980 defeat. I had the privilege and honor of meeting Jimmy Carter very briefly on two occasions: once, during the campaign and a second time, when I was invited to one of the inaugural affairs in Washington to celebrate his victory. I was one of several thousand guests and, obviously, Jimmy Carter would not remember when I shook his hand warmly with admiration and hope for the future, but I will never forget how I felt and what I told him during the few seconds I held his hand: "Mr. President, it makes me very proud to know that we elected an American to the White House who shares the moral values of the founders of our great country."

When I returned to San Francisco one week later, I wrote the following commentary in the *Philippine News:*

WEEK OF FEBRUARY 19-25, 1977 Philippine News

COMMENTARY

MORALITY AND U.S. INTERESTS GO HAND-IN-HAND

By STEVE PSINAKIS

I JUST returned from a three-week visit to Washington where I had the opportunity to exchange views with several Senators, Congressmen and officials of the new Administration. This was the first time in eight years that Washington left me with a good feeling about our government, a feeling of optimism and pride. There is a definite change in Washington since the Carter inauguration. The words of Jimmy Carter, "A new spirit, a new commitment, a new America" are echoing inside every government building and inspiring every public servant.

My discussions with the U.S. legislators and officials of the Carter Administration covered many varied subjects but concentrated on the effects of the new approach to our foreign policy based on morality, openness and respect for human rights.

Under Dr. Kissinger, U.S. foreign policy was conducted on the basic assumption that morality was generally in conflict with the interests of the United States; consequently it was necessary to weigh morality versus U.S. interests and decide which was of greater importance. Dr. Kissinger inevitably decided that U.S. interests rated higher than morality and therefore arrived at foreign policy desisions based on short term economic and political expediency.

Since the Kissingerian foreign policy decisions were frequently inconsistent with the moral values of our people, it was obvious that foreign policy had to be conducted in secrecy. As we now know, the excuse always given by Kissinger for the need for secrecy was "U.S. national security." This is the same excuse given by Nixon for all of his own wrongdoings.

The emergence of Jimmy Carter with his strong convictions on morality has shaken Washington, the U.S. and the whole world. It has given hope to those who yearn for truth, justice and freedom and has brought despair to those who rule by lies, injustice and suppression of freedom.

Jimmy Carter has focused on an important ingredient which comes with morality, and that is "openness" in our government. When government policies are based on morality, there is usually no need to be secretive; the American people will approve, support, and be proud of their leaders. When government policies are immoral and unjust, there is obviously need to conceal them from the people.

The most significant change in U.S. foreign policy resulting from Jimmy Carter's emergence is the rejection of Kissinger's theory that morality and U.S. interests are in conflict. On the contrary, many officials in Washington with whom I have been meeting during the last three weeks are becoming more aware of the fact that "morality and U.S. interests go hand-in-hand."

It is now becoming clear that a foreign policy which disregards the "right of life, liberty and the security of person" of the peoples of other countries cannot possibly be to the best long term interests of the United States.

It is now becoming clear that a foreign policy which supplies arms to corrupt, ruthless and unpopular dictators, arms used to oppress the peoples of other countries, cannot possibly be to the best long term interests of the United States.

It is now becoming clear that a foreign policy which is not based on the moral values of our people and results in the loss of respect and prestige of America throughout the world, cannot possibly be to the best long term interests of the United States.

Finally, it is now becoming clear that the long term interests of the United States can only be protected if our foreign policy is based on our sincere concern for the welfare of the people of other countries rather than the collaboration with their oppressive rulers who exploit the people and violate their human rights. In short, it is now becoming clear that "morality and U.S. interests go hand-in-hand."

In my recent discussions with officials in Washington, we analyzed the results of our past foreign policy. In Indochina we supported corrupt and oppressive regimes to supposedly protect our national interests and to prevent the spread of communism. We ended up by losing these countries to communism along with all of our economic and military interests in these countries. In Africa, we supported oppressive colonial powers and minority rule until revolution and bloodshed forced us to change policy. In Portugal we supported dictator Salazar when the Angolans were fighting for their freedom, and forced the Angolans to embrace Castro and the Soviet Union.

In Chile, South Korea, the Philippines, Argentina and other dictatorial governments, the two past administrations have been supporting the oppressive regimes at the expense of the welfare and human rights of the people. It is finally becoming clear from actual experiences that because our past foreign policy has been both immoral and against our national interests, the U.S. has been losing its allies to its adversaries. It is also becoming clear that our real allies are the people of other countries and not their rulers, like the Marcoses, for instance, who remain in

power by force against the will of the people. Therefore the only way to maintain our allies in the long term is by maintaining the friendship of the people and caring for the people's welfare and human rights.

The change in Washington, brought about by the moral leadership of President Carter, is already very noticeable and the whole world is beginning to see "A NEW SPIRIT, A NEW COMMITMENT, A NEW AMERICA."

Yes! I was disappointed with Jimmy Carter's defeat, but I told an equally disappointed Presy: "This is the beauty of freedom and democracy. We are disappointed, but we are in the minority. Most Americans disagree with us; that's why Reagan is in the White House. Now we have to hope that the majority was right and that Reagan will make a good President. We will support him when we believe he is right and criticize him when we think he is wrong. That's another beauty of freedom and democracy."

"That's true," Presy agreed. "I remember very well how, despite your admiration for Carter, you criticized him more than once in your columns for signing the U.S. Bases Agreement with Marcos and for several other foreign policy decisions."

"Yes, I remember it very well," I said, "that's why America is the great country that it is. It's sad that relatively few Americans realize how lucky they are, in spite of our problems. If they only knew what it's like to live under dictatorships like that of Marcos or under communist regimes like that of the Soviet Union."

"It has been one of our major problems," Presy said. "It's so hard for the average American to believe or even understand what is happening in the Philippines under the criminal Marcos regime. Usually, when you try to make an important point, you have to inflate the truth a little to drive your point home. In our case, when we describe the repression and corruption of the Marcos regime, we must *deflate,* not inflate, the truth because the actual truth is so unbelievable, even when it is well documented.

'How right Presy was,' I thought.

Imelda was now gloating about Reagan's victory and boasting about the support he had expressed to her for "President Marcos and the martial law regime." She had good reasons to be happy, but she was treading on dangerous ground. Reagan will be more sympathetic and supportive to Marcos than Carter, but if either she or Marcos believe Reagan can change the course of events in the Philippines, they are mistaken. I tried to explain.

"Mrs. Marcos, if there is one point I'll try to make clear to you today, it's this: What is happening now in the Philippines is happening because of the *Filipino people*—not because of Carter, Reagan, any foreigner, and certainly not because of me, to whom you have given such prominence. No individual can change the course of events in your country, only the Filipino people can. It is true that if you choose the course of violence, Reagan's support of your regime may result in more bloodshed—but the *outcome* will be the same. In fact, I believe that if Mr. Marcos were to tighten his grip because of Reagan's election, he would only convince more Filipinos that force is the only way to freedom. Now, you have twice mentioned your husband's firm decision to lift martial law next month. From what I read in your papers and from what I hear from the opposition, the announcement of the lifting of martial law in January indicates another—how do you say it?—Lutong Macoy? A deception. How can you talk of sincerity when your husband announces the lifting of martial law and at the same time your IBP (National Assembly) is passing so-called legislation giving him more power than he has now under martial law? You cannot think very much of your people if you believe that such a move can deceive them." I said calmly but decisively.

"The President is sincere," she said, returning to the defensive tone she had had earlier. "The lifting of martial law is the first major step toward normalization. The President cannot suddenly change everything in one step. It has to be a gradual change. He has to maintain enough power to assure our people of an orderly transition."

"I don't believe that anyone would argue against the need for an orderly transition," I assented. "What people will argue against is insincerity and deception. For a major step to be considered sincere, the opposition must be consulted and must agree. Mr. Marcos alone cannot decide that his step is sincere when the entire opposition considers it an outright farce. The road to normalization, if it is to come through peaceful means, has to come through agreements achieved at the conference table between Mr. Marcos and the opposition."

"But the President agrees on the benefit of dialogue. He invited the opposition to talk, but they don't want to talk. They are divided and can't make up their minds."

"The last time Mr. Marcos invited the opposition to a dialogue was in connection with the bombings—in connection with what you refer to as "terrorist activities." It was more of an *accusation* than an invitation."

"Of course," she replied. "When the opposition engages or encourages terrorism, what do you expect the President to do? You heard Ninoy's speech? How *should* we respond to such threats?"

"Mrs. Marcos! Did you read Ninoy's speech or did you believe the propaganda and the distorted stories in your own newspapers? Ninoy's speech was asking you—*pleading* with you would be more accurate—to avoid violence by dismantling the martial law regime voluntarily through peaceful means. He was only informing you that he had talked with the leaders of young, dedicated, idealistic Filipinos who were preparing to use force if Mr. Marcos continued to ignore the people's cry for freedom and justice. Unfortunately, your husband's reaction was rather foolish. He twisted Ninoy's words; he called him crazy; he called him a dreamer; he called him a man who lived in a world of fantasy. But what happened? Less than three weeks after Ninoy's speech, he was proven right, and Mr. Marcos looked like the man living in a world of fantasy."

"But what did you gain by a few small explosions?" she asked, without attempting to question the main point of Marcos' reaction or the distortion of Ninoy's speech.

Before answering her question, which I felt was only a way of sidetracking the conversation, I stopped for a second to assess the direction of our discussion. I was satisfied that by now Imelda understood she was talking with someone who would not hesitate to tell her exactly what he was thinking, no matter how unpleasant it was for her to hear. But I was not yet satisfied that our discussion was heading in a constructive direction.

"I am glad you asked what was gained by the few small explosions. Before I respond to this extremely important question, let me first clarify how most guerrillas feel about violence."

"Yes, I would be very interested in hearing their views," she said eagerly.

"Not surprising to me at all, I found that most, if not all, the activists I talked to condemn the use of violence and abhor the use of terrorism."

"Why, then, have they taken to violence and terrorism?" she interjected.

"Because they condemn violence and abhor terrorism," I emphasized. "For eight years they have been subjected to the violence and terrorism of your repressive regime. They want it to stop. You have managed to convince ordinary peace-loving Filipinos that the only way to stop your violence is to respond with violence. For eight long years they've used every peaceful approach and failed. Every time they tried to ask for their rights peacefully, you responded with more of your regime's institutionalized violence. They agree with you, as I do. Let's stop the violence. This means that you should stop the violence, and then they'll have no use for it either."

"It's not fair, Steve, to say that we have institutionalized violence. The little violence that has occurred by some overzealous military has been the exception to the President's policy. Whenever incidents of mistreatment of prisoners have been reported, we acted swiftly. Many soldiers and officers have been dismissed or disciplined when we obtained evidence of misconduct . . . "

Imelda obviously planned to continue, but I interrupted. For the first and only time throughout the five-and-a-half-hour meeting, my voice betrayed some of the anger I felt.

"Mrs. Marcos, you are not talking to some foreign correspondent at a formal press conference in Malacanang (the Presidential Palace in Manila). You are talking to me in the privacy of your suite. Don't talk to me about isolated cases. When your secret agents can raid *any house at any time* and arrest people without warrants, jail them for years without filing charges, deny them legal counsel, extract confessions through inhuman tortures, *that is* institutionalized violence. When your military bulldozers can scoop away the poor homes of villagers to build a factory for one of your business friends, *that is* institutionalized violence. When your secret agents can pick-up a citizen at night and the next morning return his mutilated body to the town square, *that is* institutionalized terrorism.

"Need I go on, Mrs. Marcos?" I asked. When I realized how angry I had begun, I quickly brought my anger under control.

"These things are *not* happening in my country. You must be listening to the lies of communists who want to take over the government. You should come to the Philippines and see for yourself. These things are not happening," she repeated defensively.

"I don't have to go to the Philippines to see. I know what is going on there. Many people more qualified than I have gone there, have seen, and have reported: people from Amnesty International, for one; International Commission of Jurists for two;

International Red Cross for three; and hundreds of other individuals and organizations. Besides, your own official decrees stipulate and, in fact, legalize your institutionalized violence. By decree, if you strike, you can be arrested; by decree, if you demonstrate, you can be arrested; by decree, if you assemble, you can be arrested; by decree, if you criticize the government, you can be arrested; by decree; by decree; by decree. All these decrees are issued by one man when *only* in his opinion are they necessary. Now *that is* institutionalized violence. What do you want me to come and see?" I asked and suddenly stopped.

Imelda froze. Apparently she was not quite ready for this. Although I had brought my anger under control, the words had an anger of their own. She paused for a few seconds. I waited for her to speak.

"Our country was in a state of chaos before the President declared martial law. Our people needed to be disciplined. I agree there have been some excesses. The President has tried to minimize the excesses and is now moving ahead with normalization. He wants to turn over legislative powers to the Parliament. He wants to end rule by decree. He wants to lift martial law. Martial law has served the country during a period of crisis. Now he is preparing to lift it. But he wants to do it voluntarily and peacefully."

"I am very pleased to hear this, and I hope it's true. I was only answering your question of why the guerrillas abhor violence and terrorism. You've told me: 'let's stop the violence.' I am telling you that it's the greatest news I've heard in a long time. By all means, let's stop the violence, now that we know who has been resorting to violence for eight years."

"Steve, it does not help to argue about what has happened in the past. Let's admit we all make mistakes. We must look toward the future. If we made mistakes, let us learn from them and not repeat them in the future. Let us now work in good faith to solve the serious problems confronting us," Imelda said, recovering her composure and speaking in her well-known "compassionate" tone.

"Now," I said, "let's return to the question of what was accomplished by the few small explosions."

CHAPTER 10

The First Signs of Revolution

Imelda's question gave me the opportunity to return our dialogue to the key issue.

"You ask what was gained with the few *small* explosions?" I said. "Before we get into this question, let me say that I do appreciate your obvious willingness to discuss candidly these matters that are sensitive and difficult. On the other hand, let me also say that it would be far more useful and prudent if we were both willing to be honest rather than attempt to bluff each other. I do not think I could fool you, and it might be safe for you to assume that you could not fool me either. You know exactly why you wanted to see me, rather insistently, and I also have a pretty good idea. Let us please agree to be honest with each other. If we are not, Presy's and my original impression that we would be wasting your time and ours will prove correct." The tension reappeared in Imelda's face. I continued:

"Your question attempts to dismiss the 'small bombings' as an insignificant event. Yet, both you and I know differently. The situation is serious. That's why you are here talking to me. For reasons that might be right or wrong, you consider me an important member of the revolutionary movement. That's why you want to talk to me." I watched her and was both surprised and pleased she made no effort to refute my statement. 'Maybe,' I thought, 'she is *really* willing to look at the facts.' I went on:

"What is happening today in the Philippines is the beginning of a violent revolution, which, unless it is understood and attended to very soon, will reach an irreversible point. If that happens, it will not only cause your destruction, but it will also cause destruction to your country that will set it back for years. Surely, no one sensible wants this to happen. Look at the examples of Iran and Nicaragua."

My last remark gave her an opening. The comparison of Iran and Nicaragua had been made before, and she was prepared with an answer.

"You are not saying that the Philippines is similar to Iran or Nicaragua before the Shah and Somoza were overthrown. In both these countries, the people were suffering. They were unhappy with their leaders. In our case, you must come and see for yourself; the President is popular and appreciated. We have done so much for our people. The poor are so much better off today. The per capita income has increased from only $210 when we took over to $780 today. The great majority of the people are behind us; they don't even want martial law to be lifted. It is only the few disgruntled elements and few ambitious politicians who are causing all the trouble." She was planning to continue, but this time I cut in as she hesitated.

"I am not saying that your situation is only similar; I am saying that your situation is exactly the same as Somoza's or the Shah's in one very vital respect. You are treating the initial signs of an impending explosive revolution as insignificant. That's how Somoza and the Shah looked upon the first signs of the revolutions that caused their downfall along with the destruction of their countries. By the time they realized that the initial dissent had developed to a full revolution, it was too late. The course was irreversible. In that respect, your situation is identical. Incidentally, I can show you newspaper clippings quoting both the Shah and Somoza saying what you just said: 'We are very popular with our people. There are only few disgruntled elements–communists and anarchists–who are causing the trouble.' Now, I agree with you that the blowing up of three or four toilets *per se* is not necessarily the beginning of a revolution. But again, it may very well be. You should examine who is doing this and why."

I was now satisfied that the conversation was centering on the main issue. Imelda appeared to be listening with interest. She made no sign of wanting to comment as I paused for a second, so I continued.

"If you reach the conclusion, which many of us know to be correct, that indeed the events during the past year or so are the first signs of a revolution, then there is only one possible time and only one way to stop it."

"How can we stop it?" Imelda asked, without arguing against its existence.

"Firstly, by acting soon, before it becomes irreversible and secondly, by looking at the true facts and giving the people what they want so desperately that they are ready to kill and ready to die for it."

"Your impression of what is happening in the Philippines may not be accurate. I travel all over the country, and I can feel the pulse of the people. They are happy, and their standard of living is steadily improving. The farmers have their own land; their homes have electricity; we are producing enough rice so we can now export; we have peace and order. I cannot believe that my people are as unhappy as you make them appear."

"It is quite possible that you want to see the truth but cannot. That's what happens when repressive regimes are feared by their people. You know, those who are organizing your trips around the country have to make sure you are impressed with the reception you receive. If you're not, they're out of a job. It is not really difficult to gather several thousand people to greet you and cheer you when you visit some barrio. This can create the very impression you ascribe to me. On the other hand, it is difficult to dismiss the events on April 6, 1978 as an orchestrated affair. How can you possibly believe that you are popular and loved by the great majority of your people—or that your opponents are only few disgruntled elements—when all of Manila burst into a spontaneous noise demonstration against you? Nothing comparable had ever happened in the Philippines. How can you account for that?" I suddenly stopped my monologue and waited for an answer.

Imelda seemed stunned. She was listening attentively and obviously had not expected an abrupt and specific question. After a hesitation, Imelda managed to say, "It could have been the fever of the campaign. You know how the Filipinos are about elections."

"Why then should they scream *against* you instead of *for* you?" I insisted.

"Well, Manilans have always been for the opposition," she responded.

"If that is the case, why did the results show such a resounding defeat of all twenty-one opposition candidates? Are you admitting that the election was rigged?"

"Well," she answered lamely, "Manilans are traditionally with the opposition, but they are not always the majority."

I overlooked her contradictory answers. I was not trying to humiliate her. I was only trying to help her see what her supporters were trying to prevent her from seeing. I simply said, "Perhaps you will at least agree with me that the 'disgruntled elements' are not just few, but *quite* a few—in Manila anyway." I did not wait for a comment. She seemed to be listening with interest.

"Mrs. Marcos, you are an intelligent woman. Your husband is thought to be a brilliant man. One need not be intelligent or brilliant to see the obvious, if one wants to see it. When you ask yourself why Presy and Steve oppose you, you may want to deceive yourself with the answer: 'because I hurt their family; I imprisoned their brother; I took their money. When you ask why Ninoy, Manglapus, Tanada, Salonga, Diokno, Rodrigo, Macapagal and other politicians oppose you, you may want to deceive yourself with the answer: 'because they are envious and just want to take my place.' Your answers may be right in some of these cases, because, with such people, there is certainly the possibility of a selfish motive. But, Mrs. Marcos, if you really want to find out whether the recent events in Manila are the first clear signs of revolution or the activities of a 'few disgruntled elements,' please consider this question: 'why would a bright, well-educated man, a man who has no reason or motive to have anything against you personally; a man who has no political ambition; a man who is a staunch anti-communist; a man who is a devout Christian from a family of priests and nuns; a man like Eddie Olaguer; why would he oppose you? Why would a man like Olaguer tell you 'I have taken arms against you because you've hurt my people enough.' You find the answer to this question, and I am sure you will find out whether you are looking at the first signs of a real revolution."

"I really appreciate your views, Steve, although I can't say that I agree with everything you are saying. You have a clear way of making your point. I wish you could have a good talk with the President. It might be very useful. Maybe you could meet somewhere. In Hong Kong or somewhere," she whispered, as if she were thinking aloud rather than talking to me.

I felt that I was getting through to her. I could not believe that she would be so patient if I was not reaching her at all. Neither could I imagine that her apparent interest was only an act for my benefit. This pleased me but did not make me forget for one second who she was.

"Mrs. Marcos, first you must understand that dictatorial regimes like yours can be destabilized and overthrown. It happens all the time. During the past four years alone, thirteen or fourteen dictatorships, quite similar to the martial law regime in the Philippines, have collapsed for one reason or another—some through relatively peaceful means and some through violent revolutions. Let us look first at your main source of strength, the military. The main reason you view the martial law regime as stable is the support you now enjoy from the military. The military as a whole is a formidable force of two hundred thousand armed men and women that no other force can presently confront and defeat."

"Precisely," she interrupted, sensing perhaps an admission of the opposition's weakness. She continued, "there is no one group in the Philippines today or anywhere who can organize in the future to defeat our military. What are all these threats of revolution? Who is going to mount the revolution?

"Well, this is the point that dictator after dictator fails to see. Please understand that no one in the opposition expects to organize an army of two hundred thousand to fight against *your* army of two hundred thousand. The opposition, at least the sector of the opposition working for your overthrow through the use of force, knows what you don't seem to understand or don't want to admit: The military is *not* yours. The two hundred thousand soldiers are ordinary Filipinos doing their jobs. Today, their superiors order them to point their guns at the Olaguers, so they point their guns at the Olaguers. Tomorrow, if their superiors, whoever they may be, order the same soldiers to point their guns at Marcos, they will do just that. The point is very clear and has been proven time and time again. It is not the two hundred thousand soldiers that are *yours.* It is only a General Ver, a General Ramos, General Olivas, and a few Ilocano generals who are *yours.* For the time being, the orders of these generals are to point the soldiers' guns at the Olaguers. But two things can happen at any moment. First, these few generals can be eliminated. The new generals may issue different orders, and the two hundred thousand strong army, which you throught was *yours,* will now point their guns at you. Secondly, all of these generals, Ver, Ramos, Olivas, or anyone else, now realize that their support keeps you in power. They can turn against you and throw you in jail."

"But the leaders of our military are loyal and trusted men," Imelda insisted.

"Maybe so today. The fact is they know they have you in their hands. If, for instance, Ver and Ramos walked to your office with only three or four of their men and told you, 'Okay, Ferdie and Imelda, you are under arrest. We're taking over!' What would you do? Who could you call on to help you? The two hundred thousand soldiers?" I stopped and waited for an answer.

"Our generals would never do that. They are loyal and happy," she said, without attempting to respond to my question.

"But that is not the point, Mrs. Marcos. The point is that they *can* do it, and they know it. You are at their mercy. Do you think that Park Chung Hee expected his equivalent of General Ver to shoot him down like a dog? Of course not. Park felt his general was as loyal to him as you believe Ver is to you. All you really need is one such miscalculation, and it's all over. The bottom line is this: those working for your overthrow through force know very well that they don't have to confront and defeat an army of two hundred thousand soldiers. They know the soldiers are basically with the people, and, in any event, they will follow the orders of their superiors. All the revolutionaries have to do is take care of the small clique who, at the present, gives the orders."

"Our military is strong and unified. It can crush any possible challenge by subversives. This talk about division within the military is not true." Imelda insisted, refusing to address the main point.

"I can remember another contemporary dictator in my native land, Mr. Papadopoulos," I went on patiently. "He was in a much more stable and secure position than you and Mr. Marcos are today. And yet, one nice evening a *trusted* colonel, in fact one of the very colonels who had helped him pull the military coup—Colonel Ioannidis—ordered just two dozen of his men to arrest Papadopoulos at his house. That was all. The next morning, the so-called stable Greek dictator found himself in jail, where he still is today. That's what happens when the men with the guns, the military, get politicized and get a taste of power. The civilians running the government become their pawns. You have mounted a tiger, and it's hard to get off without being mauled."

"Steve, you are comparing situations in Iran, Greece, Nicaragua, and Korea with the Philippines. Our situation is not the same."

"Well, Mrs. Marcos, I do not expect you to admit your weakness vis-a-vis the military. Nothing would be gained by admitting it to me. My only hope is that you will understand the situation and realize, first of all, how vulnerable you are to the whims of a few generals who, for the time being are serving your purpose. Secondly, you should realize that when you say the military is *yours,* you are really only talking about a few generals and not two hundred thousand soldiers."

"You are right. I will not agree with you on this point, but I am listening to what you are saying."

"The fact that you are listening to my lengthy presentation is in itself a good sign. I do not expect you to admit that the military can be as much of a base of your strength as it is a threat to your staying in power." I decided to change the subject.

"Okay, let's forget the military for a while, and let's look at the revolutionaries. Here, I think, we may find it easier to agree."

"Yes, this is an area where I am particularly eager to work with you. I hope we can make progress and arrive at some conclusions," Imelda said eagerly. "Our aim is to stop the violence and find solutions to our internal problems without bloodshed. Violence will not serve the interests of either side. One thing is certain. Washing our dirty linen in public is no good. We must wash our dirty linen in private."

"Well, before we even discuss the possibility of working for a peaceful solution, it is necessary to realize where the revolutionaries stand. I hope I can make you understand that what is now happening in the Philippines is the first clear sign of a revolution that may explode anytime. If we cannot agree on this point, there is no need to talk about stopping any violence. There would be no violence to stop. I am sure you're not worried about the blowing-up of three or four toilets." I was tempted to say, "I heard, however, that many of your business executives have been taking their own potty to the office instead of using their toilets," but decided against being so blatantly sarcastic.

"It is true, Steve, that the violence that recently erupted has cause us serious problems. There is no point in denying it. It doesn't take much to scare tourists away. Just give the Philippines a bad name, and the tourists will disappear. Certainly the ASTA bombing has been very damaging. I also agree that foreign investors can be easily scared away. I've talked with some of the American bankers and they have expressed concern. Ninoy talked to them also, and they don't know what to believe. The bombings have been exaggerated in the foreign press, and some people really believe we are about to have a revolution."

"Of course, many people think so. They are not stupid. They have seen the same signs in other countries. They can recognize the problem, perhaps more easily than you. That's how revolutions start. They don't suddenly flare up out of nowhere without any warning."

"The President understands this. That's why we are concerned and want to solve the crisis in time. We don't think we are on the verge of an imminent revolution, but certainly there are signs of some unrest. We want to find the cause and solve the problem."

"Let us then, Mrs. Marcos, define some of the strengths and weaknesses of the revolutionaries. The weaknesses? Money, logistics, and numbers. It's hard to raise money and difficult to find arms and explosives locally and/or to smuggle them from overseas, and it's even more difficult to find people ready to give up everything, including their lives, for their country."

"Exactly," she said with some self-assurance. "We already know how explosives were smuggled into Manila. We confiscated several items in their original packing, and we know the technique. Besides many of those arrested confessed without any pressure."

She was planning to continue, but I broke out laughing.

"I am sorry for laughing. You probably think I am laughing at your statement of 'getting confessions without any pressure.' " I said, still laughing.

"I am sorry, Mrs. Marcos," I said, controlling my laughter, "but you made me recall a very funny incident."

"Why don't you tell me? It must be amusing," she suggested.

"It is indeed. I was planning to discuss this point with you anyway because it relates to one of the strengths of the revolutionaries, but you made me think of a very funny conversation I had with a friend."

"I am anxious to hear it," Imelda said with a confused smile on her face. She wasn't sure whether I was making fun of her or not.

"Well, your statement of 'getting confessions without pressure' is funny enough in itself. We both know how many of the confessions have been extracted—but that's not what made me laugh—it was your knowledge of the smuggling techniques for the explosives," I said. I couldn't help chuckling some more.

"Well, it's true," she said without smiling, "we've confiscated many of the smuggled explosives and arrested several of those who brought them in and several of those who received them. You and I know this is true," she said rather spitefully, as if she wanted to say, 'you see, you're not so smart. We're smarter than you.' I wanted to laugh but somehow managed to control myself.

"Mrs. Marcos, a few weeks ago, I was talking with a friend who confirmed exactly what you just said. That is, you *have* confiscated quite a few explosives in their original packaging and some of those arrested confessed."

"You see," Imelda interrupted, triumphantly. "What's so funny about that?"

"Well, this friend, who incidentally is one of the freedom fighters, was telling me how helpless you must feel cutting off the supply line of explosives from abroad. He explained that some of the explosives are smuggled in by ordinary tourists in their very ordinary-looking suitcases and packages. He said they are inside sealed cans of food; inside sealed cigarette boxes—not just sealed cartons of cigarettes but sealed packs of cigarettes inside sealed cartons; sealed toys of all sorts in their original packing; all kinds of gifts—some wrapped, some not; food containers; medicine bottles; hi-fi speakers; TV sets; etc."

"Exactly," Imelda said, "we know about all this."

"That's precisely why I laughed before and why my friend and I broke into uncontrollable laughter when he was narrating the story. You *know,* but you can't do anything about it. 'What can the idiots do?' my friend asked me. 'One out of three thousand passengers is bringing in something. In order to find it, they have to break up every box, every can, every toy, every pack of cigarettes, every TV set, every speaker, every everything of two thousand nine hundred and ninety-nine people who would raise the greatest hell with the customs inspector. My friend and I broke out in hysterical laughter at the thought of it, and your comment about the explosives reminded me of it again. Don't you find it funny?" I asked mischievously.

Imelda didn't know whether to laugh, protest, agree with me, or disagree. It was clear she felt awkward. She didn't reply. She smiled half-heartedly. I went on, "I will tell you this, even though I am a little embarrassed," I said, "but this was the funniest part of his story. My friend said they even smuggled blasting caps, which are as big as a regular cigarette, inside the padding of Kotex. The pads were sealed inside their original box. 'Can you imagine,' my friend had said amidst hysterical laughter, 'Imelda's secret agents at the airport or on a passenger liner opening every lady's Kotex box and looking inside the cotton padding of every sanitary napkin?" I was hardly able to finish the sentence without laughing.

Imelda also laughed, as if she had no other choice. It seemed unreasonable not to find the incident funny. However, at the same time, she could not hide the anger in her eyes. She knew every single word I said was true.

"That's one of the strengths of the guerrillas," I said. "You cannot cut their channels of supply. If you decide to place a thousand agents at each entry point to break open every little item in *every* suitcase of *every* passenger, the guerrillas would have caused you more damage than the explosives they attempt to smuggle in. There wouldn't be another passenger coming to Manila. You know it and they know it," I concluded. There was no longer anything funny, either in what I said or in the manner in which I said it. The atmosphere suddenly became tense again.

"This is quite true," she said. "We cannot stop the smuggling completely but the *amount* of arms or explosives that can be smuggled in this manner is quite small."

"That's correct," I agreed. "They can't smuggle too much, but that's one more strength, if you will, of the revolutionaries. They don't need much. Look what a small one-pound package can do. That's all, I was told, they used at the ASTA Convention."

"I agree that the guerrillas have caused significant damage, and I accept that they can cause much more. We are concerned and we want to find a way to unify the nation and prevent more violence. Let's talk about how we can accomplish that instead of . . ."

I interrupted, "No, Mrs. Marcos. Before we talk about preventing more violence, let's make sure we both know and understand where the revolutionaries stand, what they are trying to accomplish, and what they are able to accomplish. I think first we have to understand the problem before we attempt to find the solution. We talked about the weaknesses of the guerrillas, and now we are talking about their strengths."

It was obvious that Imelda preferred to change the subject. She was visibly uncomfortable listening to the "strengths" of the guerrillas. I didn't feel any satisfaction in pressing the point just to make her uncomfortable. There was nothing to be gained by it. But I felt it was imperative for her to understand that, firstly, the Destabilization Plan could be implemented with very modest logistics and even more modest manpower. Secondly, both the needed logistics and the manpower were either available or could easily be made available, and, thirdly, under the prevailing conditions in the Philippines, a well-planned and executed Destabilization Plan is all that is necessary to cause the collapse of the artificially propped-up martial law regime.

I felt this was a vital issue that had to be clarified and fully comprehended. I had read the Philippines government propaganda attempting to ridicule the impact of the guerrilla successes, and I had been surprised at the success of the propaganda. I had found that most uninvolved Filipinos were swayed by the constant bombardment of the controlled media in the Philippines; many believed the successes of the guerrillas were nothing more than the foolish and ineffective activities of few naive and amateur romantics.

As a matter of fact, I participated in many meetings composed of well-informed and politically-involved Filipinos who also, to my surprise, understood neither the effect of the guerrilla actions to date nor their potential to overthrow the regime through their Destabilization Plan. Therefore, it was not unreasonable to assume that Imelda may have had the same erroneous impression. In fact, this was more likely in Imelda's case since she is known to be quite isolated from the realities in her country.

There was no doubt that she was scared of what she had seen so far of the urban guerrillas and of their successes during the previous 12 months. Otherwise she wouldn't be talking to me and listening with patience and, at times, with great interest. But I could not be certain that she understood the imminent danger of a violent overthrow of the martial law regime.

I continued on the same subject, "the third weakness of the guerrillas is numbers. It is difficult to find many people willing to pay the price of being a guerrilla. Also, the risk of infiltration makes it difficult to screen volunteering guerrillas. So the number is small. On the other hand, this is also the strength of the urban guerrilla approach. In most cases, the fewer persons assigned to a project, the better. How many guerrillas do you need to prepare, say, ten time bombs?" I asked rhetorically. "One," I answered. "How many guerrillas do you need to plant the ten bombs in different buildings in Manila within a 12-to-24-hour period? Two, maybe three. How much havoc can ten simultaneous explosions cause? Well! This, you already know. How many guerrillas do you need to plan and execute one or two assassinations of one of your businessmen or one of your foreign tourists? Two or three guerrillas. What would be the effect of assassinating, say, one of your close business associates, one Japanese tourist, and one American multinational executive? Well! We don't know *yet,* but we can imagine. Anyway, we may all find out quite soon. As you know from the copy of the destabilization plan you captured in Olaguer's house and from Ninoy's speech, the second step of the plan is 'symbolic assassinations.' "

I felt I had made the point quite clear. "Do you still think that what has been happening the past twelve months or so is just a wild dream of a few amateur subversives or would you now concede that it could be the first sign of a real revolution?"

"I do not deny that the situation is serious and could get worse. Our duty as good Christians is to look for solutions to prevent violence, destruction, and bloodshed in my little country. The President is in the process of returning the country to its full democratic processes. We must all help do it peacefully. I know you can help if you really want to. The guerrillas must be made to understand that patience is the better part of valor," she ended with an inappropriate cliche. I was at least partly satisfied with her answer. I didn't really expect her to concede that the martial law regime was about to collapse. Her admission that 'the situation is serious and could get worse' was good enough. I was also pleased that she was now using the word "guerrillas" instead of "terrorists."

CHAPTER 11

Two of Ours for Two of Yours

Imelda was on the receiving end, and I was pleased she was not always attempting to argue against the obvious. There was no doubt she was listening with interest, but I could not be sure how much she was really absorbing.

'Is it possible,' I asked myself, 'she really wants to hear and learn the truth? Is this perhaps why she was so insistent on seeing me? Because she knew I would tell her the truth as it is?'

'Very doubtful,' I answered spontaneously. 'That's too much to hope for. But then again, even if there is one chance in ten that she really wants to learn, I owe it to my friends—the Olaguers, the Tanadas, the Aquinos, the Avilas, the Alverez' and to so many other courageous Filipinos, I owe it to all these people to try.'

"Mrs. Marcos," I said, "Ninoy mentioned to me yesterday that during your discussion, you told him he and I have sent assassination teams to the Philippines to kill members of your family, members of your Cabinet, high military officers, and business people closely identified with your government."

"That's correct," she confirmed, "we have evidence that several of our people are being monitored by activists, and we have every reason to believe they are marked for assassination. Besides, Ninoy said in his speech that the next step after the bombing is the assassination of our people. I asked him to please tell the guerrillas to stop this kind of action before it starts, and I would like to ask the same of you."

"I also understand," I said, "you told Ninoy something like 'if you get two of ours we'll get two of yours and what will that do for either of us?' "

"Well, of course," she snapped. "What do you think we will do if you start killing our friends? Just take it and do nothing? After all, we are in a much stronger position to act than you."

"Mrs. Marcos," I said with determination, "please allow me the favor of explaining this point at length. It's very important you understand exactly what is happening so that no matter what action you decide to take, you will take it wiith full knowledge of the facts."

"I am here to listen, Steve, and I appreciate your coming. I would not be here if I didn't think it was important. You know I am a very busy person, and I would not spend hours talking with Ninoy and with you unless I thought it would be helpful in solving our problems." She sounded sincere but again appeared slightly nervous, almost embarrassed. I wondered if she had any notion of what I was about to tell her. After all, we were talking about killing each other's people—maybe even about killing each other.

"Thank you, Mrs. Marcos. I really do appreciate your attitude, and I am beginning to feel glad that I came to see you." I used as gentle a tone as I could because I had prepared myself for this part of my discussion, and I knew it was going to be tough on her. I was hoping I would be able to tell her the truth in a sincere way. I did not want to leave the impression I was responding to her threat with another threat, because that was neither my intention nor the truth.

"Last month," I continued, "you brought Presy's mother and her brother, Manolo, to the Palace and gave them the same message—something like: If we were to hurt your people, you could play the same game. My poor mother-in-law was terrified; she has been terrified for the past eight years since you threw her son, Geny, in jail. If you were trying to scare her, you were wasting your time; you can't possibly scare her any more than she already is. If, on the other hand, you were trying, through her, to scare Presy and I, you were again wasting your time. Neither our mother's fear, nor your threats to us, will change anything. You've tried this before, and we were surprised you didn't know any better than to try it again."

I spoke gently, but with a sincerity I was confident would show clearly in my face. I was neither sarcastic nor dominating. I assumed my tone was effective because Imelda appeared to be relaxed and listening. I continued on:

"You now come and tell Ninoy and me that if our guerrillas kill your people you will get even by getting us and our friends. Okay! First of all, Ninoy, as you know, has a soft spot for you. He thinks of you as the person who allowed him to come here for his heart operation, and he is truly grateful. Ninoy did not wish to debate this point with you because you may have felt insulted, but *I must.*

Firstly, let me stress that neither Ninoy nor I have sent any squads from the United States to assassinate your people. You must believe, and, more than just believe, you must understand what is happening in your country is the work of *Filipinos* in the *Philippines.* Certainly, many of us here admire their dedication and support their struggle for liberation, but we are not the ones doing it or even causing it.

"Secondly, it is true that the Destabilization Plan of the revolutionaries, with which you are familiar, calls for selective assassination of personalities symbolic of the oppression, tortures, foreign support for your regime, and corruption of your family and friends. The assassinations are part of the overall plan. No one from here has ordered the assassinations, and certainly no one from here can order them stopped. If the plan needs to continue, the assassinations will take place. The only way to stop the assassinations is to stop the plan, and the only way to stop the plan is to take away the cause that has convinced ordinary, peace-loving Filipinos to resort to a revolutionary plan. Only you and your husband can remove the cause peacefully. I will come back to this point later.

"Thirdly–and this is the most important aspect–your threat to kill us in exchange for your people, a threat also voiced in Manila by Johnny Ponce Enrile and others, is either a bluff or not a very wise move. I would like to believe it is a bluff. I will explain."

Imelda appeared engrossed. I continued, "Suppose the revolutionaries proceed with their plan and assassinate two of your people–let's say, Disini and Colonel Abadilla. What is their objective? Certainly not vengeance. Their objective is to give a clear warning to all those whom Disini and Abadilla symbolize. Disini is a businessman who stands for the greed and corruption of the business community surrounding the palace. Colonel Abadilla is a notorious killer and torturer of political prisoners and a military officer promoted and decorated by your husband for his efficient service. He symbolizes the ruthlessness and repression of the martial law regime."

I didn't have to think hard to pick out Abadilla and Disini as the best possible symbols of Marcos' terroristic tactics and corruption. Colonel Abadilla is the most notorious torturer and killer of political prisoners. What makes Abadilla's case unique is that despite, or rather because of, his known reputation, Marcos has repeatedly promoted him and actually decorated him for efficient and loyal service, thus making it clear to the Filipino people that Abadilla's conduct is not only condoned but, in fact, rewarded.

As for Disini, although the business cronies and frontmen of the Marcos-Romualdez families are numerous, Disini stands out in a class all to himself. The international press has reported extensively on the many "business schemes" and on the "wheelings and dealings" of Disini.

The January 23, 1978 issue of *Time* magazine reports: "Since the President imposed martial law in 1972, his relatives and cronies, as well as those of his glamorous wife Imelda, the governor of Manila, have been amassing huge fortunes. Their blatant influence peddling has prompted one amazed diplomat in Manila to observe: 'It's incredible what they've taken over.' No one, however, can quite rival the meteoric rise of Disini, a Marcos buddy whose wife is a cousin of Imelda and former governess to the First Couple's three children."

All of the presigious U.S. news publications *(New York Times, Washington Post, Newsweek, Los Angeles Times, Chicago Tribune,* etc.) have reported "the exploits" of Disini. His notoriety as a symbol of the palace corruption has also attracted the attention of the prestigious news media in Europe—the *Economist* of London, *Der Spiegel* of Germany, *Le Monde* of France, and others. A portion of the January 23, 1978 *Time* article is reproduced on the following page.

When I mentioned Abadilla and Disini as typical examples of the regime's repression and corruption, I felt Imelda knew what I meant. However, I thought it was also important to let Imelda know that we understood her vulnerability.

"Suppose the guerrillas do away with Abadilla and Disini. What is their objective?" I repeated the question for emphasis. "The objective is to serve notice to all the Disinis and Abadillas around the

THE PHILIPPINES

Tales from Disiniland

How to succeed in business if you know the right people

Two hours' drive west of Manila in Bataan province, a sprawling 620-megawatt nuclear power generator is rising on a cliff overlooking the ocean. Its $1.1 billion price tag makes it the most costly single venture in Philippine history. It also represents a record-breaking financial windfall for the country's champion wheeler-dealer, Herminio Disini, 41. His total commissions from the project could top $40 million.

What makes Disini's services so valued? It might be his very close friendship with President Ferdinand Marcos, a connection that, according to veteran observers in Manila, was invoked to win a major share of the government's nuclear plant construction contract for Disini's client, Pittsburgh's Westinghouse Electric Corp. Allegations about the suspicious nature of Disini's services recently prompted the U.S. Export-Import Bank, which is providing much of the financing for the project, to ask the Justice Department to determine whether Westinghouse made improper payments to a foreign business agent. . . . .

Disini, of course, is not the only Filipino who has been known to profit from a personal relationship with Marcos. Since the President imposed martial law in 1972, his relatives and cronies, as well as those of his glamorous wife Imelda, the governor of Manila, have been amassing huge fortunes. Their blatant influence peddling has prompted one amazed diplomat in Manila to observe: "It's incredible what they've taken over." Marcos' sister Elizabeth Marcos Keon, for example, is governor of Ilocos Norte province, and Benjamin ("Kokoy") Romualdez, Imelda's brother, who owns the *Times Journal*, one of the capital's major dailies, is governor of Leyte province and heads the League of Provincial Governors and City Mayors. Roberto Benedicto, a frequent Marcos golfing partner, has acquired three television stations since martial law was imposed (giving him a total of four) and is chief of the Philippine Sugar Commission.

No one, however, can quite rival the meteoric rise of Disini, a Marcos buddy whose wife is a cousin of Imelda's and former governess to the First Couple's three children. In the past six years, Disini has transformed an otherwise undistinguished company, Herdis Management & Investment Corp., from a small cigarette-filter manufacturing plant into a conglomerate empire of 33 separate enterprises with assets totaling about $200 million. . . . .

Herdis' extraordinary expansion seems in large part to be the result of favored treatment by Philippine officials. Not only has Disini received government guarantees for his loans—totaling $160 million—but favorable tariff treatment has also permitted his cigarette-filter business to become a near monopoly.

It was this cozy relationship with officials that Disini apparently used on behalf of Westinghouse. For a while, reported TIME's Bernstein last week, it seemed that the nuclear plant deal had been locked up by Westinghouse's chief competitor, General Electric. The Philippine National Power Corporation had finished preliminary feasibility studies by early 1974 and had signed a contract with G.E.'s local consulting firm. According to knowledgeable Philippine businessmen, Marcos then unexpectedly intervened and stunned a number of advisers by ordering that the profitable contract be awarded to Westinghouse instead. . .

Disini bragged that Herdis and Asia Industries will bring him a 7% fee on the $616 million that Westinghouse is being paid to construct the single Bataan plant. A Westinghouse spokesman insisted last week that the commissions being paid are within "corporate policy guidelines. Westinghouse denies it has made any improper payments relating to the Philippines nuclear plant."

Apparently not content with his sales commissions on the nuclear deal, Disini acquired the Philippine Summa Insurance Corp., which promptly won a portion of the $693 million policy sold to the National Power Corporation to cover the Bataan plant. The ambitious entrepreneur also bought controlling interest in the consortium of firms that are constructing the generator under contract from Westinghouse. . . . .

TIME, JANUARY 23, 1978

palace. Even though there shouldn't be any need to explain the effect such assassinations would have among your friends, I will anyway. All the Disinis are rats who care for their skin first and their ill-gotten wealth next. When they finally realize that their lives are in danger, they will run like rats and rush to abandon the sinking ship. Many will leave the country after taking as much of their wealth out of the Philippines as they can. The economy will get worse–it's already pretty bad. In fact, as you know, many of your so-called friends in the business community are already moving vast sums of money out of the country."

Imelda didn't like what she was hearing, but I had the impression she knew it was the truth. I continued.

"As for Abadilla, he is a dirty stain on the reputation of the honorable Filipino soldier. The ordinary Filipino soldier hates Abadilla as much as those who have been tortured by him and his men. The army, in general, will rejoice at Abadilla's death rather than retaliate. The same thing is true of the foreign multinationals, the foreign tourists, etc. As soon as it becomes clear that these people's lives are in danger and that you are in no position to protect them, they will disappear. They have no reason to risk their lives, no commitment to anything except to themselves, to their businesses, and to their pocketbooks. Therefore the damage inflicted on your regime will be significant. This is the objective of the Destabilization Plan." I spoke without pausing. I did not want to risk interruption.

"Now, let us look on the other side of the coin. Suppose after the death of your two people, you turn around and kill two members of the opposition or two of the known guerrilla leaders. What will be the effect? First of all, you'll get damaging publicity. No one could probably prove it was you, but everyone will point the finger at you. Therefore, publicity-wise you will lose, not gain. Now, how about the effect on the revolutionaries? Do you think it will discourage them? On the contrary, it will inspire them and increase their resolve. There will be ten more who will rise to take the place of each murdered rebel. Instead of reducing the guerrillas, you will help multiply them. You see, Mrs. Marcos, there is a great difference between the elite surrounding the palace and the revolutionaries fighting for freedom. The elite have a lot to lose and don't want to risk anything, least of all their lives. The revolutionaries, on the other hand, have given up everything for their cause and are already risking their lives. They are beyond the point of being scared or intimidated. That's the big difference. Can you imagine what would happen if, God forbid, someone shot the son or granddaughter of Senator Tanada, especially for the fifty thousand peso price you put on their heads? God help you. You'll never be forgiven for such a thing, and you can be sure there will be thousands to rush to take their places. Sometimes I don't understand your husband. I thought he was a brilliant man. The worst thing he could have done was to put a price on the lives of Tanada's son and granddaughter."

About two weeks after the ASTA bombings, the headline stories in the Manila papers announced the ₱50,000 REWARD for each of four alleged "terrorist leaders." Two of the four were Renato "Nats" Tanada and his daughter, Karen, son and granddaughter respectively of former Senator Lorenzo M. Tanada. Senator Tanada is the 83-year-old Filipino statesman, by far the most courageous and most respected member of the opposition. The "Grand Old Man," as most refer to the renowned statesman, was himself arrested soon after the April 7, 1978, fraudulent election. He had headed a group of demonstrators carrying a symbolic coffin to mourn "the death of Philippine democracy." Marcos released Tanada a few days later due to the support generated for him by the international press and the Carter administration.

Imelda's expression betrayed geniune concern when I spoke of the rewards for the Tanadas. "I was not in favor of offering rewards for the capture of the Tanadas," she protested. "It was Enrile and some of the hardliners in the military. They have been embarrassed and humiliated by a bunch of kids. They told the President repeatedly that everything was under control and all the urban terrorists had been arrested, but they were embarrassed when more bombs exploded."

"This is precisely the point I was trying to explain earlier. There is *no way* to eliminate the urban guerrillas by force. For every one you catch or kill, ten more will take their place, and you'll never know who it will be. It might be a secretary, it might be an executive, it might be a farm hand, it might be a student, it might be even a nun or a priest."

"The President and I are fully aware of this, but some of the hardline generals don't agree. You know, before the ASTA Conference, we held several meetings to evaluate the guerrillas' threat, but no one in the Security Council seriously considered cancellation. It would have been embarrassing and would have been interpreted as a surrender to the rebels. Enrile laughed at the April 6th threat and said he hoped the terrorists would try it. He would catch them, he said, before they got within a mile of any of the foreign convention delegates. The security measures were very strict. Johnny didn't count on an insider planting the bomb—Doris Baffrey, one of our own government employees from the Tourist Department. You can imagine Johnny's embarrassment. You know how the Filipino feels about what we call 'losing face.' I am sure you can understand how angry the military were, particularly those who were in charge and responsible for the security of the ASTA convention."

I have always believed that Defense Secretary Juan "Johnny" Ponce Enrile is the most unscrupulous high-ranking official in the Marcos government. He always tries to play every side off against each other, meanwhile appearing friendly to everyone. He consistently tries to "buy insurance" from the opposition to save his neck, while at the same time carrying out Marcos' most unscrupulous schemes. There are many "bad eggs" in the present government, but Enrile, in my opinion, tops them all. If he felt it would be in his own interest, he'd betray Marcos and Imelda as easily as he would betray any member of the opposition. Nevertheless, I would not place the blame for the rewards on Johnny but on the dictators themselves. If Marcos and Imelda were not in favor of them, the rewards would never have been offered.

I had reason to believe Enrile was willing to betray Marcos and, in fact, even propose his assassination. I had this impression because in 1976, a person whom at that time I believed enjoyed Enrile's confidence, was used as an "emissary" between Enrile and myself during our "explorations" for the restoration of democracy to the Philippines. The "emissary" was under the impression that I was acting as a spokesman for "certain forces" that was a combination of the Philippine opposition and the U.S. CIA. The emissary told me that Enrile was under the same impression.

Due to my "inexplicable" and sustained involvement with the Philippine situation and my support for the effort to restore a democratic government in the Philippines, many assumed—and still assume—that I am a CIA operative. As a matter of fact, my own brother-in-law, Geny Lopez, once told me that "Jake and I are concerned about your loyalties in case of a conflict in the interests of the Philippines and America. We know your love for the Philippines, but, if push comes to shove, will you support the interests of the Filipino people or, *as a CIA man,* will you have no choice but to take the side of the United States?"

I was initially furious with Geny's unjustified comment linking me with the CIA. I told him I was *not* associated with the CIA, but I later realized my answer would be identical even if I were with the CIA. Nevertheless, I was disappointed in his judgment and his friend Jake's judgment. Eventually, I came to accept the fact that many find it convenient to interpret "my keen interest in the Philippines as part of my work with the CIA."

During discussions with the emissary, we examined and considered several alternatives. Enrile's possible involvement entered into the picture when the emissary suggested that the quickest and most efficient way to restore democracy would be a "bloodless coup" spearheaded by Enrile and implemented by his "loyal military supporters." The plan was discussed in general terms, and the emissary agreed "to discuss the matter with Enrile and get back to me."

After a silence of two months or so, the emissary informed me that "the matter had been discussed" with Enrile. According to the emissary, Enrile had essentially told him he was interested in the "elimination" of Marcos, that he would not attempt to arrest Marcos as long as Marcos was alive, but that Enrile was willing to take over the government if our group (the group they assumed I was in touch with) first "eliminated" Marcos. Enrile was quoted as having said, "as long as Marcos is alive, I will not risk going after him myself, but if your group would eliminate him, then I would be willing to take over the transition government and call for free elections within six months."

According to the emissary, Enrile made it clear that he had ambitions of becoming the head of the next democratic government, and he asked if, in exchange for his cooperation, our group would be willing to support Enrile's Presidency. He further requested a meeting with a trusted high-ranking "representative" of our group. The meeting would explore the different plans and possibilities. Enrile assumed that the representative would be a member of the CIA or the U.S. State Department, but, according to the emissary, Enrile would not deal with me because of "the bad blood between us." During Geny's and Serge's hunger strike, I had publicly denounced Enrile as the "lowest sort of scum responsible for the betrayal of the two hunger strikers."

I had told the emissary that I could possibly arrange such a meeting for Enrile, but I must first obtain more specific information from him. I also said that "the group would not, under any conditions, support the Presidency of Enrile or anyone else. Their only goal is to help restore democracy to the Philippines so that the people can freely choose their own leader through the process of free elections." I did, however, suggest that if Enrile was instrumental in restoring democracy without bloodshed, he would certainly have gained the respect and appreciation of the people, and, at least in this regard, his chances for the Presidency through free elections would improve.

I also asked the emissary to tell Enrile that the opposition leaders I was in touch with did not approve of the "elimination" of Marcos, because, among other objections, they felt it might create chaos and result in a bloody struggle for power. In such a case it was possible that some group other than Enrile's would seize control. Consequently, if the people I represented were to cooperate with Enrile, it would only be on the premise that there would be no assassinations, only arrests, by Enrile's military loyalists.

The emissary agreed to convey the message to Enrile and again "get back to me." Several more months passed, and, in December of 1976, I had another meeting with the emissary. I was then informed that Enrile "was not ready to move against Marcos in a bloodless coup," because, among other reasons, "Enrile's loyal group in the military was not as strong as we perhaps thought. Marcos, Enrile had said, had replaced most high-ranking military officers with Ilocanos, whose loyalty belonged strictly and solely to Marcos." Thus ended the "explorations" with Johnny Enrile.

There was no way I could be certain that the emissary was in fact communicating the messages back and forth between Enrile and me, but I had good reason to believe he was.

Returning now to my conversation with Imelda about Enrile, I was tempted to tell her my experience but decided against it. Firstly, she might have thought I just wanted to intrigue, knowing her dislike and mistrust of her Defense Minister. Secondly, it was not really pertinent to the main subject of our conversation.

"Mrs. Marcos," I said, "it really makes no difference who proposed the reward for the Tanadas and who approved it. The responsibility rests on the *head* of your regime. That's your husband. I just pray that someone does not shoot any of these four Filipinos for the 50,000 pesos you offered, because, I am sure, it would be an injustice that would never be forgiven."

"This problem of the Tanada children must be solved soon," she said. "It *would* be a tragedy if something really happened. I'll talk to the President about it as soon as I return to Manila."

"I hope you do something about this soon," I assented. "Now returning to the subject we were discussing, this business of two of yours for two of ours, I believe the bottom line is that if two or more of your people get assassinated, you get seriously hurt and weakened. If you retaliate and assassinate two or more of the opposition leaders, you do not balance things out. On the contrary, you get hurt more, while at the same time you strengthen the revolutionaries. Now, please tell me. Don't you think this is a more accurate analysis of the effects of assassinations on both sides?"

All this time Imelda had just been listening. She made no effort to interrupt or to protest. I had the gut feeling she knew I was not threatening, but I was telling her the truth as I believed it to be. She might not agree with everything I said, but she knew I believed in what I was saying. What is more, I felt that she saw some of the more obvious points of my presentation.

"Well, it is difficult to say," she answered. "Some radicals may realize we mean business and get discouraged, but it's quite possible that others may get radicalized and join the underground. In any event, this would be terrible, and we must prevent it from happening." Her tone was calm and realistic and her answer, I thought, as close to accepting the truth as could be expected under the circumstances.

I decided to make the point even clearer. "Well, you have Eddie Olaguer in jail. He has admitted during pre-trial interrogation that he has taken arms against you. He restated the same thing during his formal trial. Why don't you put him against the wall and shoot him?"

"Oh, No, No, No," she protested, "we don't want to do that."

"What do you mean No, no, no?" I persisted. "The man had admitted to the deed you are trying to prove in your military courts. Why continue the trial? Just shoot him."

"No, No," she repeated. "That is not the answer."

"Well, of course, you're right," I said in agreement. "It's really *not* the answer. You shoot Olaguer and the next day there will be hundreds or thousands taking his place. That's the whole point," I said with finality.

"You know, Steve," Imelda said in a warm, almost a motherly tone, "I love my little country and people. I want to find ways to prevent bloodshed. No one will gain from violence. We must all do our best to solve our country's problems *peacefully*. There is nothing I would not do to help my country. The President is a kind and compassionate man. He is often misunderstood. We have made so much progress during the past eight years because the President used a firm hand. You remember how it was prior to 1972? Almost total anarchy. A strong hand was needed. The Filipinos are not ready yet for American democracy. They are like children who need the discipline of a strong father. We want to give our people everything, but we should not give it to them all at once. Look what happens to little children who have indulgent parents giving them everything they want. The children get spoiled because they are not mature enough to utilize what the parents give them."

"You are quite right, Mrs. Marcos," I agreed. "Young children need the discipline of their parents, but the children grow up and become independent. When the parents continue to impose their will on grown-up, independent children and attempt to regulate their lives through more discipline, the children revolt. Besides, normal people become parents through love and the will of God. They do not become parents by force. No father has the right to grab a child that is not his and force his will upon it, all in the name of love."

"Steve, I understand my people better than anyone. I study them all the time and even conduct experiments. I want to give my people not only everything they need but also everything they want to make them the happiest people in the world. But I know I should not give it to them all at once; it must be gradual. I have actually tested this by conducting an experiment. Let me explain. I found a small barrio of about fifty to sixty families where the people were very poor and just struggling to survive. I studied their lives and habits. They would work all day in the fields, from grandparents to grandchildren, trying to provide for their mere existence. But you will be surprised. They were not unhappy people. It was a happy little community. They all loved and helped each other like one big family. They were content being busy. They also managed to enjoy themselves. Every Saturday night they would have their barrio fiesta—roast their pig, sing, dance, etc. The crime rate in that barrio—theft, rape, murder, etc.—was way below the national average; crime was practically non-existent. Well! I thought this barrio was ideal for my experiment. I gave these people everything you can imagine. I gave them electricity; I gave them a complete water system with tap water in every house; I started a small industrial project where everyone would be employed at high wages; I built a school and sent them a teacher—the children were now at school instead of in the fields; I gave them almost everything they could never expect to acquire in their whole lives. What do you suppose happened? Do you think they were happier now?"

"I don't know. What happened?" I asked, even though I half-guessed her answer.

"On the contrary," she said, "they now had all these things and didn't know what to do with themselves and their time. They were jealous of each other—of who had the better TV or the better house; they started to fight and steal, even to kill each other. In a short time, this community changed from a group of the most peaceful, contented, hard-working people to a barrio with the highest crime rate in our country. You see what happens when you give immature children too much too soon? That is why we want to give our people as much as possible, but *gradually.*"

I listened with interest and studied her face. She seemed quite sincere. I said to myself: I suppose she really did conduct such a foolish experiment. I saw no point in trying to debate her experiment or to explain why I felt her conclusion was erroneous. I was not there to prove who could win more points. I was there to tell her the truth about the explosive situation in her country in a way in which probably no one else could tell her. Maybe, just maybe, she would understand the real problem and decide to work for its solution.

CHAPTER 12

You Are Always Welcome

Considering the subjects under discussion, the atmosphere was quite relaxed. If someone listened to our conversation without knowing our backgrounds, he might have easily assumed that Imelda and I were two old friends just chatting casually about our differences.

I appreciated this atmosphere. I knew that if our meeting were an emotional confrontation, nothing could be accomplished. With the kind of dialogue we were now having, there was hope we could establish a constructive line of communication. I had no great illusions, but I did have hope. I felt that, so far, some of my touchy points had registered.

I wanted to bring the discussion back to the main issue but Imelda looked eager to continue. I had done most of the talking up to that point and didn't want to appear that I was trying to lecture Imelda, since lecturing was precisely what I was not prepared to accept from her. Furthermore, it had become clear that the meeting was open-ended and would be long.

I took the pack of cigarettes out of my pocket as she finished describing her "experiment"–I had not smoked until now–and asked, "Would you mind if I smoked?"

"No, not at all. Please go ahead," she answered. "I am sorry, I didn't offer you anything. Would you care to take something?" she asked attentively.

"A cup of coffee would be great, if it's not too much trouble."

"Colonel," she turned to the man standing behind her. "Colonel, have some coffee and cookies sent up."

"Yes, Mam." I finally heard the voice of the Colonel. A few minutes later, a huge silver tray arrived containing servings for coffee, tea, and at least one hundred assorted cookies. Looking at the huge tray, I smiled, thanked the Colonel and helped myself to the coffee. Meanwhile Imelda resumed the conversation.

"I don't know why Presy feels bad about me. We were such close friends. I always liked and respected her. When she left Manila with you, we were on good terms. When you visited Manila years later, I welcomed you both and treated her like the old friend she was."

I felt Imelda was now moving in an unproductive direction. I didn't mind avoiding a debate on the merits and demerits of her barrio experiment, but I couldn't feel honest if I remained silent about the facts surrounding our last and only meeting in the past eleven years.

From September 1972 until early 1974, my father-in-law, Eugenio Lopez, Sr., patriarch of the Lopez family, had been yielding to all of Marcos' demands in an attempt to gain the freedom of his imprisoned son, Eugenio, Jr. (Geny). Imelda's brother, Benjamin "Kokoy" Romualdez, had been visiting the senior Lopez in San Francisco almost every month since late 1972, submitting the Marcos' demands, which, if complied with, would presumably secure Geny's freedom. By early 1974, Lopez had given away all his multimillion-dollar properties to Marcos' associates, but Geny was still in jail.

By March of 1974, the senior Lopez's terminal cancer was so advanced that doctors were giving him only a few more months to live. His only remaining wish was to see his eldest son freed before he died.

Presy and I decided to help. We volunteered to go to Manila and try to find out what more Marcos wanted to release his prime hostage. Presy called the palace and talked to both Imelda and Marcos.

"Please come and see us. It will be great to see one of my best friends," Imelda had said on the phone. She had passed the phone to her husband and Marcos had said, "You are always welcome here. Do come and see us."

So Presy and I went. During our two-week stay in Manila, Imelda allowed us to see her twice, both times in social gatherings surrounded by dozens of other guests. We told her we would appreciate a private meeting with her and her husband to discuss the reason for our trip. We were not granted a private appointment by either Imelda or Marcos. Finally, I sent Marcos a letter, hand-delivered by a friend who had access to Marcos, telling him that, regrettably, we considered our mission a failure and were returning the next day to San Francisco.

Hours before our scheduled departure, Kokoy Romualdez suddenly appeared to "invite" Presy and Geny's wife, Chita, "to see the President on his yacht." They saw him for a few minutes, during which Marcos said, "it would be better if your father came to see me personally to discuss this sensitive matter."

In spite of his grave condition, old man Lopez did go to the Philippines to see Marcos. It was the last time he would see his beautiful country. He returned to San Francisco a few weeks later without a resolution. He had seen Marcos only once.

A few months after his father fruitless visit, on November 12, 1974, Geny Lopez decided to embark on a hunger strike "to focus world attention to the plight of all Filipino political prisoners." From his prison cell, he smuggled a letter to his parents—in the underpants of his wife—informing them of his decision to "stake one's life for His (God's) principles." Geny wanted to free his father from the bond caused by his detention. The letter read:

November 12, 1974

My very dearest Nanay and Tatay,

Please be assured that I have thought over very completely my decision. I believe I am very fortunate in that I am being provided the opportunity to test the ultimate proof of my love for God—the willingness to stake one's life for His principles. Not very many are given this chance. My commitment to Our Lord is total. If He wills to cut my life short through this fast, then it simply means that I shall be reunited with Him that much sooner. Isn't this the objective of our existence anyway? I am at peace with all—even with those who have persecuted us.

But by this act, I hope to end the humiliation and punishment that both of you have undergone for the past two years. Also, I hope to restore some of the dignity that rightfully belongs to any man and which you have been deprived of. You have demeaned yourselves, you have been embarrassed—you have suffered enough. It is now time to speak up. I can only guess what you have undergone, Tatay. You have always been a fighter. My detention neutralized you. But the voices that have been stilled must now awaken. We must now fight for what is right. You must now be like that Spanish general at the Alcazar who did not mind seeing his son die. They can no longer harm me. What I have, nobody can take away.

You have always fought and stood for principles. This is what our enemies do not have. So how can they win? Do what you like. Do not worry about me.

Geny

The hunger fast had a worldwide impact. It was the greatest embarrassment to Marcos since the imposition of martial law two years earlier. By the tenth day of the hunger strike—in which Geny's cellmate, Sergio Osmena, III had also joined—Marcos decided to "negotiate." He sent his emissary, Johnny Enrile, to the hunger strikers and also invited their wives to the palace, promising them that he would meet their demands to release all political prisoners not facing formal charges, *if* Geny and Serge ended their hunger fast. They believed Marcos and stopped their fast. They were deceived.

Geny and Serge were taken to a military hospital, and, after a short period of recuperation, always under heavy security, they were thrown back in jail.

Before the end of the year, even the desperate old man Lopez lost all hope of seeing his son again. He had nothing left to trade for Geny's freedom except his soul. Marcos now wanted a declaration of support for his martial law regime, both from the father and the son. Neither of them was willing to endorse it.

Moved by his son's letter urging him "to fight," old man Lopez decided to engage in his last battle. On December 31, 1975, he broke his two-year silence and issued a long press statement describing the gruesome details of how Marcos had been blackmailing the Lopez family for more than two years. During January and February of 1975, the dying old man gave several press interviews despite his health condition. He presented convincing documentation proving that all three of the major business enterprises owned or controlled by the Lopezes were extorted from them by the Marcos-Romualdez families.

One of the newsmen who interviewed the Lopez patriarch several times was the nationally-known "intelligence" editor of *Parade* magazine, Lloyd Shearer. (*Parade* is a Sunday supplement to more than 100 major newspapers in the United States.) Shearer's March 2, 1975 article read as follows:

THE WASHINGTON POST March 2, 1975

PARADE MAGAZINE

Extortion in High Places

By Lloyd Shearer

In September, 1972, Ferdinand Marcos, President of the Philippines, declared martial law. Now comes word that Marcos and his wife's family, the Romualdezes, are about to become the two wealthiest families in the Philippines via a series of incredible financial manuevers.

Eugenio Lopez, Jr., 45, former publisher of "The Manila Chronicle," was arrested in the Philippines on Nov. 27, 1972, and jailed without a trial or any formal charges. Marcos' henchmen said he was implicated in a plot to assassinate Marcos, which Lopez and his family claim is not true.

What the Lopez family claims **is** true is that Marcos is holding Eugenio Lopez, Jr. as a hostage until the Lopez family signs over all its vast holdings in the Philippines.

Eugenio Lopez, Sr., former president of the Manila Electric Company, says, "I have already given up to the Marcos Foundation my holdings in Manila Electric which are worth at least $20 million. The Marcos Foundation had made to me the ridiculous down payment of $1500 and claims they will pay some more if the company ever makes any money. Meanwhile they control the company which is worth some $400 million.

"I signed over my holdings in the hope that President Marcos would release my son and let him join me here in San Francisco. But to date, Marcos has refused. He still holds my son captive in the Philippines and claims he will try him in a civil court.

"I accuse President Marcos of holding my son hostage so that he can blackmail me and my family into silence and have his front men take over all our business enterprises in the Philippines.

"Only recently the Marcos front men took over our family's six TV and 21 radio stations. They paid nothing for them. The front men Marcos is using are controlled by Gov. Benjamin Romualdez of Leyte province, who is the brother of Imelda Romualdez-Marcos. Mrs. Marcos' uncle is also the Philippines' ambassador to the U.S. Both families run the country.

"I am an old man of 74. I am ill with cancer. I would like to have my son beside me, to see him once more before I pass on. The report that Geny [diminutive for Eugenio Lopez, Jr.] was involved in an attempt to assassinate Marcos is ridiculous. After all, Marcos was an old friend of ours. We supported him and Imelda until we realized his true aims.

"My family has agreed to all of the Marcos demands to secure the release of our son. I have signed away the Manila Electric Company, the largest corporation in the Philippines. I have signed away the largest TV-radio chain in the islands, the ABS/CBN broadcasting networks; also "The

Manila Chronicle," one of the major daily newspapers in the country, was forcibly leased to Governor Romualdez, Imelda Marcos' brother. I told him that he could take over all the assets of Benpres, my holding company, at no cost, in exchange for the freedom of my son and the safety of the rest of my family. But no sooner do I comply with one of their demands then they come up with another.

"First, they demanded that my family keep quiet about everything and never criticize Marcos or his martial law. Then they asked me to visit the Philippines in order to prove that I was no political opponent in exile, threatening Marcos' position. I did that, too, in April, 1974. I have been blackmailed into silence, into giving up millions of dollars in my company assets. Enough is enough. I refuse to be blackmailed further. The Marcos and Romualdez families have bled me dry.

"It was lucky for me and some of my family that we were traveling in the U.S. when Marcos declared martial law.

"Ferdinand and Imelda Marcos have a young daughter Maria who is a sophomore at Princeton University in New Jersey. How would they like it if the United States Government suddenly held their 'Imme' hostage? That is not how civilized governments are supposed to behave. I, Eugenio Lopez, Sr., an old man, now appeal to public opinion. I have no other source to help me regain my son."

The *Parade* article sent shock waves to Manila. It was the first "raw article" to appear in prestigious U.S. newspapers exposing the corruption of the Marcos-Romualdez families and their crude extortion schemes.

Marcos realized that if *Parade* could not be made to apologize for its accusations and retract its statements, other newspapers in the United States and in other countries would rake over the gruesome details of the Lopez blackmail and would have a field day on this very damaging evidence.

I later learned that an emergency meeting had been called immediately by Marcos to decide on the course of action. Firstly, additional staff was assigned to the Philippine Embassy in Washington to handle the flood of inquiries from the United States Congress and the American news media. Secondly, a team in Manila was assigned to prepare a lengthy and confusing legalistic document of how the Lopez properties were allegedly acquired "legally" by Filipino companies unrelated to the Marcos-Romualdez families. The 120-page bound report was prepared within a few days and hundreds of copies were hand-carried to Washington, D.C., by a Philippine government official. Copies of the document were distributed by the Philippine Ambassador in Washington to hundreds of U.S. Congressmen and Senators, many of whom had officially raised questions about the article. The actual letter of inquiry made by California Congressman Fortney H. Stark, Jr., is reproduced below. It is similar to the inquiries made by many U.S. Congressmen and Senators.

March 12, 1975

His Excellency
Eduardo Z. Romualdez
Ambassador Extraordinary and Plenipotentiary
Embassy of the Philippines
1617 Massachusetts Avenue
Washington, D. C. 20036

Dear Mr. Ambassador:

I was surprised by the article "Extortion in High Places" in the Parade section of the Washington Post. The charges made are extremely disturbing.

The article states that President Marcos has held Mr. Eugenio Lopez's son, Eugenio, Jr., in jail without trial or formal charges. How has this occurred in a country which recently released its political prisoners?

I have also read that the President holds open-dated resignations from Philippine judges. What implications does this have for Philippine justice?

I would appreciate hearing your comments on this matter.

Sincerely,

Fortney H. Stark, Jr.
Member of Congress

FHS/jhc

The response of the Marcos government to the hundreds of inquiring legislators is typified by the following letter sent by Ambassador Romualdez to Congressman Thomas Rees:

EMBASSY OF THE PHILIPPINES
WASHINGTON, D. C. 20036

12 March 1975

Dear Congressman Rees:

In further reference to your letter dated March 6, 1975, on the subject of Messrs. Eugenio Lopez, Jr. and Sergio Osmena III, please permit me to furnish you with the following:

1. A Press Statement of the Secretary of Public Information of the Philippines replying to an article in the March 2nd issue of Parade Magazine which dealt with the case of Mr. Lopez' detention as well as certain transactions involving the Lopez properties in the Philippines, and

2. A pamphlet entitled "Meralco Foundation - Benpres Transaction" which clarifies the transfer of the Lopez interest in the Manila Electric Company (Meralco) to the Meralco Foundation; this was the subject of a brief prepared by one Gerald Hill, a lawyer in San Francisco retained by Mr. Eugenio Lopez, Sr.

I trust the foregoing materials will assist you in any further consideration you may wish to give to this matter.

Please accept assurances of my high regard and esteem.

Sincerely yours,

EDUARDO Z. ROMUALDEZ
Ambassador

Enclosures:
As stated.

The Honorable
Thomas M. Rees
United States House of Representatives
Washington, D.C. 20515

In addition to the responses by the Ambassador in Washington, one of Marcos' cabinet members, Francisco S. Tatad, was assigned to respond personally to many U.S. legislators and newsmen who were considered particularly important.

Tatad's direct responses from Manila are typified by the following March 21 letter to Congressman Matsunaga of Hawaii:

Department of Public Information
Manila Philippines

21 March 1975

Rep. Spark Matsunaga
House of Representatives
Washington, D. C. 20515

Dear Congressman Matsunaga:

I am writing on behalf of His Excellency, President Ferdinand E. Marcos, to acknowledge your letter of 4 March, expressing your concern about certain allegations that have been made against the President, his wife's family and the Philippine Government in the Parade issue of March 2, 1975.

It is unfortunate that neither the American press nor the American Congress seems to have been spared of the barrage of anti-Philippine propaganda, which seems to have had the effect of misleading otherwise well-meaning American individuals.

Fortunately for us, the Philippines remains an open - rather than a closed - society, and events can be verified objectively by any observer who comes to the country without any fixed biases and conclusions. We are confident that through objective investigation, the distortions and misrepresentations that have been made and continue to be made about my country will eventually be rectified.

For the moment, we wish to assure you that we are more sinned against, than sinning, in the Parade article of March 2 and we are sure Parade itself realizes this by now. I am enclosing herewith a copy of a reply I sent to Parade to correct its false and malicious allegations against President and Mrs. Marcos.

We hope that in a small way the truth about those allegations will help inform the "indignation" which, as you say, is "mounting across America."

With all best wishes.

Very sincerely,

FRANCISCO S. TATAD
Secretary of Public Information
Republic of the Philippines

Thirdly, and most importantly, a team of lawyers was assigned to study the legal steps Marcos could take to intimidate the management of *Parade* magazine and, hopefully, force an apology and a retraction.

Following the meeting of the lawyers, Marcos dispatched the following urgent cable to the Editor of *Parade,* Jess Gorkin, through his Information Minister:

Jess Gorkin
Parade Magazine
733 3rd Avenue
New York City, NY 10017

WE BELIEVE PRESIDENT AND MRS. MARCOS AND MY GOVERNMENT DESERVE AN APOLOGY FOR FALSE AND MALICIOUS

ALLEGATIONS IN PARADE ISSUE OF MARCH 2 STOP THOSE WHO HAVE BEEN MISLED ARE ENTITLED TO KNOW THE TRUTH STOP WE TRUST YOU WOULD TAKE TROUBLE TO GATHER FACTS FIRSTHAND BY SENDING SOMEONE TO MANILA OR AT LEAST ALLOW EQUAL SPACE FOR REPLY WHICH FOLLOWS BY NEXT CABLE THANKS

FRANCISCO S. TATAD
SECRETARY OF PUBLIC INFORMATION
REPUBLIC OF THE PHILIPPINES

A 7-page cable from Tatad to Gorkin followed the next day. The lengthy cable contained an obfuscated legalistic explanation of the "sales transactions" and accused *Parade* of having "unceremoniously maligned the Philippine President and Mrs. Ferdinand Marcos." It also accused *Parade* of having made "blatantly false and offensive charges against them without verification, much less comment, from their side."

The cable ended by requesting the publication of Marcos' lengthy cable and by demanding an apology. "You have done President and Mrs. Marcos and the Filipino people an undeserved and unconscionable wrong—for which the least you can do is to extend to them a proper apology," the cable concluded.

In addition to the direct cables from Manila, Gorkin was visited in his New York office by Ambassador Romualdez. In the meantime, to further intimidate the *Parade* management, one of Marcos' newspapers in Manila reported that the aggrieved parties had decided to file multimillion-dollar libel suits against the Lopez family and against *Parade* magazine.

Responding to the threat to file a suit against the Lopezes, I issued a press statement calling the threat a bluff and challenging Marcos to file the suit in the U.S. Courts. "We consider any move by Marcos to bring legal action in the U.S. or international courts a welcome development," my statement read.

Overwhelmed by the bombardment of cables and the visits

from high Philippine government officials, Jess Gorkin appeared concerned about the possible consequences. He contacted me and expressed his and his board of directors' concern. I assured him the article was accurate and the official documentation in my possession would back up all the statements made in the *Parade* article.

Gorkin was not convinced. He asked me to fly to New York to clarify my position and then fly to Philadelphia to convince *Parade's* lawyers that there was no danger of a libel suit. I flew to New York and briefed Gorkin. I then flew to Philadelphia and had a gruelling 8-hour session with *Parade's* lawyers. They were all convinced their article was accurate and backed up by irrefutable evidence. The following day Ambassador Romualdez revisited Gorkin in New York to get his reply.

"We stand by our article" Gorkin told Romualdez. "We don't see the need for an apology or retraction, or even publication in our magazine of your lengthy response. However, in the interest of justice and fair play, we are prepared to arrange at our expense a nationally-televised press interview. A panel of well-known reporters will interview your representatives on one side and Steve Psinakis on the other side. The interview will be live and unrehearsed. Mr. Psinakis accepted the offer. Would you also like to accept?" Gorkin asked.

"I will have to consult with my government in Manila," Romualdez responded and left.

The offer was rejected, and Marcos never pursued his threat of filing a libel suit either against *Parade* or against the Lopez family.

I will always be grateful to Lloyd Shearer for studying the facts and writing the March 2, 1975 article. I will similarly always be grateful to Jess Gorkin for upholding the values of the free American spirit and the tradition of our free press.

This exposé of the blackmail by the Marcos-Romualdez families, was to be old man Lopez' "Last Hurrah." Four months later, on July 6, 1975, the ailing patriarch succumbed to terminal cancer. From his deathbed, just three days before he died, he issued a last appeal; he pleaded with Marcos to send his son "under guard" to the hospital for a final farewell. The appeal was denied.

These thoughts about her treatment of Presy's family raced through my mind as I talked to Imelda. Certainly she was making a mistake to remind me how well she treated Presy and I during our April 1974 visit to Manila. Still, I realized there was nothing to be gained by reminding Imelda what really happened prior to, during, and after our 1974 visit to Manila.

"Mrs. Marcos," I said somberly, "both Presy and I have nothing but sad and unpleasant memories of our encounters with you and your husband during our 1974 visit to Manila. It's best we leave that subject alone. The only good thing we can associate with our efforts to secure Geny's freedom was his sucessful escape three years after that visit. I am sure you now wish you had let Geny and Serge out on your own."

Soon after Marcos and Enrile betrayed Geny and Serge and threw them back in jail after their hunger fast, the two cellmates reached a new decision. "We must try to escape," they told each other. "It's now clear that Marcos will never let us out as long as he is in power, and, if he falls, he'll have us killed before he goes."

With the help of Geny's best friend, Jake Lopez, Geny's wife, Chita, and their two eldest sons in Manila, and with the help of a few of us here in the United States, several escape plans were studied over a period of two years. The final plan was attempted on the night of September 30, 1977, and, 33 hours later, the two prisoners had gone from their cells in Manila through four different countries, finally landing at the Los Angeles Airport in California.

Various accounts of the escape appeared in many newspapers around the world. The most interesting and accurate newspaper account I have come across was written by a young reporter named Stu Cohen of the Boston *Phoenix*. Stu interviewed Geny and I for several hours, and the story he wrote from those interviews was published on November 8, 1977. It read:

THE BOSTON PHOENIX November 8, 1977

The Great Escape

From Manila to LA in 33 hours: How two prisoners of the Marcos regime broke out of a Filipino jail

by Stu Cohen

Lingayen is a small, sleepy town in the northern Philippines. It sits on a cove and there's an airstrip, about 400 yards from the waters of the South China Sea. Not a very busy place, the Lingayen airstrip usually plays host to the private planes of wealthy Filipinos and tourists, bound for Baguio and other resorts to the north. Nothing much in the way of amenities: a little shed that provides a bit of shelter from the sun, a windsock and a runway that points out over the sea to Hong Kong and China.

At 7:40 on the morning of October 1, five men waited at the airstrip, scanning the horizon. They talked to some children who were playing nearby and amused themselves by watching the antics of a company of soldiers doing their morning calisthenics on the far side of the runway; to anyone who cared to notice, they were simply five men of varying ages, probably prosperous, probably off on a pleasure trip.

They had been waiting for more than an hour when, at 7:45, a speck appeared on the horizon. As it grew, the aircraft's blue-and-white markings identified it as the one they were awaiting. The plane—a twin-engined, six-seat Cessna 320—came in across the sea and touched down lightly on the runway, rolling towards the waiting group. And then a curious thing happened.

The pilot reached the runway's end and turned the ship's nose back toward the ocean; without stopping, he opened the Cessna's door. Moving quickly but deliberately, the five men jumped into the plane; the door closed; the pilot increased his speed and the plane took off again, rising out over the cove, heading for Hong Kong.

For two of the passengers, Eugenio

Lopez and Sergio Osmena, it was the first day of freedom in five years. After two years of planning and almost six months of intense preparation, Lopez and Osmena had escaped from the maximum-security prison in which they had been held since being arrested by the government of President Ferdinand Marcos. And now, nearly 11 hours after their jailbreak, Lopez and Osmena were on their way to Los Angeles **via** Hong Kong and Tokyo.

Neither Eugenio Lopez, Jr. nor Sergio Osmena III is your average political prisoner. At the time of his arrest, in November 1972, scarcely a month after President Marcos invoked martial law "Geny" Lopez—a small, ebullient man of 48—was the publisher of the **Manila Chronicle,** the country's second largest daily. In addition, his combined Alto Broadcasting System-Chronicle Broadcasting Network (ABS-CBN) owned six television and 22 radio stations and was the largest media organization in the Philippines. His uncle, Fernando Lopez, had been Marcos' vice-president and the Lopez family was powerful and solidly entrenched in Filipino society. So it was with more than a little surprise that "Geny" Lopez found himself in prison. "How I became a political prisoner," he said with an ironic laugh in a **Phoenix** interview last week, "I'll never know."

But a political prisoner he was, charged with plotting the assassination of the president. Sergio Osmena III (now 33), accused of the same crime and housed in the same prison, was also the scion of a powerful family. From a power base on Cebu (in the south), Osmena's grandfather had become president of the wartime government-in-exile; Sergio's father had run against Marcos in 1969. "Modern dictators," said Lopez, "don't round up one or two million people and put them in concentration camps—they arrest symbols in order to cow the rest of the population."

And as "symbols" neither Lopez nor Osmena was subjected to the physical brutality that has become commonplace in many of the world's political prisons. Incarcerated in a maximum-security section on the Fort Bonafacio military base in suburban Manila, the two were segregated from other prisoners but allowed a variety of privileges.

There were weekly visits from family members and daily food packages from Lopez's wife, Conchita. There was a garden behind the double cell in which they lived, and a patio with a variety of recreational equipment, including weights and a punching bag. And until they staged a hunger strike in 1974, there were occasional "home passes" as well. But, Lopez remembers, "The loss of freedom was itself a form of torture."

Two years ago, as their imprisonment dragged on, Osmena and Lopez began talking about escape. The tentative plan at that time centered on the "home passes," but the passes were suddenly canceled. "And so the plan—the idea—lay in limbo for a while," Lopez told the **Phoenix,** "until last April, when Jake Lopez (Augusto Lopez, a lawyer and no relation to Eugenio) said 'You know, since your hunger strike you've become symbols for the opposition in this country and I think you should make an attempt to escape—even if it doesn't succeed, well,at least you made one.' So my wife and I and Serge discussed this very carefully because we knew that, well, first we had to answer the question, 'Were we willing to lose our lives?' I think making that decision really simplified things. I mean, there were no more hassles about the risk and all of that. We were willing to die—of course, not foolishly, but using our talents to the best of our ability. And second was the commitment to the cause of freedom. We could see the tyrant who was oppressing our people, we could see that civil and human liberties were being violated grossly."

In the subsequent months, as the idea grew into a detailed plan, it came to involve family members and friends in the Philippines and Lopez's brother-in-law, Steve Psinakis, a naturalized US citizen (born in Greece) and an engineering consultant in San Francisco. Through coded messages between Manila and the US, Psinakis developed an intricate and well-financed plan to get Lopez and Osmena out of the Philippines and into the US. But the more immediate problem was how to get them out of Fort Bonafacio.

This was, admittedly, not the same as freeing them from a medieval dungeon. The maximum-security area (see accompanying diagram) is essentially a fenced-off area inside the military base. They would have to cross two fences, but the chief difficulties would be getting out of their quarters unseen and then traversing the open ground of the prison: the area is ringed with lights and watched constantly.

"We accepted the fact that we had only one chance, one attempt; we would not have another," Lopez says. "We agreed that it would be made on September 19. And then my wife said that perhaps we should postpone it to the 22nd, because the 21st was the fifth anniversary of martial law and on this day the president usually releases some political prisoners and on the one percent chance that he was feeling benevolent, he might just let us go. I was not very sanguine about it and, as you might have expected, no releases were made."

Meanwhile, in Los Angeles, Steve Psinakis had purchased the Cessna that would land at Lingayen and had found someone to fly it. The pilot would be Reuven Jerzy—a US citizen, an airplane salesman, a figher pilot for the Israeli side in the Six Day War—and a friend of the Osmena family.

As September 22 approached, however, the plane was laid up with engine trouble and a typhoon was moving across the South Pacific. Lopez and Osmena rescheduled the escape for Thursday, September 29, at 9 pm.

By that rescheduled date everything seemed to be in order for the planned escape.

Reuven Jerzy had arrived in Manila several days earlier. Accompanying him in the Cessna was Angel Slater, a friend from California, who was posing as the pilot's fiancee. To the authorities, they were merely two flamboyant American tourists who intended to fly to the northern resorts for some fishing. However, when Slater called the States to advise her family that they had arrived safely, she was told, according to plan, that her mother had been seriously injured in an auto accident and that she was needed at home. The next day she boarded a commercial flight for Los Angeles, **via** Hong Kong; Jerzy was to follow her in the Cessna later. Slater arrived in Hong Kong, left the flight, checked into a hotel and waited for Steve Psinakis.

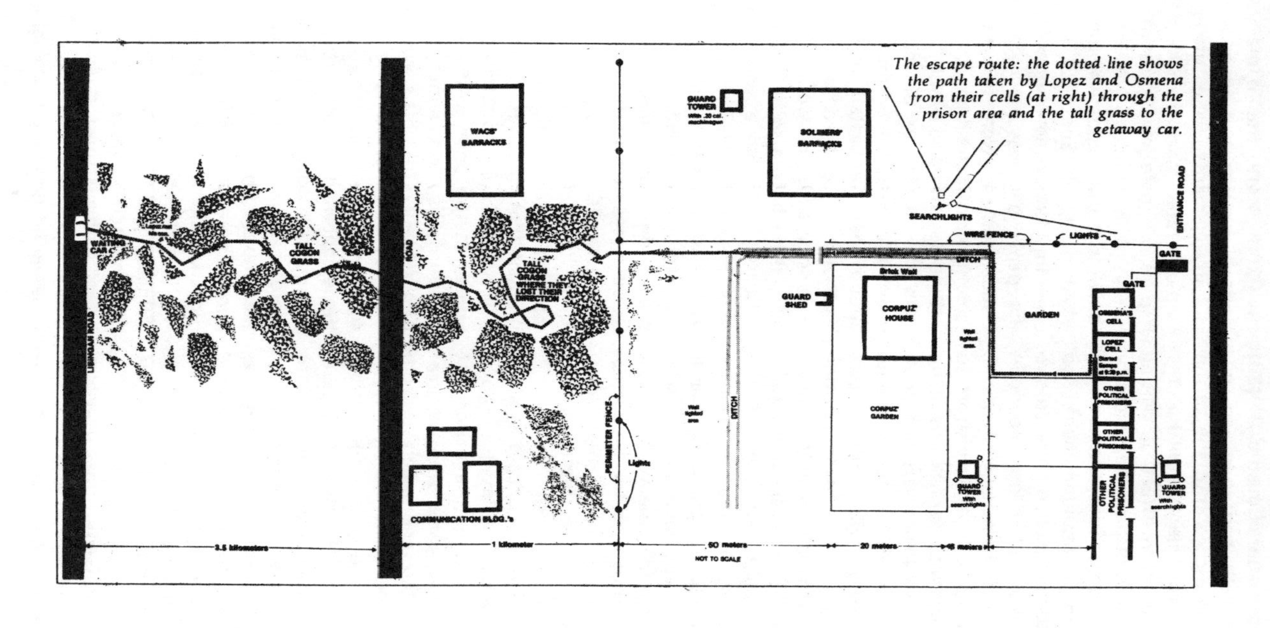

Diagram of the Fort Bonifacio Military detention center showing the Lopez-Osmena prison cells and their escape path to the awaiting car.

During the preceding three months, Lopez's older sons, Eugenio III (25) and Rafael (20) had smuggled supplies for the escape into the prison by taking advantage of a quirk in the security system in effect of visiting days. After establishing their identity at the main gate, visitors were driven to a building containing men's and women's dressing rooms, an adjoining bathroom and a large room in which the actual visits took place. Security officers ferrying visitors to this building returned to the main gate, and the visitors were left unattended for several minutes until a second jeep arrived with those officers who would search them. During these few minutes, Lopez's children would hide whatever contraband they had brought behind the toilet in the bathroom. After an uneventful search, the second group of guards would leave and one of the sons would retrieve the object. When their father was brought in for the formal visit, the guards again left them alone; in this way, three cutting tools were passed to Lopez.

On another visit, Lopez was given two sets of khaki denim clothes of a kind often worn in the prison. At about the same time, the two prisoners requested and received from the prison administration cans of brown, black and green paint, ostensibly for some of their furniture. Osmena painted the denims into camouflage suits. On those occasions when Lopez and Osmena were removed from the prison to attend hearings before a military tribunal, they hid the tools and camouflage suits in the punching bag on the patio.

Conchita and Geny Lopez devised a code for last-minute messages, employing the paper bag in which she sent food to him. If the parcel for the 29th bore the name "Geny Lopez," he was to understand that all arrangements were made; "E. Lopez" would mean that the attempt had to be postponed for another 24 hours; plain "Lopez" would let him know that the escape was uncertain.

"At noon on Sept. 29 the food came in," Lopez remembers, "and on the paper bag was my name, Geny Lopez, and so I went to Serge and I said, 'Tonight's the night.' "

It would not be so simple.

On the afternoon of that day, a guard informed Lopez that a dental appointment requested weeks earlier had been approved by President Marcos and that he would be picked up a little before six in the evening.

"Can you imagine that?" Lopez says, breaking off his account. "For such a common thing as a dental appointment we needed presidential approval." Psinakis smiles and agrees.

Lopez says he told the guard he was ill and would reschedule the appointment for another time. "The guard reported this to his officer and I thought that that was the end of it."

At about 6:15 that evening, a guard arrived at the door with a bottle of vitamin pills, the same kind Mrs. Lopez used. The bottle was marked "E. Lopez." According to the prearranged code, the message meant the escape had to be postponed for 24 hours. Lopez was astonished, therefore, when his sons—on a visit the next day—asked, 'What happened? We were waiting out there all night last night.' What **had** happened was that the officer to whom Lopez's "illness" had been reported took it upon himself to provide the vitamins. Lopez told his sons, "Well, all right, that's water over the dam." The escape would be made that night, September 30, and Lopez and Osmena spent the afternoon making final preparation.

That night at 9 o'clock, Serge and I donned our camouflage suits and we escaped through my bathroom window (see diagram). The window had iron grilles welded to a steel frame, which in turn was nailed to a wooden one. The day before we had pried loose all of the nails. The window remained in place—it had been undisturbed for five years and it was very snug.

"So we took it out and then there were six glass louvers, which we removed one by one, and then we cut the wire screen. I went out of the window first; Serge handed me the glass louvers, then he came out. I propped him against the wall and he pulled the steel frame back into place with a rope that he had looped over the shower head, using the shower head as a pulley. It again fit very snugly. I started handing him the glass louvers one by one. We replaced five of the six but stopped at that point because we were making too much noise."

In each cell bed, Lopez and Osmena left pillow dummies with wigs and arranged the glass louvers so as to obscure any passing guard's view into the rooms.

"That night there was a full moon. It was very still and there was no wind. It seemed that events were conspiring against us, you might say." Once they were out of the window, only shadows protected them from discovery by the guard in his watchtower. They waited about 30 minutes, heard no movement from the tower—"You know, on a still night like that any movement you make is really magnified a lot"—and decided the guard was asleep. They crawled along the edge of their garden, sheltered in the foot-wide shadow of the woven mat fence. After cutting through the mat and the barbed wire behind it, they entered another compound (marked "Corpuz" on the accompanying diagram, since Philippine Communist leader Victor Corpuz and his family were imprisoned there). As they rounded the corner, Sergio, who was in the lead, saw a guard shed, an obstacle they had not counted upon. "You see, there is a drag-racing oval near the base, and my sons would go out and mix with the crowd. Standing on the roofs of the parked cars, they had taken telephoto pictures of the area to give us an idea of the terrain. But in the pictures we had, this shed appeared to contain a water pump." When they discovered the mistake, "We both agreed that we would remain there until midnight, when the shift changes. We thought maybe the guard might walk back to the barracks without waiting for his relief or that he might fall asleep.

"But that didn't happen: at 12 o'clock we could still hear the guard rattling around with his tin cup. So Serge suggested that we wait until one. Finally at five minutes to one, I said, 'You know, we still have a long way to go and it's going to get light at five o'clock, so I think we should make our move now.'

"So I started crawling along a small ditch which was about six inches deep. I crawled up to a grassy area and waited for Serge, but by 2:30 he had still not arrived."

Osmena had waited for almost 30 minutes to follow Lopez along the ditch. But the longer he waited, the more noise the guard made. Finally, about an hour later, the guard quieted down and Osmena began crawling.

Still waiting, hidden in the tall **cogon** grass, Lopez made up his mind: "I had to make a decision as to whether I would leave Serge or not, but I shoved that to the back of my mind. I began crawling back for about 20 yards and then I heard the swishing of grass and sure enough, it was Serge. 'Just follow my tracks,' I told him.

"Using our pruning shears, we began cutting our way through the thick grass. We made our break through the chain-link perimeter fence of the prison area and started running and stumbling—losing our way for a time—and walking for about 40 minutes to meet my sons.

"They were supposed to meet us at a certain place with a car and a change of clothes but they got impatient and decided to come a bit closer. For the first time in all of this I really got scared, because Serge suddenly said to me 'Look, somebody's coming.' We both dropped down on our bellies and, sure enough, I could see the outlines of a person. I could not imagine who it could possibly be except a soldier; who else would be around a military camp at that hour of the morning? But finally, I realized that it was my son, Rafael. He saw us and said, 'Dad, let's get the hell out of here. Serge and I got into the trunk of the car and were driven to a deserted alleyway in suburban Manila, where we were met by Jake the lawyer—the fifth member of our group—who was driving another car." They drove to a family-owned building in Manila (the plant for the now-suppressed **Chronicle**); while Lopez and Osmena changed clothes in the basement, Jake Lopez called the pilot.

"So," Geny Lopez continued. "at 4 a.m. we drove to this unattended airstrip at Lingayen. We got there at 6:30." By 7:45, he and his sons Eugenio III and Rafael, along with Jake the lawyer and Sergio Osmena, were on their way to Hong Kong where Steve Psinakis was waiting for them.

Leaning back in his chair, listening to his brother-in-law's story with obvious relish, Psinakis comments: "Now, although this is by far the most dramatic part of the escape, in terms of danger to life, what is perhaps as intriguing is how we got through four countries—the Philippines, Hong Kong, Japan and the US—without being detected. There have been dramatic escapes from Fort Bonafacio before but no one has, to our knowledge, gotten 10,000 miles away in 33 hours."

Psinakis had arrived in Hong Kong with four legitimate US passports: his own, his two-year-old daughter's and six-year-old son's, and that of a California friend, Bill Chapman. When Angel Slater met him in Hong Kong, she turned over her passport as well. The sixth would be Reuven Jerzy's ("If he hadn't made it, I wouldn't have needed the passports anyway").

The Cessna landed in Hong Kong during a period when five major commercial flights also arrive. Jerzy handed his passport to Psinakis and the five fugitives mingled with the crowd and worked their way into the lounge for passengers awaiting connecting flights, thus avoiding the scrutiny of immigration officials. Psinakis had already booked six seats on a Japan Air Line (JAL) flight to LA **via** Tokyo; then he and Jerzy wandered over to the ticket counter.

"I gave the clerk six tickets and six US passports—I had bought the tickets in names to match the passports—and said that my kids were doing some last-minute shopping with their relatives. We were checked in and the clerk gave me six boarding passes. We walked away from the desk and I gave Reuven both his passport and Angel's—she was booked to leave the following morning on a Pan Am flight—and then I went to check through immigration normally, as if I were traveling alone. No problems. I went into the transit lounge, gave each one a boarding pass—that's all you need to get on the plane from the lounge. The flight was called, we got on the plane and that's how we got out of Hong Kong.

"As the plane lifted off the runway, that was the first time we relaxed; we embraced and had the kind of emotional reaction that you would expect. And then, this guy," he continued, gesturing at Lopez, "had a few drinks to celebrate his freedom and he was out cold. The others remained awake.

"We thought that this was the end of our hassles. I had picked a plane which would go straight through to Los Angeles with only a brief stopover for refueling in Tokyo. Normally, during such a stopover, you simply remain in the plane." Again, however, it began to look as if "events were conspiring" against the fugitives.

"Coming to Tokyo, half an hour before we were due to land," Psinakis said, "the pilot made an announcement that due to tight security all passengers would have to disembark and go through a passport check. At that time, there was a hijacking of another JAL plane going on. Shit—this was the only place where we hadn't anticipated any problems and now we were in danger of getting caught.

"Had we been stopped in Hong Kong, it wouldn't have been very good, but we thought the US and British governments, being 'human-rights conscious,' would help us get out. But in Tokyo we faced the possibility of being shipped right back to Manila because Marcos and (Japanese Prime Minister) Fukuda are very close."

Moments after the captain's announcement, Psinakis's panic subsided. "I got my cool back a little and told all of these guys to pretend they were asleep. We were in the first-class compartment and I called the steward and said, "Look, these are my children and their uncles here.' " (Psinakis, at 45, could easily pass as the father of Lopez's sons, who are in their 20s.)" 'We've been traveling all day,' I said, 'and we're really tired; we picked first-class in order to get some sleep and I'd appreciate it if we don't have to get off the plane in Tokyo.' The steward said he'd check with the captain, and came back a few minutes later and said, "All right, you all have permission to stay on the plane, but an immigration officer will come in to check you here.' So I thought, 'Well, that's half the battle, anyway.'

"Sure enough, when we landed in Tokyo an immigration officer came in and saw these five guys asleep. I tried to use a bit of psychology on him by putting my finger up to my lips and whispering, 'Ssh,' and saying, 'This is my group; these are my children and their uncles.' He checked the passenger manifest and saw Psinakis—three people' and the names 'Slater,' 'Jerzy,' and 'Chapman.' He asked for the tickets and I had all of them. Next he wanted the passports."

Psinakis clearly could not hand over four passports, two of them for children, for six adult men. Continuing the bluff, he handed over his own passport and said, "Look, we're all together and they're asleep—I'd prefer not to wake them to get theirs.' And it worked: the immigration official said, 'Thank you very much' and walked out." Geny Lopez was still out cold; the other four opened their eyes slowly and gave a collective sigh of relief.

As the plane came within the sight of the California coastline, Psinakis remembers, there was unrestrained emotion. "It was great to see **that** coast," Lopez says.

If the scene in Tokoy airport had been one of tension and drama, the Los Angeles stop was welcome comic relief. "I got up first in line at the immigration check," Psinakis said, "and the others were behind me. I gave my passport to a young woman who stamped it and welcomed me back to the US. Then she called, 'Next,' and I said, 'Well, I have a little problem here; these people behind me just escaped from a prison in the Philippines and they have no papers.' Of course, she was a little surprised.

"The young woman brought her supervisor in and we all went into a corner of the immigration area. At first the fellow was a little excited; he kept saying, 'Oh, oh, you mean these men have no passports? Well, we'll pack them in the first plane and send them back home.'

"I asked the immigration people to call Benjamin Fleck, the US State Department's head of Philippine Affairs, and even gave them Fleck's home number. Because of my lobbying for the Movement for a Free Philippines, I knew Mr. Fleck quite well and he knew who Geny and Serge were. Ben Fleck later told me that when the call came and he learned that Lopez and Osmena were in the US, he almost fell off his chair."

Fleck immediately telephoned senior State officials Richard Holbrooke and Philip Habib, both of whom were in New York for the UN General Assembly. The word came back to LA that Psinakis and his party were to be given over to the custody of the JAL manager and to appear before immigration officials on Monday morning and formally request political asylum.

Monday morning, the Immigration and Naturalization Service granted Geny Lopez, his younger son, Jake the lawyer and Sergio Osmena a 90-day "parole" allowing them to remain in the US until a final decision about political asylum could be made. (Lopez's older son, Eugenio III, is already an American citizen, having been born in Boston while his father attended Harvard Business School.) Sources in Washington report that the likelihood of political asylum's being granted is "very high."

Conchita Lopez and the younger Lopez children remain in the Philippines, but Mrs. Lopez has, since the escape, been issued a new passport without any difficulty. President Marcos has said that she and the children are free to leave at any time; Psinakis and Lopez believe the case will generate so much publicity that the Marcos government will be effectively prevented from taking any reprisals against those still in Manila.

How President Marcos learned about the escape represents the final irony ("I like that part," Psinakis says amid much laughter). When Benjamin Fleck called Holbrooke and Habib in New York, the escape had still not been reported in Manila. Also present at the UN was a large Philippine delegation, including Marcos' wife, Imelda, Defense Minister Juan Ponce Enrile and a retinue of some 87 people, among whom were friends of the Lopez and Osmena families. Ponce Enrile was informed of the escape by the US State Department; according to a friend of the fugitives who was present at the time, the defense minister then called Manila and spoke directly with Marcos.

Two hours later, the president of the Philippines reportedly called back to say the story was correct: two prisoners were indeed missing from Fort Bonafacio.

When the escapees landed safely in Los Angeles, Presy told me, "Poor Tatay [Daddy] could not obtain Geny's release when he was alive, but he must have succeeded in getting the help of our Lord when he joined Him in Heaven."

The escapees on Capitol Hill: Lopez, Jr. and Osmena, III in Washington, D.C., visiting Congressional leaders after their escape. Left to right: E. Lopez, Jr., Senator R. Manglapus, Congressman P. Burton, S. Psinakis, and S. Osmena, III.

CHAPTER 13

Fifteen Years Is Long Enough

Imelda apparently agreed that it would be best to drop the subject of our Manila visit and her "friendly reception" for Presy and me. She changed the subject nicely by asking if I would like some cookies with my coffee.

"It would be nice to see Presy again. I hope we can meet soon," Imelda said warmly. "We worked so hard together during the 1974 campaign. Presy knows how hard I work. I have kept the same pace all these years. There is so much that has to be done for my little country and not enough time to do it. I wonder if I will be able to accomplish all my goals for my people. Our country is just now developing."

"I do not think, Mrs. Marcos, that it is possible for any head of government to ever feel that he or she has finished what had to be done. There is always more to be done and more that should be done to improve the life of the people. This is true not only in developing countries like the Philippines, but also in the developed countries. Certainly President Ford did not step down for Carter because he felt he finished what he had to do for America.

And Carter did not step down for Reagan for this purpose—come to think of it, neither did Franco after ruling Spain for about forty years, or the Somoza family after forty-four years and three generations.

"Heads of governments do not step down because they feel they have finished their work. They step down because their people feel someone else should be given a chance to do better. In free countries like the United States, the people change their leaders through the ballot. In countries where that freedom has been taken from the people, as in Nicaragua, the leaders are changed by the bullet."

Imelda got the point but chose to continue on her own trend of thought. "When you have a developing country needing so much attention to put its house in order and to make progress," she continued, "the disruptions caused by new governments every few years are counterproductive. The President has undertaken several long-term programs vital to the country. So have I. If a new set of leaders were to take over suddenly, all the gains of the New Society would be lost. All the plans in progress will be interrupted and maybe never continued. Any change in our government must be made gradually. Our programs must continue. Let me give you an example?" Imelda said questioningly. I did not respond, so she continued:

"I am now in the midst of the most exciting project of my life. I believe we have solved the energy problem of the country. We have developed a gasifier engine which can generate power and electricity by burning Philippine wood, from the ipil-ipil tree. It's my philodendron project—a dendron is a Greek word for wood, you should know. My assistant," she mentioned a name I didn't quite catch, "invented a method of extracting the tar residue from the ipil-ipil tree, and *you cannot imagine* how clean the gasifier engine runs. You should see it."

Her voice and expression were beginning to show genuine excitement. It seemed like our previous discussion was forgotten. "You cannot imagine what this means for my people. It all started from the idea of the wood-burning engines we used for our busses during the Japanese occupation. The Filipino is very ingenious about such things."

'That was a correct statement,' I thought.

"In addition to generating electricity," she continued, "we have also developed a nice, clean, compact car engine, using wood instead of gasoline. I called Henry Ford and asked him to study using our engines in the Ford Fiera cars being assembled here in the Philippines. But that is only one of its uses. The main achievement is in solving our serious energy problem. You know the ipil-ipil tree grows this big in three years," she made a gesture with her hands, showing a diameter of eight to ten inches. "In any other country of the world, it takes twelve years for the tree to grow so big. I plan to have millions of acres of ravaged land reforested with ipil-ipil trees. You know, in less than ten years we can generate more than five million kilowatts: that's the total present power needs of the *whole* country. My staff estimates that in twenty years we can plant enough trees to generate a total of thirty-five million kilowatts of electric power. All we have to do is cut down what we need, and the trees will be ready again in three years. I have one of my best generals in charge of this project: General Pedro Dumol."

I watched her as she talked with real excitement, and it was absolutely clear she believed every word she was saying. Although she was looking straight in my eyes, I had the impression she was now talking to herself, as if in a trance, without realizing I was still there. I was soon to be proven wrong.

I tried to calculate some of these figures in my head. Theoretically, they were possible, but practically, they were impossible. 'What a coincidence,' I thought. 'Here she is, talking about unrealistic solutions to her country's energy problems, and she is telling her dreams to me, *of all people,* a man whose *profession* is electric power production.'

Ironically, I had met Imelda and her husband through my wife's family, the Lopez family, who at that time controlled Meralco, the electric power company supplying the Metro Manila area with electricity. I had specialized in the design and production of electric power, and, during the sixties when I occasionally met with Imelda, I was the Operations Manager of Meralco.

"Do you realize, Steve, what this means for my little people?" she continued with the same excitement, "Billions of dollars in savings and independence from foreign oil," she said, answering her own question. I was grateful she did; I wouldn't know how to begin if she really expected me to respond to her question.

"The oil imports are killing us, and we're having all kinds of problems with Meralco. Power interruptions and brown-outs are now almost a daily occurrence. You know? Since you left Meralco, the company has gone down the drain."

I was stunned. I could not believe that she was really talking to me and, least of all, that she was aware of my profession. How could she be describing to me in detail her exaggerated "philodendron" project? It was now more clear than ever she really believed every word she was uttering.

It was true that Meralco had gone down the drain after I left the Philippines, but my departure had nothing to do with the deterioration of the power company. When I left Manila in 1969, the company was in the hands of Filipino engineers with better qualifications than mine to manage and operate the power company. I learned the cause of Meralco's problems years later from several of its employees who visited me in San Francisco. Their story was always the same.

After Meralco was taken from the Lopez family in 1972, Imelda's brother, Kokoy, along with other Marcos cronies and some army generals, took over the management and operation of the company. This new breed of totally ignorant managers brought the formerly efficient power company down to the level of their own incompetence.

One typical, but factual, story from an old Filipino chief engineer of one of the Meralco power plants went like this: "I was on duty that Tuesday evening when we detected a small steam leak starting in one of the boiler tubes. I immediately ordered the supervisor to shut down the generating unit for repairs. I was informed by the supervisor that he was under direct orders from the general not to shut down any of the units. I called the general at his home and explained the problem. He asked how serious the leak was, and I told him it was small and had just started, but if we did not stop it in time, it could explode and cause serious damage to the whole unit. The general told me not to shut down the unit. When I tried to protest and asked why, the general snapped at me: 'You should know better; President Marcos ordered yesterday that there would be no more brown-outs. How can you ask to shut down the unit and embarrass the President. You should make the repairs next weekend when the shutdown will not cause any brown-outs.' 'Yes, Sir!' I replied. Four hours later, the leaky tube exploded placing the whole unit out of commission for three weeks instead of the one or two days needed for the repair of the leaky tube."

I realized the strong analogy between this situation at the power company and the first signs of the revolution. 'Would Imelda also wait,' I wondered, 'like her Meralco general and do nothing until it explodes? Can she understand she is incapable of ordering the revolution *not to explode* any more than her general could order the same of the leaky tube? The answer to this question,' I told myself, 'will be known in the next few months.'

Imelda's dendro-thermal energy project is not necessarily a bad project. Wood-fueled power plants and wood-fueled cars are nothing new. As Imelda herself stated, wood-fueled cars were used in many countries during World War II when gasoline was scarce.

The ipil-ipil tree may, in fact, have good burning qualities for this purpose, and a well-organized program to develop the potential of dendro-thermal energy in the Philippines appears to be a worthwhile project. But between a modest, practical project and Imelda's grandiose plans, which she was now relating with genuine excitement, there is a great gap. I couldn't help feeling sorry for this new general, Pedro Dumol, whom Imelda placed in charge of this project; he must be facing a tougher job than her Meralco general.

Imelda went on with this subject for at least fifteen more minutes. She was quoting figures in millions of acres of land to be planted with ipil-ipil trees—mountainsides, valley, useless lands. She was quoting numbers of jobs to be created by this project: many thousands of jobs. She was quoting billions of dollars to be saved: many billions.

As she continued, totally engrossed in what she was describing, I was thinking how easy it is for a person in her position to lose touch with reality. It was disconcerting. She talked about her 5-, then 10,- then 20-year program for the dendro-thermal energy project. The description of her project started when she was trying to explain how counter-productive it is to elect a new government before the old one has a chance to finish the programs it had started. Was she trying to tell me she expected to rule the Philippines for 20 more years so she can complete her ipil-ipil project?

"Mrs. Marcos, your project sounds very interesting. It could be a significant contribution to the energy program of the Philippines." I meant what I said, but I saw no point in attempting to explain that she was projecting far beyond the limited practical application of the ipil-ipil dendro-thermal project. "What really amazes me is your own incredible energy and enthusiasm about the projects you undertake." I also meant that. "I was thinking, while you were just talking, that if you made up your mind to devote a portion of your inexhaustible energy to study the current political crisis in your country, you would easily understand the problem."

"But I *am* doing this. That's why we are here."

"It would certainly be a waste to ignore your energy, but there are many ways you could help your people besides heading the government."

"Steve, I would really feel so helpless and depressed if I could not work for my people."

"There is no reason why you could not always keep helping your people in areas where they would need and want your help."

"When I was a little girl living in the province of Leyte, I was given the task of making the coconut oil for the lamps of our house and those of our neighbors. I used to work so hard grating the coconuts, squeezing the oil, and distributing it to our neighbors for their oil lamps. I thought of myself as 'the light of my people.' Without me, they couldn't see at night. I felt useful, needed, and proud. Then, one day, electricity came to our area. I became so depressed. I was no longer needed. I was no longer the light of my people."

As she narrated her childhood story, there was no question that she was reliving the experience. "I understand your feeling," I said, compassionately.

"Now I am in a position to really give everything I can to my people. That is why I am always involved in so many projects."

"You know, Mrs. Marcos, you and your husband have ruled the Philippines for fifteen years. I think that in your hearts you both believe you have done well for your people. History will be the ultimate judge of this, long after you and I are gone. We can never resolve this issue here, particularly since we know we disagree."

"We are not afraid of history's judgment. We have a clear conscience. So many in our family have served the country well for many many years," Imelda said proudly.

"That's part of the problem, Mrs. Marcos," I commented, "almost every brother, sister, cousin, nephew of yours and/or your husband's is either a high government official or the chairman and president of ten or more large corporations each. You have virtually converted the whole country into a family possession, both politically and economically."

"We are being accused of nepotism, but we are proud that so many people in the President's family and my family have been asked to sacrifice their private lives in order to serve our little country and people," she said with her studied humble expression that invariably brings tears in her eyes. I looked for the tears but saw none. I just stared at her for a moment and wondered why she used my "little" people so often and what exactly she meant by "little," although I did have an idea or two that I kept to myself.

"Well, of course, Mrs. Marcos," I said. "How can you not be accused of nepotism? Your brother, Kokoy, is the governor of your province and was concurrently Ambassador to China, in addition to owning or heading some 70 or 80 private business enterprises; your uncle, Eduardo, is Ambassador to the United States; your husband's sister, Elizabeth, is governor of her province of Ilocos Norte; your husband's brother, Dr. Pacifico, is in the Ministry of Health and owns or heads some 40 or 50 private corporations; your cousin, Disini, has taken over more than 30 of the largest corporations in the Philippines; your husband's fraternity brother, Roberto Benedicto, holds several government-appointed posts and owns or heads the largest number of so-called private business enterprises in the Philippines; even your 24-year-old son, Bong Bong, is vice-governor of his province. These are facts, as you well know. Shall I go on?" I asked.

She appeared stunned as I rattled off the names of her relatives and friends with their respective government positions and even the number of "known" private businesses each of them owned or headed. She paused, a little confused, and then said: "How can you blame me or the President because many in our family have dedicated themselves to public service or have excelled in business. Is that supposed to be a crime? Frankly, we're very proud of our family's contributions to the political and economic development of the country."

I saw no point in pursuing this subject any further. Obviously, Imelda was not about to admit that the government appointments of the Marcos-Romualdez family members were not based on merit, and neither was she going to admit that the hundreds of corporations now owned by the two families and their cronies were acquired through extortion and corruption.

"Well," I said, "the issue of whether you have done well for your people is irrelevant to what your people now want and deserve. Fifteen years is long enough. The people want the right to choose their leaders freely. Please try to understand that. Give them back this right peacefully, or they'll have to take it by force."

CHAPTER 14

Sincerity Is the Key

"You must believe, Steve, that the President intends to return the country to normalcy as soon as possible, but you do agree, I believe, that this cannot be done overnight. The first step is to lift martial law; this has been the most irritating issue. Elections will follow, but there must be a period of adjustment before elections are held. The problem is that the opposition is not cooperating. Everything the President recommends, they reject for the sake of opposing him. In the meantime the underground is exploding bombs and preparing to assassinate our officials. We are in a serious crisis. How do you get out of it?" Imelda did not ask the question rhetorically. She addressed it to me and expected an answer.

"The problem you have with the political opposition is credibility," I responded. "They have all become cynics. After feeling deceived for eight years, how can you blame them for not believing you now? It's like the boy who cried wolf to fool the people; he did it so many times that when the wolf came and he yelled for help, nobody believed him."

"How can we overcome this critical problem?"

"The burden of proving your sincerity is on *you.* If Mr. Marcos is indeed sincere, he has to recognize that the opposition will not accept his sincerity at face value. Mr. Marcos must be ready to accept the justified doubts of the opposition. He can only prove his sincerity by what *he does* and not be what he says he will do. This will obviously take a little time."

"That's what I was telling you earlier," Imelda replied, jumping on this point. "We need time to remove the measures of our emergency government and return all the democratic processes. Do you think the politicians and the rebels understand that?"

"I think they do. But the problem with the political opposition and the problem with the rebels is quite different. The solutions are also different."

"What do you mean?" she asked with genuine interest. It appeared to me that our discussion was now taking a useful turn—a dialogue, not just a defense of our respective positions or accusation of each other's actions.

"In a case of the political opposition, the problem is your credibility. This also applies to the general public. Total normalization will take some time. All gradual steps you propose will be initially viewed as nothing more than cosmetic changes—you know there have been enough of those. If you are really sincere, actions will speak louder than words, and your credibility problem will be gradually solved. But to help establish your credibility, the opposition must participate in deciding the steps to be taken."

"You know some of the hardliners in the opposition refuse to even talk to the President. How can we overcome this? Who do we talk to?"

"I am certainly not qualified to name who you should talk to among the political opposition leaders. I admit that this question presents a problem, but I do not think it is a serious problem. The serious problem, in my opinion, is still your credibility."

"If that is true," she said, "then where do we go from here?"

"The key to the solution of the present crisis is *sincerity,*" I said, emphasizing the word as much as I could. "Sincerity. If you can convince the political leaders, the people in general, and the rebels that you are sincere, I am sure almost everyone will be willing to cooperate with you during the process of normalization. Now, considering what has happened during the past eight years, I admit you must be patient; no one will assume you are sincere until there is concrete proof. You must expect this."

"The lifting of martial law is concrete. How can the President convince them that he is sincere?"

"Not very easily," I answered forcefully. "First of all, as I mentioned earlier, I, for one, do not get the impression that the announcement of the lifting of martial law is sincere. First, the decision was made unilaterally by Mr. Marcos without consultation with any of the respected leaders at home. Secondly, the constitutional amendments introduced during martial law, the decrees issued by Mr. Marcos, and the legislation passed or being proposed by the Interim National Assembly grant more powers to the Presidency than Mr. Marcos has under the provisions of martial law. Naturally everyone, including myself, views the lifting of martial law as another meaningless maneuver."

"But it is not a meaningless maneuver. It is the first major step. All the other needed steps will have to follow gradually, one by one. Not all at once."

"Mrs. Marcos, I think we are getting into an area where it is difficult for me to be of much help. I am neither qualified, nor do I have any right, to negotiate on the specific steps toward normalization. All I can say on this issue is that you must, I believe, find a way to deal with the political leaders honorably, and you must convince them that you are sincere. The best chance you have to convince them of your sincerity, is *to be* sincere."

"You must realize," I continued, "that just as you need

some reasonable amount of time to complete the normalization process, the people will also need time to be convinced that the steps being taken are different from those they have witnessed for eight years."

"I know the President wants to open a dialogue with the opposition. I hope a dialogue can start soon. How about the rebels? You said the problem is different."

"Very much so. However, I believe the solution is easier, although the dangers are much greater. Before I go into the specifics of the problem with the revolutionaries or its solution, I should repeat that, there too, the key to success is *sincerity.* You must convince the revolutionaries that you are willing to implement voluntarily and peacefully the reforms they expect to achieve through the use of force . . ."

Imelda interrupted me suddenly. "But will the rebels wait while we implement the reforms?"

"My answer is the same as it was for the political leaders. I believe the rebels will cooperate and will wait only *if* and *when* they are convinced you are sincere. However, I think you can demonstrate your sincerity to the revolutionaries much easier and much faster than to the politicians."

"We know you have many direct contacts with the rebels," Imelda said confidently. "We have intercepted several of your communications. If *you* are also sincere, you should be willing to help us."

There was no need to refute my communications; we both knew it was true. "I am more than just willing to help, if I can. However, I am sure you have an inflated impression of my influence with the revolutionaries. My personal contacts are quite limited. I am in touch with very few of them. I know there are many more groups committed to the overthrow of your regime, but I don't know where they are or who their leaders are."

In my eagerness to convince Imelda that her perception of my role was exaggerated, I caught myself drifting away from her question. I corrected my error. "I am really more than willing to help if I can believe that Mr. Marcos is sincere and I can be of some help. One thing I want to assure you, I am now glad I came to see you."

"So am I," she injected.

"I feel there is a good chance that some benefits will be derived from our meeting–if nothing else, at least a little better understanding of what is really happening."

"I think much more can be gained if you want to help."

I felt she was now flattering me, but I wasn't about to play the role of the shy, modest youth. I just ignored the compliment. "The problem with the revolutionaries is different," I repeated. "First of all, let me make it clear that the rebel groups are not under the direction of any one political leader. It is true that many of the groups rally around Ninoy. As you know, in one of their communiqués, the April 6th Liberation Movement openly solicited Ninoy's leadership. Consequently, Ninoy has significant influence on them, but it would be wrong to assume that he can simply order them to do what he wants and expect them to blindly obey. Ninoy can exercise moral leadership, but he cannot act as their military commander. This simply means that whatever he might want them to do, he would first have to explain it to them and convince them, rather than simply order it to be done."

"We really think his involvement is more extensive," Imelda interjected as I paused.

"Maybe so!" I countered, "but at least believe me when I say that *nobody,* including Ninoy, can simply issue orders to them without reasonable cause. They just wouldn't follow. Now, you asked me how their problem and its solution is different from that of the politicians. Well, they are in the front line, so to speak. They are being hunted, arrested, tortured, and even killed.

Last week, two of the rebels from Tondo were killed. Last month, dozens were arrested. At this very moment, many are being hunted, some of them like game trophies with prizes on their heads. Many are being tried by your military tribunals. Others are being mistreated in your jails and forced to sign confessions without being allowed to see a lawyer. We have reliable reports that several of the April 6th rebels who were arrested have been and are being tortured. Now these are facts you and I know."

"Well, *they* started the trouble," she protested. "What are we to do?"

"We are talking about what you can do to show the rebels your sincere intent to implement meaningful reforms. You can and you should change your attitude toward the revolutionaries. Stop the hunting and the new arrests; stop the mistreatment of those arrested; discontinue the trials of subversives–especially the Light-a-Fire, the April 6th, the Kalaw-Rondon groups and others. Release gradually and quietly detainees held for alleged subversion. These are all steps that can be taken almost immediately in 'the spirit of unity and reconciliation' that Mr. Marcos has so often claimed. These are all steps that can directly reach the revolutionaries. *Then,* Ninoy and some of us can talk to them about sincerity. Unfortunately, the lifting of martial law, elections, and the like appear too far down the line as far as the rebels are concerned."

"I understand what you are saying," Imelda commented, "but this cannot be just a one-sided approach. There must be sincerity and give-and-take on both sides."

I had lost track of time. I had not looked at my watch at all. There was no reason to. I was willing to stay with Imelda for as long as I felt some progress was being made. I had come to the conclusion that our discussion was useful. I did not know then and do not know now, if and how the progress being made would eventually manifest itself, but I did feel progress was being made.

I was sincerely glad I had gone to see her. Ninoy was right, I thought. Presy and I were wrong.

Suddenly, I heard a door open behind me and saw Imelda stand up with a broad smile on her face. I stood up and turned around to see who it was.

"Welcome, son," Imelda said. "Come in, come in."

It was Bong Bong Marcos. During the past few months, Bong Bong had been studying at the Wharton School at the University of Pennsylvania. About one month earlier, the papers in Manila headlined stories of alleged plots by U.S. rebels to kill Bong Bong. Brief newspaper reports on the alleged plots had also appeared in the U.S. press because Marcos had officially requested protection from the U.S. government. As with all other recent Manila reports on "terroristic activities," my name was again somehow implicated in the alleged plots against Bong Bong. He stood there at the open door for a few seconds smiling at his mother but not saying anything or coming in.

"By all means, come in Bong Bong," I said laughing. "I promise not to kill you." All three of us laughed as Bong Bong now entered the room and greeted his mother.

It occurred to me that I had been there with Imelda for nearly two hours (I was guessing, since I still had not looked at my watch) without any interruptions. 'Imelda must have left instructions not to be disturbed,' I thought.

I shook Bong Bong's hand and asked him about his school work. He said he was doing fine but was looking forward to getting it behind him and going home.

"Are you going home with your Mommy for the Christmas vacation?" I asked.

"Yes," he smiled, "but I prefer not to go in the same plane with her," he said, with an expression that implied he had some mischievous plans of his own that could do without a chaperone.

"I know what you mean." I smiled back. "When I was your

age, I really didn't want to travel with my mother, either."

We all exchanged pleasantries for a few minutes. At one point I told Bong Bong, "Your mother is inviting me to come to the Philippines, but I am a little hesitant. I don't think I would enjoy her jail very much." Again we all laughed.

"Perhaps you'd rather go to Bong Bong's jail in Ilocos Norte," Imelda said, still laughing. "His is not as bad as mine."

"That's not hard to believe," I said. "I'll keep it in mind."

Bong Bong stayed and chatted for five or ten minutes and then excused himself.

Later, Ninoy told me that Ramon Jacinto was still outside the suite waiting for his meeting with Imelda when Bong Bong arrived. Ramon said that when Bong Bong asked the security officer who was with his mother, he was told it was Steve Psinakis. Bong Bong had said "Oh! This is the fellow who is going to kill me. I want to see him." When Ninoy told me this, I smiled. My comment to Bong Bong when I first saw him at the door turned out to be more appropriate than I had expected.

When Bong Bong closed the door behind him, I asked Imelda in a half-serious, half-joking manner: "Tell me, Mrs. Marcos, do you really think rebels here in the United States are plotting to kill your son?"

"Oh! We're quite sure of it. It's not something we made up, and it's not just propaganda against you," she said, very seriously. "As a matter of fact, the FBI informed us of the danger. The U.S. Embassy in Manila reported that suspicious characters had been closely watching Bong Bong's moves. Why would they do that if they didn't want to hurt him? If not kill him, at least kidnap him?"

"I suppose it's possible. I know there are Filipinos whose hatred for your regime is so great that *anything* is possible. But I can assure you that those I know in the guerrilla leadership would be set against hurting Bong Bong, particularly here in the

U.S. The rebels are gradually gaining the recognition and sympathy of the American press. They are beginning to be viewed as what they really are: patriotic guerrillas, not terrorists. Your campaign to depict them as terrorists and senseless murderers is failing. Any action against your son here in America—whether kidnapping or assassination—would be denounced by the American public and would turn the press around in your favor. I don't think any legitimate member of the opposition would approve or encourage any such action against Bong Bong. On the other hand, the danger is always there. Your regime has been responsible for the torture and murder of so many people. How do you suppose their relatives feel?"

"The President is not responsible for whatever excesses have occurred. He has tried to discourage the military from overreacting whenever they arrest new subversives."

"Try to tell this to the fathers, mothers, brothers, and sisters of those who have died at the hands of Colonel Abadilla and other military torturers. You know, even if Mr. Marcos had not specifically ordered the tortures and the murders, it is still his command responsibility."

"But the President cannot be responsible for every soldier?" she protested as fear registered again on her face.

"I believe you are wrong, Mrs. Marcos," I countered quite calmly. "The head of a repressive regime whose leader has such absolute power *is* responsible and *must* be held responsible for the actions of his military torturers."

"I know," she said, "that many of you view the President as a cruel and ruthless leader, but he is really a kind and compassionate man. He is only a strong leader whose firmness at a time of our national crisis has been misunderstood."

"I pray that what you say is true. Few, if any, Filipinos would agree with you, but if you are correct, your husband must now prove it through his actions. Anyway, I don't think your son would be in any danger here from the legitimate rebels. And speaking of killings, tell me, Mrs. Marcos, has Mijares been killed?" I popped the question unexpectedly. Imelda appeared stunned. The insinuation of my question, considering Mijares' background, was that Marcos had ordered Mijares' murder.

"How should I know?" she snapped. "Mijares had more enemies than you can possibly imagine. He was the lowest kind of snake that ever lived."

It was clear that Imelda hated Tibo Mijares. She spoke of him in the past tense—she had said *was*—as if she knew he was dead.

"Tibo was a thief, a compulsive gambler and a loser, and, worst of all, a cheap extortionist." Imelda continued: "He was not a newspaperman; he was a blackmailer. From the old days when he covered the Congressional events, he would ask the Congressmen for money in exchange for a favorable commentary in the paper. Worse than that, he would threaten to write an unfavorable article about some Senator or even some businessman unless they gave him money. He was a cheap extortionist, and anybody could have killed him." Imelda's distaste for Mijares was much too evident.

"If you knew all this about Mijares," I asked, "why did your husband make him his top media man as well as the official press censor of the martial law regime?"

She didn't like the question and had no ready answer. "That's another story," she said, skirting the question. "The fact is, speaking of scums, you couldn't find a worse one than Mijares."

From what I knew of Mijares, as well as from my personal dealings with him, I generally agreed with her description of his character.

Primitivo "Tibo" Mijares was a Filipino newspaperman and a two-term president of the National Press Club. However, he developed notoriety only after the imposition of martial law. Marcos had made him his top media man and his press censor. It was known that Mijares was one of the very few who could walk into Marcos' office at almost any time without an appointment. As chairman of the "Media Advisory Council," he controlled virtually all the political news and propaganda of the martial law regime. This was the case up until late 1974, when he arrived in San Francisco with Imelda's advance party to prepare for her forthcoming visit.

In San Francisco, Mijares secretly contacted the *Philippine News* editor, Alex Esclamado, and implied he was preparing to defect from the Marcos government.

Alex could not contain his excitement. He told me about his talk with Mijares and arranged for a second secret meeting between the three of us–Mijares, Esclamado, and myself. "Imagine what Mijares' defection will mean for our cause," Alex announced exuberantly. "Can you imagine what a blow it will be to the Marcos regime? Tibo probably knows as much as anyone about the political shenanigans and corruption of the palace."

During our secret meeting, Mijares confirmed his decision to defect. I was almost as excited as Alex. This was really big news. We planned his defection strategy and on February 20, 1975, Mijares formally announced his defection during a press conference in San Francisco. He castigated Marcos and explained how "the dictator" planned the imposition of martial law because he "never intended to relinquish power." Mijares claimed that he "personally participated in the fabrication of the results of the January 1973 and July 1973 referenda." He also said that the referendum scheduled for the following week, February 27, 1975, was also rigged and "the results will show about 90% support for Marcos' martial law regime." Mijares' prediction was on the button. The announced results of the February 1975 referendum showed 90.6% approval for the continuation of martial law.

Mijares' defection was indeed very damaging to the "Conjugal Dictators." His disclosures about "the illegal political maneuvers," about the "many scandals," and about the "corruption of the First Family," attracted the attention of the U.S. press. But the greatest damage to the Marcos regime occurred when Mijares revealed that Marcos had attempted to bribe him.

Congressman Donald Fraser, Chairman of the House International Relations Subcommittee, invited Mijares to testify during the Subcommittee's June 1975 hearings on the Philippines. Marcos offered Mijares–through the San Francisco Consul General, Alconcel–a $50,000 bribe not to testify. In his panic, Alconcel deposited the bribe money in a San Franciso bank, and, with the help of my lawyer, Gerald Hill, we were able to obtain an actual copy of the $50,000 check from the bank.

The bribe attempt was reported in most newspapers throughout the United States. The Washington syndicated columnist, Jack Anderson, assigned his top investigative reporter to this case, and he reported the details of the bribe attempt in four of his columns. Anderson's July 2nd and 3rd columns read as follows:

THE WASHINGTON POST Wednesday, July 2, 1975

Marcos bribe offer cited by witness

By Jack Anderson and Les Whitten

President Ferdinand Marcos, the Philippines' strongman, offered a witness a $50,000 bribe the other day not to testify on Capitol Hill about corruption and tyranny in the Philippines.

The witness, Marcos' former press censor Primitivo Mijares, was prepared to tell the uncensored story of the Marcos regime to a House International Relations subcommittee.

On the eve of his testimony, Mijares received a personal call from Marcos in Manila urging him not to testify. Then an aide got on the phone and offered him the $50,000.

The money actually was deposited in a San Francisco branch of Lloyds Bank of California in the names of Primitivo Mijares and Ambassador Trinidad Alconcel, the Philippines' consul general. Thus Mijares couldn't withdraw the $50,000 until the consul general countersigned the check.

Mijares not only went ahead with his testimony but informed Chairman Don Fraser (D-Minn.) of the bribe attempt. Fraser's office notified the Justice Department, which is investigating.

We have confirmed that $50,000 was deposited in the names of both Mijares and Alconcel in savings account No. 0662-460-62 at Lloyds Bank of California. The bank's records show that Alconcel removed Mijares' name from the joint account on June 18, the day after Mijares testified.

For a foreign head of state to attempt to bribe a congressional witness is unprecedented. The amazing story began a few months ago when Mijares walked out of Malacanang, the presidential palace, after three years as Marcos' confidant and propagandist.

By Mijares's account, he simply became disgusted with Marcos and sought asylum in the United States. An approach was made in May to persuade him to come home. A colonel in Marcos' presidential guard, Romeo Ochoco, looked up Mijares in San Francisco.

Over coffee and doughnuts in a 24-hour restaurant, they talked about a book that Mijares is writing about the Marcos dictatorship. He plans to call it "The Conjugal Dictatorship of Ferdinand and Imelda."

The colonel was soothing. "He said Marcos would talk to me about my complaints," recalled Mijares. But the former press censor felt he knew Marcos too well to trust him.

The colonel's visit was followed by a series of telephone calls from Ambassador Alconcel, who had heard that Mijares would be a star witness at Fraser's hearings on U.S.-Philippines problems.

The consul general tried to persuade Mijares not to testify and, when Mijares refused, to "pull the punches." In return, the former censor was promised that Manila would "help" him.

He flew to Washington, nevertheless, to testify and checked into a downtown Washington motel. Not long afterward, on June 16, he received a call from Manila.

"It was Marcos," Mijares told us. "He started out by calling me by my nickname, 'Tibo.' He asked me not to testify, because of what it would do to his 'New Society.'

"I told him it would be difficult to back out since I was already under the committee's jurisdiction. He told me his assistant would tell me something, that they had something for me."

Then presidential aide Guillermo de Vega got on the line, according to Mijares, and began speaking in a mixture of Tagalog and Spanish to confuse possible wiretappers. The aide said $50,000 would be awaiting Mijares in San Francisco if he didn't testify. But if he went ahead with his testimony, the aide warned, it would be "a declaration of war."

Mijares held firm. Two hours before he was scheduled to take the stand, he received a call from Alconcel imploring him not to testify and reiterating that the money would be on hand in San Francisco.

But the onetime censor, having renounced his former way of life, took the witness chair and testified in detail about vote fraud, corporate theft, payoffs, illegal jailings and general corruption.

Mijares laid all these crimes right at the door of Marcos, his family and his cronies. Nor did Mijares spare himself in his testimony.

THE WASHINGTON POST Thursday, July 3, 1975

Ex-aide reveals Marcos' corruption

By Jack Anderson
and Les Whitten

Earlier this week we reported that Philippine President Ferdinand Marcos offered a former confidant, Primitivo Mijares, a $50,000 bribe not to tell the U.S. Congress what he knows about corruption in the Philippines.

Now we can reveal the story that Marcos tried to cover up. It is another Watergate scandal, Philippine version—a story of high crimes and misdemeanors, ranging from abuse of power to misuse of government funds.

The story is told in a 24-page memo that Mijares submitted to the House International Organizations Subcommittee. In the memo, Mijares confesses his dirty work for Marcos.

The memo details how Marcos won reelection in 1969 using some of the same tactics that Richard Nixon utilized in 1972. Mijares describes the Marcos campaign as "the dirtiest election ever held in the Philippines."

Marcos used "goons, guns and gold," his former confidant charges, to win the election. The strategy was to create an atmosphere of disturbance, which called for Marcos' strong hand to control.

Marcos, according to the memo, "had military personnel infiltrate the ranks of demonstrators to explode bombs in their midst and to instigate the demonstrators into committing acts of violence."

Philippine air force infiltrators allegedly lobbed "heavy explosives in front of the (U.S.) consular offices," and "armed forces psychological warfare units" conducted bombings on Manila's water system, city hall and the bathroom of the Constitutional Convention. The violence was "later blamed by Mr. Marcos on the Maoist People's Army."

The incidents that Marcos secretly encouraged, Mijares alleged, had their innocent victims. When a bomb exploded inside a department store, for example, "a family man who was buying a gift for a child observing its birthday was blown to bits." A conscience-stricken police sergeant later confessed he had planted the bomb "on superior orders," claims Mijares.

To improve his press notices, Marcos allowed "heavy borrowings from the Philippine Bank," according to the memo, so a toady could buy up a "media empire." Allegedly the pro-Marcos media collected "part of their salaries . . . from the president's contingent fund."

These tactics worked so well, charges Mijares, that the reelected Marcos continued using them to assume dictatorial power. Under the Philippine constitution, Marcos was limited to two terms, but he had no intention of retiring.

He continued to stir a crisis fever. He staged "a supposed landing of combat weapons," for example, "along the coast of Digoyo." Mijares claims the weapons were planted by "a special operations group of trusted military men," but Marcos loudly blamed "a foreign power" and "Maoist guerrillas."

There also was a faked ambush, Mijares charges, involving a Philippine official's car. By exploiting these incidents, Marcos had the country psychologically ready for his proclamation of martial law on Sept. 21, 1972.

With a great show of benevolence, he proclaimed a "smiling martial law." He quickly restored order and gave the citizenry respite from turmoil. He also closed down opposition newspapers and jailed recalcitrant editors and rivals.

Marcos asked a constitutional convention to put a stamp of legitimacy upon his dictatorship. But when the delegates showed a little independence, the memo states, he "caused the arrest and detention in military stockades of delegates" and "bribed floor leaders of the convention with money and favors."

To make doubly sure the convention gave Marcos the powers he wanted, alleges Mijares, the results "were manufactured by a group headed by the president's favorite brother-in-law, Gov. Benjamin Romualdez."

Mijares had personal knowledge that the convention vote was rigged, he writes, because "I was a member of that group." Just as John W. Dean III later confessed his role in the Nixon scandals, Mijares describes how he ordered the takeover of a newspaper, investigated an Associated Press reporter, prepared phony stories on revolutionaries and committed other outrages on Marcos' orders.

Mijares' memo then tells how Marcos' "military regime has gone absolutely corrupt." The dictator parcelled out to his cronies the licenses to smuggle in luxury goods and to smuggle out sugar, copra, lumber and cement, charged Mijares. Military supporters have been given lucrative rackets in Manila to run as they please, he adds.

Through front men, according to Mijares, Marcos has taken over agricultural lands in northern Luzon, the Visayas and Mindanao. He allegedly controls oil concessions, a huge export business, a free trade zone in Mariveles and a claim on some buried World War II Japanese treasure in the Sierra Madre.

Mijares claims that Marcos has misused some of the $100 million in U.S. aid he gets each year. The greatest part of U.S. medical aid, for example, "goes to the United Drug Co., the biggest pharmaceutical firm in the country, which is owned by a front man of the president," alleges the memo.

Yet the State Department, swears Mijares, has thwarted Marcos' democratic opponents by supporting "the Philippine martial regime."

Marcos, of course, denied he had attempted to bribe Mijares. In a lengthy report prepared hurriedly in Manila and hand-carried to the United States by Philippines Foreign Undersecretary, Jose Ingles, Marcos had to confirm that he gave Mijares the $50,000 because the evidence of the actual cancelled bank check, which we possessed, made it impossible to deny this fact. However, the report claimed that the $50,000 given to Mijares was unrelated to his Congressional testimony. The report claimed that the money was not intended as a bribe, but for the purpose of starting a pro-Marcos newspaper in San Francisco.

Marcos' claim that the $50,000 payment "was unrelated to the U.S. Congressional hearings," appeared ridiculous and unbelievable considering the fact that the payment was made just two hours before Mijares was scheduled to testify and withdrawn immediately after Mijares went through with his testimony.

The Marcos report further claimed that Mijares was a "double agent" and was supplying Marcos with information about a plot on his life and Imelda's life by a U.S.-based group headed by me and my wife, Presy. The lengthy Philippine government report also claimed Mijares had received three more payments totaling $45,000 that "were authorized by President Marcos on the understanding that this nominal fee would ensure a continuous flow of information on the (Psinakis) assassination conspiracy."

As in the case of the Marcos report on the Lopez blackmail exposé, the Philippine Ambassador in Washington submitted copies of the Marcos report on the Mijares bribe attempt to hundreds of U.S. Senators and Congressmen who had been outraged by the "despicable Marcos attempt to interfere with U.S. Congressional hearings." A copy of the report was also submitted to the Fraser Subcommittee. Fraser acknowledged receipt of the report and included it in the Committee's official records. This fact would later become "a legal technicality" that would save Marcos from a six-million-dollar libel suit.

The Marcos-fabricated and libelous accusation against Presy and me contained in the "Ingles Report" was published only by the two Philippine government propaganda organs in the United States. No other American newspaper published the baseless Marcos accusations.

On the basis of the publication of the Marcos accusations in two propaganda newspapers circulated within the United States, Presy and I filed a six-million-dollar libel suit in the U.S. Federal Court against Marcos, General Ver, Consul Alconcel, and a few other "conspirators." The libel suit, filed on August 15, 1975, was progressing, and, after several hearings on the defendants' petition to dismiss the suit, the federal judge ruled against the defendants. However, the submission of the Marcos report to the Fraser Congressional Subcommittee provided the "legal technicality" that enabled the defendants to win a dismissal of the case through an appeal to the Appellate Court. According to U.S. law, any statements considered part of official proceedings of Congressional hearings can be published by the media and no libel actions can be taken against the publication. Thus, the Marcos conspirators got off the hook not on the merits of the case but due to this legal technicality.

SAN FRANCISCO EXAMINER Saturday, August 16, 1975

Philippines' Marcos sued here for libel

Philippine President Ferdinand Marcos and six of his government officials were named in an $8 million libel suit filed in federal court here yesterday.

Defendants include San Francisco Consul General Trinidad Alconcel, named recently in a $50,000 bribe offer to a former Marcos aide to not testify before a Congressional committee. Marcos and the other defendants are accused of preparing a false report of an assassination plot against Marcos, which they sent to columnist Jack Anderson and to the Filipino Reporter, a newspaper in San Francisco.

Steve Psinakis and his wife Presentacion, filed the suit. He is 40, an American of Greek descent, and operates an import/export business. His wife is the daughter of the late Eugenio Lopez Sr., a Philippine financial tycoon who died last month. He had lived in self-imposed exile here after a falling out with Marcos.

San Francisco Examiner story on the filing of the libel suit.

In the meantime Marcos had become very concerned about our libel suit. He had filed a formal petition with the U.S. State Department for his exclusion from the suit. Documents obtained in January, 1981 through the Freedom of Information Act reveal several communications between the U.S. and Philippine governments on Marcos' efforts to be dropped from the suit. With the recommendation of Henry Kissinger, on September 26, 1975, the State Department requested U.S. Attorney General, Edward H. Levi, to "cause an appropriate suggestion of immunity to be filed with U.S. District Court for the Northern District of California" for Ferdinand Marcos as a head of a foreign state and "for foreign relations reasons." The Attorney General followed the State Department's recommendation and Marcos was granted "immunity" from our libel suit on October 29, 1975.

When Presy and I were reviewing the many documents we recently obtained from the State Department under the Freedom of Information Act, Presy commented: "Poor Ferdinand and Imelda; they must have nightmares everytime they think of you, and, lately, they must be thinking of you quite often."

The Mijares bribe attempt did not end with the $50,000 payment from Consul Alconcel. The publicity of the bribe attempt gave Mijares and the anti-Marcos forces in the United States a big boost in their propaganda offensive against the illegal activities committed in the United States by Marcos and his agents.

At about the same time, September 1975, there was another case filed against Marcos' agents in San Francisco and Los Angeles for illegal activities involving theft of MFP documents and harassment of anti-Marcos organizations. Alex Esclamado and I were spearheading that case. We had raised a great deal of interest among Congressional leaders who were pressuring the State and Justice Departments for action.

Another investigation on the illegal activities of foreign agents in the United States had been initiated independently by Senator George McGovern's Subcommittee. I had visited McGovern's legislative assistant, Mike Glennon, several times and submitted documentation on the cases against Marcos, the most important of which was, at that time, Mijares' case. Mike Glennon was in charge of the Senate Committee investigation.

With all this activity going on and Mijares' case still in the limelight, Marcos decided to increase the bribe offer to Mijares even though he had *already* testified before the Fraser Subcommittee. This time, Mijares was offered $100,000 to leave the United States and to agree not to publish his book entitled, *The Conjugal Dictatorship,* which Mijares had announced was ready for publication.

Mijares took Alex Esclamado and me into his confidence on this second bribe attempt. We planned our strategy together. By this time, we had enough "circumstantial evidence" to conclude that the State Department, under the direction of Henry Kissinger, was exerting every effort to block investigations that would prove embarrassing for the Filipino dictator. A conviction against Marcos and his agents would have made Kissinger's job of granting massive U.S. aid to the Marcos regime very difficult.

Esclamado, Mijares, and I discussed the strategy of how to obtain irrefutable evidence on the second Marcos bribe offer to Mijares. We decided to have Mijares pretend he was willing to accept an offer—but not just $100,000. He was to call Marcos at his palace and negotiate for a higher amount. We would invite the FBI to witness the call and confirm the bribe offer "directly from the horse's mouth."

The call to Malacanang Palace was set up for July 6, 1976. I called special agent Mike Henry of the San Francisco FBI office and asked him to come to my house that evening to listen in on the call to the palace. We were shocked when he said he didn't want to listen in on the conversation. Mike Henry was the FBI agent assigned to investigate this case.

"But Mike," I said, "this is the perfect opportunity to obtain first-hand evidence on the bribe attempt."

"I am sorry. I don't think I should listen in myself," Mike told me. "You go ahead with the call and submit an appropriate report to the Bureau."

"But Mike," I protested, "that won't do any good. A report

would be just one more allegation. I know Marcos is guilty of the bribe attempt. I don't need the evidence for myself. I want you, the FBI, to know the truth and get the evidence."

It was useless. The FBI would not witness the call. "That bastard," I told Tibo Mijares, "He doesn't want the evidence. He must be under orders from Kissinger to cover up for Marcos."

We were getting frantic. Tibo had arranged the call with Marcos for 5 p.m., and it was now 3 o'clock. We wanted at least one other independent credible party to witness the conversation.

Frustrated and dejected, Tibo called Jack Anderson in Washington and told him what was happening. He appeared furious with the FBI's attitude. "This is not the first cover up, and it won't be the last," Anderson said. "Anyway, I'd like verification for my own record. I've been following this case from the start."

Anderson called a law firm in San Francisco and arranged for an attorney, Mr. Sheldon Greene, to rush to my house and witness the call. By the time Greene arrived at the house it was 6 p.m.

Tibo placed the call to Malacanang Palace in Manila. Marcos was "indisposed" but his top aide-de-camp, Dr. Guillermo de Vega, who had negotiated the initial bribe attempt, came to the phone. Sheldon Greene and I listened on the two extensions. After the usual amenities, Mijares said, "Look Gimo, I am willing to leave the United States and stop publication of the book, but the $100,000 offer is not worth it. I expect to make more than that just from the publication of my book. I am willing to accept $250,000."

"I am sorry, Tibo. I am not authorized to go above $100,000. I must take this up again with the President. Only he can authorize a higher payment," de Vega said.

The July 14, 1975 Jack Anderson column reported the incident of the Mijares-de Vega phone conversation:

Mon., July 14, 1975 San Francisco Chronicle

Merry-Go-Round

New Bribe Offer In Philippine Case

Jack Anderson

WE RECENTLY reported, with detailed documentation, that Philippine President Ferdinand Marcos had tried to bribe a former aide with $50,000 not to testify before the U.S. Congress.

Marcos has now offered the witness, Primitivo Mijares, a full $100,000 if he will recant his testimony, repudiate our story and retire to Australia.

As Marcos' former press censor, Mijares had a ringside seat to the rise of the Marcos dictatorship. He has testified at House hearings about the tyranny and corruption he had seen.

★ ★ ★

IN MANILA, meanwhile, Marcos has denied he tried to block Mijares' testimony. We happen to have copies, however, of the bank transactions involved in the original $50,000 bribe.

On the day Mijares testified, a Philippine National Bank check, No. 4905, was made out for $50,000 to Marcos' man in San Francisco, Ambassador Trinidad Alconcel. The check was endorsed by Alconcel and deposited in a joint bank account in the names of Mijares and Alconcel.

After Mijares went ahead with his testimony, Alconcel abruptly transferred the $50,000 the next day to his own personal bank ccount.

Since it is a criminal offense to interfere with a federal witness, we have turned our information over to the FBI. Representative Don Fraser (Dem-Minn.), who presided over the House hearings, has also urged the Justice Department to conduct a full inquiry.

Unaware that Mijares was cooperating with the FBI, Alconcel got in touch with him again and doubled the offer. Alconcel made it quite clear he was speaking for Marcos.

To establish the connection, Mijares, an ex-newspaperman, called Marcos' office and spoke with his top aide-de-camp, Dr. Guillermo de Vega. The aide, according to Mijares, verified the $100,000 offer.

★ ★ ★

TO ESTABLISH our own verification, we retained San Francisco lawyer Sheldon Greene to listen, with Mijares' permission, to a second phone conversation with Manila. The aide, de Vega, reaffirmed in English and Tagalog his offer to "help" Mijares and didn't question Mijares' references to the $100,000 bribe.

Mijares asked, as bait, whether Marcos would go as high as $250,000. This would have to be approved, said de Vega, by Marcos personally.

Acquaintances of Alconcel in San Francisco tell us Marcos is trying to persuade him to take the rap for the bribe, leave the United States and accept a minor ambassadorship. We haven't been able to reach Alconcel for comment.

Between July 1975 and November 1976, at least one thousand letters and reports have been written and received by members of the U.S. Congress, State Department, Justice Department, and myself on the "progress" of the FBI investigation. The responses from then-Assistant Attorney Generals Benjamin R. Civiletti and Richard L. Thornburgh always reported some "progress" but no conclusion. No specific information on its status was given to the many inquiries. The typical response of the Justice Department stated: "the Privacy Act of 1974, Public Law 93-579, and Rule (6) e of the Federal Rules of Criminal Procedure place strict limitation on the type of information which can be disclosed."

On November 4, 1976, Jimmy Carter was elected President of the United States. Our hopes were now high that, with Kissinger out of the State Department by January 20, 1977, the investigation would be concluded and the truth would finally become known. However, on January 7, 1977, two weeks before Carter took office, Tibo Mijares disappeared, never to be heard from again. He was reportedly last seen at the San Francisco Airport on January 6, 1977, in the company of a certain Querube Makalintal, Jr., a confirmed intelligence agent of the Philippine government assigned at that time to the Philippine Consulate in San Francisco as the Attaché of the Philippine Bureau of Internal Revenue.

The rumors about what happened to Tibo Mijares are enough to fill a book. No hard evidence has surfaced to substantiate any of the rumors. It is, however, generally believed that he was murdered by Marcos agents to prevent the conclusion of the invesigation. Another first-hand witness to the bribe attempt, Presidential Assistant Guillermo de Vega, was murdered inside the Malacanang Palace on October 27, 1975.

Five months after the disappearance of Mijares, the following brief article appeared in the *New York Times:*

THE NEW YORK TIMES Sunday, June 19, 1977

Son of Strong Critic of Marcos Reported Slain in Philippines

MANILA, June 18 (Reuters)—The missing son of a former Philippine official, now one of the severest critics of President Ferdinand Marcos, has been found murdered, sources close to the family reported today.

They said members of the family had identified the beaten and stabbed body of 15-year-old Luis Manuel Mijares at a suburban undertaker's.

The boy's father, Primitivo Mijares, is in self-exile in the United States, where he has been making speeches critical of the martial law regime of President Marcos. He was formerly the head of the government's Media Advisory Council.

Some sources had speculated that Tibo Mijares had gone into hiding. However, the brutal murder of his son in the Philippines put an end to the speculation that Mijares was hiding and reinforced the view that he has been "eliminated."

The Justice Department finally closed its investigation on the Mijares case in August of 1978. The official Justice Department report states that "investigation conducted by the Department of Justice seriously undermined Mijares' usefulness as a key witness in a bribery prosecution and, indeed, suggested the possibility that Mijares himself may have violated Federal Law. For these reasons, together with Mijares's disappearance, the United States Attorney for the Northern District of California has declined prosecution in the case and the entire matter is considered closed."

The Justice Department investigation and its report confirmed much of what many knew about Mijares's character. Wherever he went, he left a trail of misappropriation of funds, bad debts, bad checks, petty extortions, etc. The investigation also revealed that after his February 1975 defection, Mijares did, in fact, continue to extort money from Marcos by feeding him imaginary information for which Marcos was ignorant enough to pay considerable sums. While Mijares was still receiving money from Marcos, he was at the same time lambasting Marcos in the U.S. press, causing the Marcos regime irreparable damage. It is no wonder the only natural conclusion is that Marcos had his vengeance and did Mijares in.

However, the "cover up" of the attempt to bribe Mijares still remains. I don't know of any U.S. law, or precedent, or even any logic under which our Justice Department does not prosecute a case because the character of the witness "seriously undermined his usefulness." On the contrary, I know of many cases where confessed criminals–thieves, rapists, and even professional murderers–have been (and are being used today) as key witnesses to prosecute and convict criminals. The most celebrated contemporary case is that of known Mafia hitman, "Jimmy the Weasel" Fratianno, whom the Justice Department has used in several cases.

Furthermore, the Attorney General never explained why the testimony of other witnesses, such as myself, with significant first-hand knowledge of the bribe attempt was never solicited. In fact, when such testimony was offered, it was turned down.

This is particularly difficult to explain considering the fact that even the partially confidential documents recently released by the State Department indicate that as early as July 1975, the Department knew that Marcos had indeed attempted to bribe a U.S. Congressional witness. One of the declassified State Department documents dated July 21, 1975, states:

1. The Philippine Consul General in San Francisco (the man who deposited the $50,000 to the joint account with Mijares) is a two-time bungler –first to have deposited the money in a joint account and secondly, even worse, to have withdrawn it.

2. Mijares could not accept a bribe, because, by the time he was already

scheduled to appear before the Congressional Committee, not to have testified could have resulted in his being forced to return to the Philippines.

Note: The actual document is reporduced on the following page.

Mijares' defection, the "inside knowledge" of the Marcos regime he was revealing to the American presss, and his application for asylum in the United States created almost as much of a problem for Kissinger as it did for Marcos.

Few of the "Confidential" documents I was able to obtain from the Department of State through the provisions of the Freedom of Information Act reveal Kissinger's consternation and difficulties in handling the Mijares problem. In the February 23, 1975, "Confidential" telex from U.S. Ambassador Sullivan in Manila to Kissinger commenting on the Mijares defection announced three days earlier, Sullivan writes:

MIJARES DEPARTURE NO MATTER HOW PHRASED OR DESCRIBED AND NOTWITHSTANDING HIS LOW ESTEEM IN COMMUNITY CANNOT HELP BUT BE ACUTE EMBARRASSMENT TO MARCOS. INVOLVEMENT OF LOPEZES IN HIS DECISION TO DENOUNCE MARCOS WILL BE PARTICULARLY DISTURBING. MIJARES HAS BEEN CONTINUAL SUPPORTER OF MARCOS FOR NUMBER OF YEARS AND ALONE AMONG PRE-MARTIAL LAW JOURNALISTS WAS UNQUESTIONED ADMIRER OF PRESIDENT. AS CONSEQUENCE, HE REPORTEDLY WAS ONE OF FEW INTIMATES WHO HAD DIRECT ACCESS TO MARCOS' STUDY. HE HAS PERFORMED MANY SERVICES FOR MARTIAL LAW REGIME AND UNDOUBTEDLY HAS MUCH INSIDE KNOWLEDGE THAT, IF MADE PUBLIC, COULD CAUSE DISTRESS TO GOVERNMENT OF THE PHILIPPINES. HOWEVER, MIJARES HAS BEEN CANNY ENOUGH IN THE PAST THAT HE MAY CHOOSE NOT TO REVEAL ALL MERELY TO INSURE THAT AT LEAST SOME BRIDGE REMAINS UNBURNED. ALLEGATION ABOUT REFERENDUM, HOWEVER, ALMOST DAMAGING ENOUGH IN ITSELF TO MAKE MIJARES PERSONNA NON GRATA.

x - R PPB
POL Gen - Gen
Def 15

EO 43 POL 24 Mijares EXCISE (93) (Page 3)

LIMITED OFFICIAL USE

Memorandum of Conversation

DEPARTMENT OF STATE A/CDC/MR
REVIEWED BY G.P. Harlan DATE 11/26/80
PORTIONS DENIED AS INDICATED

EXCISE

Date: July 21, 1975

1. The Philippine Consul General in San Francisco is a two-time bungler-first, to have deposited the money in a joint account and secondly, even worse, to have withdrawn it.

2. Mijares could not accept a bribe, because, by the time he was already scheduled to appear before the Congressional Committee, not to have testified could have resulted in his being forced to return to the Philippines; he could bear to appear before Marcos, but not before his wife. . .

(2) 5

USIS:GAO:JHoyt:fe

Distribution:

LIMITED OFFICIAL USE

AMB/DCM
POL
POL/R
IEA - Washington
EA/PHL
FILES (2)

Pertinent section of the actual State Department document declassified and released to Mr. Psinakis in January 1980 under the provisions of the Freedom of Information Act.

> ASSUME MARCOS WILL WANT TO KEEP THIS QUIET AS LONG AS HE CAN. IF IT BEGINS TO SEEP OUT, HE MAY WANT TO SMEAR MIJARES WITH IRREGULARITIES INCLUDING ASSOCIATION WITH LOPEZES. WHAT REPERCUSSIONS THAT COULD HAVE ON PROSPECTS OF RELEASE OF EUGENIO LOPEZ JR. IS ANYONE'S GUESS. (AMBASSADOR) SULLIVAN

The above telex to Kissinger confirms that Mijares "was one of the intimates who had direct access to Marcos' study." It also confirms that Mijares' statements "about the referendum"—i.e., his knowledge that it was rigged—was "damaging enough in itself to make Mijares personna non grata." More importantly, the telex confirms the State Department's assumption that "Marcos will want to keep this quiet as long as he can" and that "if it begins to seep out, he [Marcos] may want to smear Mijares with irregularities *including association with Lopezes.*"

This was exactly what Marcos did when news of Mijares' defection "seeped out." He tried to smear Mijares and also smear and discredit the Lopez family. A voluminous report, known as the Ingles Report, was "prepared" in 3 to 4 days and was presented to the U.S. government presumably as the findings of an "exhaustive investigation" ordered by Marcos only three days earlier. The report alleged that Mijares was a "double agent" who had uncovered an assassination plot against Marcos and his wife. The masterminds behind the plot, according to the report, were "Steve and Presy Psinakis." These fabricated accusations were published in the Marcos propaganda papers and formed the basis for our libel suit. Despite the obvious "fabrications" in the report, Kissinger's department asked the U.S. federal court to exclude Marcos from the suit.

By June 1975, Mijares had filed a formal request with the U.S. INS (Immigration and Naturalization Service) for political asylum. This created more problems for Kissinger. In another "Confidential" telex dated June 22, 1975, from Kissinger to the U.S. Embassy in Manila, Kissinger reports on Mijares' "Asylum Request." The complete Kissinger telex is as follows:

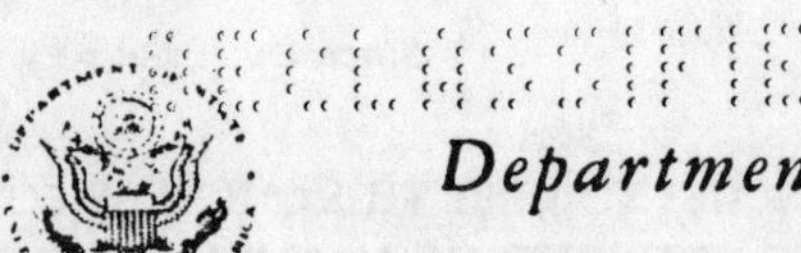

TELEG

CONFIDENTIAL

AN: D750199-0932

PAGE 01 STATE 132632

11
ORIGIN EA-06

INFO OCT-01 SS-14 ISO-00 ORM-01 SR-02 NSC-05 NSCE-00 L-01

PRS-01 VO-01 SCA-01 INR-05 CIAE-00 DODE-00 SY-02 /040 R

DRAFTED BY EA/PHL:ASWIFT:JAK
APPROVED BY EA/PHL:BAFLECK
ORM:CPAPPAS (DRAFT)
--------------------- 087930
R 062002Z JUN 75
FM SECSTATE WASHDC
TO AMEMBASSY MANILA

C O N F I D E N T I A

LIMDIS

E.O. 11652: GDS

TAGS: SREF, RP, PINT

SUBJECT: ASYLUM REQUEST BY PRIMITIVO MIJARES
1. DEPARTMENT HAS RECEIVED FORMAL REQUEST FROM PRIMITIVO MIJARES THROUGH INS FOR ASYLUM IN US.

2. DEPARTMENT PLANS TO REPLY TO INS THAT QTE IT IS POSSIBLE THAT MIJARES DENOUNCEMENT OF THE GOVERNMENT OF THE PHILIPPINES MIGHT CAUSE HIM PROBLEMS IF HE RETURNS TO THAT COUNTRY, ALTHOUGH WE ARE UNABLE TO DETERMINE WHETHER THESE PROBLEMS COULD BE CLASSIFIED AS PERSECUTION. HOWEVER, THE CONVENTION RELATING TO THE STATUS OF REFUGEES DEFINES A REFUGEE AS A PERSON OUTSIDE HIS COUNTRY OF NATIONALITY WHO IS UNABLE OR UNWILLING TO RETURN THERETO OWING TO A WELL-FOUNDED FEAR OF PERSECUTION BECAUSE OF RACE, RELIGION, NATIONALITY, POLITICAL OPINION OR MEMBERSHIP IN A PARTICULAR SOCIAL GROUP. THE KEY WORDS ARE "WELL-FOUNDED". AS A RESULT WE BELIEVE WE MUST RECOMMEND THAT MR. MIJARES NOT BE FORCIBLY RETURNED TO THE PHILIPPINES AT THIS TIME. END QTE.
PAGE 02 STATE 132632

DECLASSIFIED

CONFIDENTIAL

CONFIDENTIAL

3. WE ASSUME INS WILL THEN ISSUE MIJARES VOLUNTARY DEPARTURE STATUS AND REFER CASE BACK TO DEPARTMENT AT A LATER DATE. HOWEVER, INS DOES HAVE AUTHORITY TO GRANT ASYLUM ON THEIR OWN INITIATIVE.

4. DEPARTMENT DOES NOT INTEND TO DISCUSS MIJARES CASE WITH PHILIPPINE GOVERNMENT AND EMBASSY SHOULD ALSO AVOID ISSUE.

5. WE RECOGNIZE UNSAVORY ASPECTS OF MIJARES PAST. HOWEVER, DOCUMENTS WHICH HAVE BEEN SUBMITTED ARE COMPLETELY FACTUAL AND ON THE SURFACE SEEM TO ESTABLISH A WELL-FOUNDED FEAR. THIS IS EXTREMELY DIFFICULT CASE TO HANDLE AND WE HAVE ATTEMPTED TO CAREFULLY PHRASE WORDING OF OUR REPLY. KISSINGER

The details of the political coverups while Henry Kissinger was running the State Department will form an interesting chapter in American history, but they are not the subject of this book. What is pertinent to this book is the Mijares association with the Marcos family, his prominent role in helping Marcos terrorize the Filipino people through control of the news media, his subsequent defection to the United States, his testimony before Congress, the attempted Marcos bribe, and, finally, his disappearance.

Listening now to Imelda speak with contempt and hatred for Mijares, I found it difficult to hold back my urge to break out laughing again. 'Isn't this the kind of person who fits in so well with those who serve your family?' I thought. I wanted to ask, 'since you admit you knew the kind of "snake" and "scum" Mijares was long before martial law, how can you admit your husband brought him in the palace *after* martial law and gave him such an important and sensitive post?'

What I did say to Imelda was, "I happen to share some of your views on Mijares' character. I'd be curious to hear Mr. Marcos' explanation of why Mijares was so close until he defected. I would also like to ask your husband if he might know Mijares' whereabouts."

"I don't believe it serves any purpose to talk about someone like Mijares or to speculate on his whereabouts," Imelda concluded abruptly.

CHAPTER 15

Can We Have a Moratorium?

I lit another cigarette and took a sip of the cold coffee left in my cup. Imelda quickly put thoughts of Mijares aside and resumed her earlier warm tone.

"I really appreciate our discussion. I wonder if there is some way that you could talk with the President. I am convinced it would be very fruitful."

The idea intrigued me. A private meeting with Marcos, similar to the one I was having with Imelda, could indeed be very constructive. But I immediately saw the problem.

"Mrs. Marcos, I would welcome a meeting with your husband and would not hesitate to fly with you to Manila right now, but I am afraid such a meeting might do more harm than good, both to you and to the opposition."

"Why?" she asked, as if she considered the idea of going back with her possible.

"Well, although I consider myself as much a Filipino at heart as any native, the fact is that I am an American, and your countrymen view me as a foreigner. It would not look good for Mr. Marcos to appear negotiating the internal affairs of the Philippines with a foreigner when he *should* be having a dialogue with the Filipino opposition. Similarly, my own friends in the opposition would resent such a meeting. Although many opposition leaders, both politicians and young activists, respect my concern for the Filipino people, they certainly would and should resent any action on my part that could be interpreted as negotiation on their behalf."

"You are quite right," she said. "Perhaps you could meet another time soon when the situation has changed. In the meantime we must do what we can to stop the violence and bloodshed. We must move peacefully toward full normalization. Steve, we need some time to convince the people that the President is sincere. Can we have a moratorium?"

The question surprised me. It surprised me because I did not expect Imelda to admit the seriousness of the threat posed by the urban guerrillas. I knew she was afraid of the Destabilization Plan, and I felt our frank discussion had increased, not decreased, her fear. But still, I did not expect her to admit it by asking for a moratorium.

I was also pleased because I felt that she had wisely decided to abandon her bluffing. It was a sign she understood the problem and wanted to face the issue squarely.

"Mrs. Marcos, the question of a moratorium is a tough one with many ifs and buts. However, I am glad you are asking. I think you are on the right track."

"Why should it be so hard?" she asked. "We seem to agree that some time is needed to convince the people of the President't sincerity. The President cannot move forward while the rebels continue their bombings and killings. Please give us a moratorium for a few months."

"I am afraid I have to repeat myself once more, lest I be misunderstood or appear to misrepresent the facts. I am in no position to grant a moratorium or to speak for the rebels in any way.

Even Ninoy, as I mentioned earlier, is in no position to speak categorically for them. However, . . ."

Imelda interrupted, "I understand and appreciate that. Will you then *help us* get a moratorium?"

I was now more comfortable with her question. It indicated she was seeing the problem more clearly.

"Mrs. Marcos, I would be more than just willing to help bring about a moratorium. I would actually be proud to help if Mr. Marcos created the conditions to justify a moratorium. As a matter of fact, I'll go further. Although I have no right to speak for others, in this case I feel I can tell you that, under the right conditions, Ninoy, whose influence really counts, would be delighted to help call for a moratorium. I know how Ninoy feels on this subject. He wants to avoid violence as much as you do."

"All right then; let's have a moratorium for four to six months and give us a chance to prove the President's sincerity and intention to move toward normalization."

"The problem is not so much the declaration of a moratorium for three or four or six months. The problem is creating the *atmosphere* to justify calling a moratorium and to assure its success. This depends on Mr. Marcos. As I mentioned earlier, you are in a position to show your sincerity by taking certain concrete steps—for the rebels, almost immediately, and for the political leaders, through a meaningful dialogue."

"All right," Imelda said decisively. "I am ready to work for this with all my heart. But please understand. I have taken this initiative on my own. The President knows nothing about it. I will need some time to apprise him of our discussion and ask him to consider some of the good suggestions made here today. I want to maintain an open line of communication with you. As you know, I have established a direct link with Ninoy. I want the same with you. You can call me any time, day or night, for anything you feel is important."

"I am glad to hear this, and I appreciate your situation with Mr. Marcos," I said, although I honestly thought Marcos was aware of our meeting. I could not imagine Imelda talking to Ninoy and to me without Marcos' knowledge. Anyway, the point was irrelevant. The only essential question was whether Imelda was sincere or just simply trying to buy time.

I gave this question some thought. If Imelda and Marcos were sincere, the potential benefits were tremendous. If they were not, what did the rebels stand to lose? Not very much. One or two or three months would not change anything. The Plan could proceed effectively the following week, as well as one month or three months later. Besides, if Marcos was not sincere, it would be obvious soon enough. He would have to ease up on the revolutionaries very soon. If he continued with the hunting, the arrests, the mistreatment of those arrested, the farcical trials, etc., we would know. I decided the proposal was reasonable and should be given a chance.

"All right, Mrs. Marcos," I said with determination and honesty. "I, for one, in my limited capacity, am willing to start the process immediately. I am sure Ninoy will feel the same way. But let's make it clear that the ball is in your court. We need performance from you and Mr. Marcos before we can be in a position to really help."

"Fine," said Imelda with great satisfaction. "Now, how can you and I keep an open line of communication? Neither of us is readily available all the time. Let's establish a link between us. I can assign almost anyone to be at your disposal. Who would you like?"

"Well," I said hesitantly. "I don't know. You're catching me off guard. I'll have to think about it." I stopped and thought for a second. "Ting Paterno would be a good man. He is surely qualified and a man of integrity. However, I understand he left your government. Besides, three years ago, I attacked him for serving in your government. He may not agree to work with me."

"No, no. Ting hasn't really left the government. He is sort of a consultant. If you want Ting, it's fine with me," she said and paused pensively. "How about Zita? She is a very good friend of Presy's. She may be just the right person."

"Zita sounds fine. I just wonder if she has the background required to understand and accurately communicate some potentially complicated political issues. Why don't we give this some thought, and I'll get back to you soon. I am sure we'll find someone suitable," I assured her.

"Okay. Promise me then that you'll get back to me before Christmas. We want to establish our direct line as soon as possible. Meanwhile, if you need me and cannot reach me directly, please call Colonel Zumel any time of the day or night. He is my trusted assistant, and you can easily reach him." She turned around to the Colonel. "Colonel, give Mr. Psinakis your card and the phone numbers where he can always reach you."

The colonel pulled out a calling card and wrote down two phone numbers. He handed it to me. "You can reach me at either number most of the time, Mr. Psinakis."

Imelda seemed very satisfied—almost excited. It was evident she was pleased with my willingness to help establish a moratorium with the rebels and with my assurance that Ninoy would feel the same way.

I was pleased, too, but only guardedly optimistic. I was not at all sure Imelda understood the urgency of taking some appropriate action, particularly toward easing the problems with the activists. 'There was no way,' I thought, 'for the rebels to welcome the idea of a moratorium unless Marcos takes some immediate steps to ease the tension.' In fact, I was very concerned, since if Imelda, intentionally or unintentionally, leaked anything about an agreement of a moratorium, the guerrillas would become infuriated and retaliate.

"Mrs. Marcos," I said soberly. "I think we've come a long way in three hours. You seem pleased and so am I. We must be careful how we handle the news of our meeting. There is no way we can keep it a secret. Too many people already know we met. What do you suggest?"

"Perhaps we should keep our conversation confidential for the time being. How about a 'no comment' response to the press when they contact you?"

"That sounds like a fine idea," I said.

"Remember now, Steve. You promised to call me before Christmas about our contract. Okay?"

"Yes, I will. I'll try to call you tomorrow if I come up with any valid ideas," I reassured her. "I'll ask Presy about Zita. Maybe Zita would be suitable."

The atmosphere was now more than cordial. It was friendly. I thought that our meeting was just about over. I looked at my watch for the first time. It was 5:35 p.m. We had been talking for about three and a half hours. 'It was worth it," I said to myself.

CHAPTER 16

Imelda's Day in Court

I was about to thank Imelda and prepare to leave, but before I had the chance, she said, "Last Sunday, I had a reception here for President Nixon and some other friends. You know, Nixon is again very influential in the government. President-elect Reagan has high regard for him. He is making a comeback."

I wanted to tell her that as far as I was concerned, Nixon belonged behind bars, not in receptions at the Waldorf. But I didn't say anything. I saw no point in ruining the present atmosphere. I had done more than my share of the talking. I said to myself: 'The important points have been covered. Now be quiet and let Imelda have her day in court for the remaining few minutes.'

"We videotaped the reception with Nixon," she said casually. "Would you like to see the tape?"

She stood up (so did I) and started to walk across the room. She asked me to sit in a sofa chair in front of a TV set, and she sat in the sofa next to me. She motioned to the Colonel who immediately started the videotape machine.

The picture came into focus. It looked like a dinner party of the "beautiful people"–fancy table settings with well dressed and jeweled VIPs dining. In the middle of the head table was former President Nixon, to his right was the widow of General Douglas MacArthur, and to his left was Imelda. Several people appeared on the screen and Imelda, obligingly, mentioned their names to me, mostly important bankers and oil company executives.

At some point, Nixon stood up with a champagne glass in his hand to propose a toast to the hostess. Instead of a toast he made a speech Imelda thought would be nice for me to hear. Nixon praised Imelda, the Philippines, and, most importantly, the "government of President Marcos." He spoke of "our strong alliance" and of Marcos' loyalty to the United States and his contribution to the stability of the region.

Nixon's words reminded me of Carter's speech when the Shah of Iran had visited Washington. Carter referred to the government of the Shah as an "island of stability." A few months later, the Shah had been chased out of Iran by the revolutionaries, never to return.

Nixon ended his brief speech by committing to do everything in his power to keep the government of President Marcos strong. "That was very nice," I commented as the Colonel turned off the TV.

"Are you leaving for Manila tomorrow evening?" I asked Imelda.

"Yes. I am going straight home tomorrow. I may talk with Heherson Alvarez in the morning. Do you know him well?" she asked.

I was sure Imelda knew that Sonny and I were close associates in the MFP as well as close personal friends. "Yes, I know him quite well. He is a bright young man and very committed to his country. It would be a very good idea if you had an opportunity to exchange views with him."

"You know, Steve, I came to the States in such a hurry on this trip. I was also in New York last month on my way to Mexico. But soon after I returned to Manila, we had some serious trouble with our oil supply from Saudi Arabia. I had hardly enough time to warm my seat at home when I had to rush back here to solve this serious and unexpected problem." At this point, I just kept quiet. I didn't want to ask why, first of all, because I had heard the answer from Ninoy the day before and, secondly, because I was anxious to leave. I had to fly back to Boston that night to brief Ninoy and, if possible, fly back to California the following morning. I had an appointment in San Francisco with some out-of-town people that weekend, and I was concerned I might miss them.

Imelda continued, "during my last trip to Mexico, I just wanted to arrange for only a small oil supply contract of 10,000 barrels a day, as a back up for the oil we import from Iran. This Iran-Iraq war doesn't look good. I thought I should provide for an alternate source of supply, just in case the supply from Iraq was interrupted because of the war."

'Well!' I said to myself. 'I guess I am going to hear the whole story again.' But I didn't really mind too much. Imelda had been both cordial and patient. She had listened to me patiently for a long time without interruption. I doubted if she had done this with anyone else during the past eight years. The least I could do, I decided, was to let her have her turn. She was in a good mood and wanted to brag a little about her "troubleshooting" accomplishments.

The truth is that no matter what anyone may have to say against Imelda, one has to admit that she has been an effective troubleshooter for her husband. With her inexhaustible energy and feminine charm, she has averted many a crisis for Marcos.

"While in Mexico, instead of just providing for the small back up we needed, I negotiated a great deal with President Lopez

Portillo. We agreed to undertake a joint venture of a huge refinery in Manila with a capacity of 300,000 barrels a day, larger than our total present needs. We plan to export the excess to neighboring countries. I went home very excited and told the President and my people. I guess the press headlined the story and the Saudis learned about it. You know, the Arabs are nice people, but sometimes they act like immature babies. Can you imagine? The Saudis felt slighted because my deal with Mexico was so big. I guess they thought we were trying to show them we didn't need them—with the Mindanao problem and all. On the contrary, I value our friendship with the Saudis. Anyway, they got angry and cabled us that they were discontinuing our fuel supply from Saudi Arabia. We buy a lot of our oil from the Saudis, some 60,000 barrels. Now, that was really a crisis. I had to rush back to New York to reassure their oil minister, and then I had to fly to Saudi Arabia to talk to people there. I was very lucky," Imelda concluded with modesty. "I was lucky to solve this problem."

"Your troubleshooting missions are known all over the world. That's the best weapon of a smart wife—to make herself indispensable to her husband," I commented smiling.

A mischievous thought occurred to me. We had learned through the grapevine that Cesar Virata, the Philippine Finance Minister, was about to resign from his post because he had fallen in love with Minetta Ayala, the widow of Kokoy's former right-hand man, Tony Ayala. The news of Virata's personal love life would normally belong in the social pages of the Manila papers. However, in this case, the news had political significance.

Ministers Virata and Paterno, finance and industry respectively, were the two most respected cabinet members of the Marcos regime. They are both competent, intelligent, and reputedly honest—a rare exception in the Marcos government. The two ministers have been jointly credited for the healthy relations between the Marcos regime and the international financial institutions. Marcos has used them to his advantage.

The resignation of Paterno a few months earlier, allegedly because of his growing dissatisfaction with the regime, was a serious loss to the prestige of the Philippine government. If Virata were also to resign (because he was leaving his wife and the Philippines for another woman), the news would not be just a social scandal but an event with political implications. The information we had received was that Imelda, the everpresent troubleshooter, had flown to Washington, D.C., to see Virata and convince him to return to his wife and to the all-important Finance Ministry.

"Your mission to the Middle East was successful," I said. "Your mission with Reagan certainly appears to have been successful. I hope your mission with Virata's personal problem was equally successful," In interjected quite casually.

"Hmmmmm. Poor Cesar (Virata's first name) does have a problem, but I think the children will win out in the end. He'll come back, I think. You know, he is such a goody-goody. Maybe a little escapade will do him good."

I felt a little guilty for extracting this gossip from Imelda like this, but it was important to ascertain Cesar Virata's situation. Virata did return to Manila the following weekend and, so far, he is still the Minister of Finance. We must assume Imelda succeeded in that mission as well.

I looked at my watch; it was 6:08 p.m. "I wonder if I could place a call to Ninoy," I asked. "By now he must think you had me arrested," I laughed.

"Colonel, get Senator Aquino on the phone for Mr. Psinakis," she instructed.

The colonel used the phone near the entrance to the suite. "Mr. Psinakis," he said. "Senator Aquino is on the line." He handed me the phone.

"Hello, Ninoy. I need some help." I said in a serious voice.

"What is the problem?" he asked.

"I am being abducted," I replied, starting to laugh–so did Imelda, since she was now standing next to me.

Ninoy also laughed at the other end. "Are you still there? How was it?" he asked.

"Fine. I will be flying there tonight to report to you. What time is the last shuttle for Boson?"

"Nine o'clock," Ninoy informed me.

"I see. Eight o'clock. I better hurry up to catch it. See you later," and hung up before Ninoy had a chance to assert, "No, I said *nine* o'clock."

I wanted to leave and somehow I sensed Imelda was in the mood to continue with our chat. I was thinking of poor Sonny Alvarez; we had agreed he would wait for me downstairs at the Waldorf coffee shop, expecting that my meeting would last less than an hour. He had been waiting for four and a half hours. Besides, his wife, Cecile, must have been very worried. Earlier that morning, I had talked to Cecile, and she had expressed genuine concern for me.

"Are you going in there *all alone?*" Cecile had asked.

"Yes, why?"

"I don't know if it's wise. Remember what happened to Kim Dae Jung in Tokyo? Now he's in South Korea ready for the firing squad."

"Oh! Come on, Cecile. Nothing is going to happen. They have nothing to gain by hurting me here in New York. Don't worry," I had comforted her. However, to be very honest, I did not completely discount the possibility.

Anyway, I wanted to now leave for a number of reasons: Sonny, Ninoy, and my Sunday appointment in San Francisco. I stood by the door looking for an opportunity to bid Imelda goodbye, but Imelda was really in the mood to talk. We stood there by the door until well past seven o'clock. I was tempted to say, 'Why don't we order some dinner brought up with a little wine, but I was afraid the answer might have been, 'That's a great idea.'

I had just realized I was starving. I had only juice for breakfast, no lunch, and nothing but a half a cup of coffee two hours earlier. I glanced at the huge silver tray of untouched cookies near the couch. In my famished state, they looked like medium rare steaks, but I didn't dare move back near the couch, or I might be asked to sit down again for another five-hour session.

I really wanted to laugh. For such a serious meeting,' I thought to myself, 'this moment is really funny.'

I finally looked at my watch and acted surprised. "Oh! My! It's past seven. I'd better rush, or I'll miss the last shuttle to Boston." I opened the door and was about to thank Imelda and say good night, but she gestured and walked to the waiting room with me. I saw a number of people waiting there, among them, Ramon Jacinto. He had recovered by now and looked much better than he had when he walked out of our meeting five hours earlier.

Imelda shook my hand warmly. I noticed she had a solid handshake. I feel uncomfortable when some women gently extend their four fingertips for a handshake; I lose them in my palm and don't know what to do with them. Not so with Imelda. Her handshake was nice and firm. I also noticed that her hand was now warm; It meant she was no longer nervous.

During the last 45 minutes or so, as we were standing by the door of her suite, Imelda had done all the talking. I don't remember most of it because my mind was wandering–to cookies, dinner, wine, Sonny, Ninoy, San Francisco. I was listening just enough to be sure I didn't ignore any unexpected question.

I vaguely recall Imelda defending some of her friends who had been accused of amassing wealth through corruption. She explained, for instance, that people like Rudy Cuenca and Herminio Disini make most of their money from overseas projects and that her critics were very unfair to accuse them of using palace influence.

Then she criticized the U.S. press for its "biased reporting." She told me the story of her recent visit to the offices of *Time-Life* magazines. A *Life* magazine article written several months earlier had criticized Imelda for the flamboyant display of her extensive jewelry collection.

"So this time I went to their offices dressed in diamonds from head to toe," Imelda narrated. "They expected me to go there scared, with no jewelry at all. They were surprised. I told them: 'here it is. Here I am with diamonds all over me. Go ahead and write about it! Take my picture if you want.' You know, Steve? They were stunned. They didn't write a word about my jewelry." She seemed proud of this accomplishment.

She narrated several other stories while we were standing by the door—mostly about what she thought were accomplishments of the New Society and about some of her own projects. I had decided I would no longer debate with her, but when she mentioned, for the second time, the improvement in the average Filipino's standard of living, I felt I had to make a comment.

Earlier Imelda had stated that under their leadership, the per capita income had increased from $210 to $780—implying that the average Filipino had benefited. Now, she was not implying; she was stating rather categorically that the increased per capita income was proof of the benefits to the poor.

"Mrs. Marcos, the per capita income is the nation's total income divided by the number of its citizens," I said in a tone that implied she might not have understood the term. "If you take away the income that goes to the few elite and divide the remainder by the rest of the Philippine population, you will find that the average Filipino's income has been dramatically *reduced.* I assume, of course, you are also not forgetting the effect of inflation. All independent statistics show that under your leadership, the rich have become richer and the poor, poorer." At this point, Imelda apparently decided to reciprocate my generosity. She did not dispute my comment, appreciating, perhaps, that I had not disputed any of her other statements during the past 45 minutes.

As Imelda talked about her many projects aimed at improving the standard of living of the Filipino masses, I remembered an observation made by a man who knows Imelda as well as anyone close to her. "You know," he told me, "Imelda has been an admirer of Eva Peron and has studied every document about Eva she could lay her hands on. She has been trying to emulate Peron and find a way to gain the love and admiration of the poor and the destitute." Other reliable sources reinforced my friend's casual observation about Imelda's emulation of Eva Peron.

Coincidentally, two months prior to my meeting with Imelda, the *Los Angeles Times* featured a long article about her entitled, "Imelda: The Philippine 'Eva Peron'." The article, written by the *Los Angeles Times* staff writer, Keyes Beech (a frequent traveller to the Philippines), mentioned some of Imelda's pet projects. She had been describing these projects to me as we stood by the door of her suite. As I remembered Keyes' article, I nearly laughed when I heard Imelda's frequent use of the phrase, "my little people."

The *Los Angeles Times* feature article read in part:

IMELDA: THE PHILIPPINE 'EVA PERON'
By Keyes Beech

MANILA, Oct. 24, 1980—As the Philippine Airlines jumbo jet climbed into the hot blue sky, a Filipino reporter heaved a sigh and said, "God knows how much this trip is going to cost the taxpayers."

Imelda Romualdez Marcos, first lady of the Philippines, ambassador plenipotentiary to kings, commissars, prime ministers and presidents, was off on another of her global journeys—this time to Mexico.

There, with the charm and energy for which she is famous, she would extract a promise from President Jose Lopez Portillo to supply the Philippines with oil in case of a crisis. And, according to the controlled Manila press, which covers her activities with adoration, Mexico also promised to build a petro-chemical plant in the Philippines . . . "

Often she travels in her own plane, with a second plane as backup. "She doesn't really need a backup plane in the conventional sense," an aide said. "She takes one along because there isn't room enough on one plane for all her friends. The first lady is a very generous woman."

Many rich Filipinos, not to mention foreign businessmen, would heartily agree that Imelda Marcos is indeed a generous woman—especially with other people's money . . .

A poor but beautiful country girl once known as the "Rose of Tacloban," whose face and figure brought her the title of beauty queen of Manila in 1953, Imelda is much more than the wife of President Ferdinand E. Marcos.

As the female half of what critics call a "conjugal dictatorship," she is the second most powerful person in the country.

She is, for all practical purposes, her husband's vice president. She is governor of metropolitan Manila, which embraces about 20% of the country's population; a member of the national Assembly representing the capital region and since 1978, minister of human settlements, a Cabinet post that allows her to poke her red-lacquered nails into just about anything that attracts her.

Even more frightening to her critics is the prospect that she might succeed her husband as president and prime minister.

Her husband's political arch-enemy, former Senator Benigno S. Aquino, Jr., who is waging political warfare against Marcos from Harvard University, has compared her favorably with imperial Russia's Catherine the Great. Others see her as "another Eva Peron," the influential wife of the late Argentine dictator.

Indications are that Imelda is considerably less loved than she would like to be . . .

What is fact is that she has the kind of personality and driving ambition that leave a trail of controversy wherever she goes, whatever she does.

Her extravagant life style, her flamboyant dress, her glittering jewels, her celebrity-hunting, her hunger for the company of the "beautiful people," including unemployed European nobility, her unabashed self-aggrandizement, her lavish parties—all these things make her an irresistible moving target.

Especially so, as the Western press never fails to remind her, when her personal opulence contrasts so vividly with the stark poverty of the vast majority of Filipinos. But the Iron Butterfly, whose soft, feminie exterior masks a will of steel, shrugs off such criticism.

"I am my little people's star and slave," she tells interviewers. "When I go out into the barrios, I get dressed up because I know my little people want to see a star. Other presidents' wives have gone to the barrios wearing house dresses and slippers. That's not what people want to see. People want someone they can love, someone to set an example."

"Crap!" a Catholic priest snorted. "Pure Crap! She likes to play the role of Lady Bountiful. She has no real concern for the poor. She's on an ego trip."

Imelda's defenders charge American critics with failing to understand the Filipino culture.

A friend of the first lady who has known her since childhood—they use the same hairdresser—and sees her almost daily said candidly:

"She's a showy woman. She even looks showy in black."

Both Imelda and the president are convinced they can't get a fair break from the American press, no matter how hard they try. But several months ago they gave the red carpet treatment to a well-known American journalist and his wife by inviting them to Malacanang, the presidential palace, for a three-hour breakfast.

"The wife showed up wearing a T-shirt and denim skirt," Imelda's friend said. "All the rest of us were dressed up. Imelda was wearing a beautiful terno and I was wearing a silk suit.

"After they left, Imelda was furious. She felt insulted. She said, 'imagine that woman coming here dressed like that. Would she dress like that if she went to the White House? Of course not.' "

There are two major complaints against Imelda. One is what her critics call her "edifice complex." The other is that she and the president have used their position to enrich themselves and their friends and relatives.

The "edifice complex" has resulted in a seemingly endless series of splashy projects costing hundreds of millions of dollars.

Even her bitterest critics concede that Imelda gets things done. It's what she gets done that bothers them. Among other things, she has built a 750-room hotel, a national art center, a kidney center, a nutrition center, an eye-center, a heart center and, most recently, a University of Life, the purpose of which is not altogether clear.

A stern and ruthless taskmaster, she wants everything done yesterday—and done well. When she checked the heart center before its formal opening, she found the newly planted grass was turning brown. So were the newly planted coconut palms.

"I want them green," she snapped.

The problem was resolved with green spray paint.

One of Imelda's most spectacular achievements was to alter the Manila skyline four years ago with the forced construction of 14 new luxury hotels in time for the opening of an International Monetary Fund conference.

Critics dismiss all these projects as irrelevant to the basic problems of the country. With the possible exception of Indonesia, the Philippines has the most lopsided distribution of wealth—the greatest gap between rich and poor—in all East Asia. There is also widespread malnutrituion and social injustice in general, they assert.

There is a great deal of truth in these criticisms. It is also true that most, if not all of Imelda's projects are being used. "Of course," an American observed, "some of them cost two or three times more than they should have. But that's the way things are done around here."

What accounts for Imelda's monument-building spree and the wholesale importation of celebrities to see them?

"For one thing she wanted to put the Philippines on the map," a long-time American resident said.

"For another, there's a towering inferiority complex in this country toward tall, fair-skinned people. This is Imelda's way of combating that complex. I'm not saying it's right. All I'm saying is, that's the way it is."

Where did all the money come from? Much of it was in foreign loans—the Philippines is one of the Third World's biggest borrowers, with a current debt of more than $11 billion.

Some of the money is in the form of "contributions" from wealthy Filipinos and foreign corporations, many of them American. Donations to Imelda's good works run as high as $300,000.

Businessmen complain but pay up. Otherwise, they don't stay in business.

"I know just how much to ask of each of them," Imelda once confided, "because I see their income tax returns."

In a revealing interview with *Fortune* magazine last year, she said, "It's the rich you can terrorize. The poor have nothing to lose."

By that criterion the Marcoses have a great deal to lose. Marcos, who was a millionaire before he became president 15 years ago, is widely reputed to be the richest head of state in Asia. There is no way to prove this, but it is easy to believe.

Several years ago, *Cosmopolitan* magazine listed Imelda as one of the 10 richest women in the world. As is the case with her husband, there is no way to prove this, but it also is easy to believe.

Not even the Marcos apologists will dispute that his and her friends and relatives have grown rich under the Marcos regime, especially since he established martial law eight years ago. The reason they don't argue is that the evidence is all too abundant.

Marcos' political opponents here and in the United States have painstakingly documented, in two separate studies, the rise to riches of the "first couple" and those close to them.

One report, by a Filipino university instructor now living in the United States, estimates that the "Marcos Octopus," as it is known here, either owns or controls at least 900 Philippine companies, ranging from shipping and real estate to gambling casinos and newspapers and television stations.

Imelda's family appears to have profited more, one opposition leader said, "but perhaps that is only fair since they didn't have much money to start with."

Among the principal beneficiaries of the Marcos connection, according to the two reports:

- Pacifico Marcos, younger brother of the President, who owns or controls 50 corporations.
- Roberto S. Benedicto, former ambassador to Japan, classmate and fraternity brother of the president, 30 corporations.
- Benjamin (Kokoy) Romualdez, one of Imelda's brothers, former ambassador to Peking, who along with members of the Marcos clan allegedly owns or controls 90 corporations.

• Herminio Disini, one of the president's golfing cronies, who in six years parlayed a tiny cigarette filter manufacturing company into 30 companies with assets worth more than $200 million.

As Imelda has said, in one of her more celebrated quotations, "Some are smarter than others."

Admittedly, I found it difficult to understand how Imelda could be boasting about her projects. They have been widely criticized, not only by her opponents, but also by objective foreign correspondents and neutral observers of the Philippine scene. 'Doesn't she every read?' I wondered.

"Most knowledgeable observers," I said, "criticize you for undertaking these projects you so proudly describe as your great accomplishments. Why would they criticize you instead of praise you?"

"Oh! I don't know their motivation," she said quite casually, "I don't have the time to read trash."

"Do you consider publications like the *New York Times,* the *Washington Post,* the *Los Angeles Times, Newsweek, Time* and other such news publications as trash?" I inquired.

"Well, of course. When they have nothing better to do except waste their time criticizing me, of course, I have to believe they are trash. Anyway, as you know, the American press is biased against the President because he is strong and independent; he doesn't cower to Americans. Come to think of it, that's why the American reporters are biased," she said triumphantly as she appeared to have discovered a satisfactory answer to my earlier question.

'Oh, no,' I said to myself. 'You'd better be quiet or else you'll get into a useless two-hour argument trying to convince Imelda that it's illogical to believe all prestigious U.S. publications are conspiring against her.' Instead, I simply said, "I think it would be useful if you would read some of the critical articles about you and your husband." As I said this, I couldn't resist adding a snide remark. "But I forgot," I continued with a smile. "Your husband has decreed it a crime to write or read anything critical about either of you. You probably wouldn't want to violate your husband's decrees."

Imelda's expression suddenly changed and so did her tone of voice. "Was that called for?" she asked angrily.

I certainly thought it was, but at the same time, I didn't think it was worth engaging in a lengthy argument which would, no doubt, adversely affect the progress we had made earlier.

"Well, I am sorry for making a sarcastic remark. I shouldn't have. But your perception that the U.S. press is conspiring against you is rather irrational and very untrue. I do think it would be beneficial to read the analyses in the *New York Times* and the *Washington Post,* as well as publications from France, Germany, and England–the *London Economist,* for example.

At another point of our "standing" friendly conversation, Imelda casually mentioned her financial shenanigans with the Lopez family, hoping, perhaps, to elicit a reaction from me that would give her an opportunity to entice me with a bribe. Buying her way out of tight situations has been a SOP for her and her husband.

"I am glad the Meralco Foundation has improved its financial condition during the past two years and has been able to meet its payments to your family," she interjected. "Since your father-in-law passed away, the family had some financial difficulties. I think now that Meralco has been making its payments regularly, your financial difficulties have ended," she said as sweetly as could be, which is 'very sweetly'. "Is your family all right financially now?" she asked, almost embarrassed.

'Oh boy!' I thought. 'What a polite opening for a bribe. She never gives up,' At least she had learned enough about Presy and me to make her bribe offer discreetly. She usually just says,

"Here is what I want you to do. Now, what's your price?"

Her remark about the Meralco "payments," which were not being made to the Lopezes, reminded me of how they had come about. When old man Lopez signed over Meralco [the electric company controlled by the Lopezes] to Imelda's brother, Kokoy, in a vain attempt to secure Geny Lopez's freedom, a "purchase agreement" had been signed in Honolulu giving the "transaction" the semblance of legality. Despite exhaustive studies by Imelda's panel of lawyers to make the "agreement" appear businesslike, a quick review, even by a layman, would reveal that the document could only be an instrument of extortion.

"How can any lawyer make an agreement appear legitimate when the buyer is acquiring assets worth more than 100 million dollars and the seller receives a ridiculous down payment of 10,000 Pesos (equivalent to about $1500) and a promise that additional amounts will be paid only *if* and *when* the buyer can afford to pay?" I once asked Geny Lopez.

As expected, no payments whatsoever had been made to the Lopezes since 1972 when Imelda's and Kokoy's fronting organization, the Meralco Foundation, took over the power company. After Geny Lopez's successful escape in 1977 and his arrival to America, Presy and I tried to convince Geny and, through Geny, the rest of the Lopez family in Manila, to study the possibility of filing an extortion suit in the U.S. federal court against "the Marcos gang."

"Imagine what it will do for the cause to win a conviction in the U.S. courts confirming that the Marcoses are nothing but a bunch of criminals and blackmailers," I had told Geny. "Anyway, what do you have to lose? You are not getting anything from them anyway."

Geny seemed to be convinced, and a few months after his arrival in the United States, and after some consultation with members of his family in Manila, Geny engaged the San Francisco law firm, Goldstein and Phillips to study the matter. Judge Al Goldstein and David Phillips invited Jack Garvey, a Professor of Law at the University of San Francisco specializing in international law, to participate in the study.

A thorough review of the available evidence and the "purchase agreement" convinced the lawyers that the "transaction was a clear case of blackmail." The case presented only two problems, one legal and one financial.

The *legal problem* pertained to jurisdiction. Would the U.S. courts accept jurisdiction of a case involving foreign nationals (non-Americans) and properties located in a foreign country—the Philippines? After a careful study, the lawyers decided that there was "a very good chance" to obtain U.S. jurisdiction of the case due primarily to three criteria:

(a) The crime was committed mainly within the United States —Kokoy's blackmail of old man Lopez took place in San Francisco;

(b) The "purchase agreements," the extortion instrument, was signed in the United States—in Honolulu;

(c) American business institutions were involved and affected —many U.S. banks were creditors of the Lopez-controlled power company.

The *financial problem* pertained to the ability to collect. If the case was won by the Lopezes and a multimillion-dollar judgment was ordered, how could the Lopezes collect from the Marcoses? This problem was difficult to solve.

International law prohibits the confiscation of properties located in one country but belonging to a foreign government. In other words, assets of Philippine government banks, Philippine Embassy buildings and other such properties located in the U.S. could not be touched. Recovery of funds could only come from "private" U.S. assets held by Marcos and his co-defendents.

Although the private properties in the U.S. belonging to Marcos, Imelda, Kokoy, and the other potential co-defendants of the suit are known to swell into the hundreds of million dollars, most, if not all, are registered in names other than their real names. Consequently, the prospects of collecting a judgment were not very good.

"What do you have to lose?" Presy and I told Geny. "You're not getting anything now, anyway. You'll definitely be able to recover some of their U.S. properties, but even if you don't, what do you have to lose? You can't lose something from nothing. On the other hand, just imagine what a conviction against Marcos will do for your country. The U.S. government will have to stop its aid to a confirmed and convicted extortionist, and, without U.S. aid, Marcos will topple and your country will be free again."

Geny appeared to be convinced. He invited one of his Filipino family lawyers, Camilo Quiason, to come to San Francisco and study the matter and then agreed to send Judge Goldstein to Manila to exchange views with Geny's uncle, Fernando Lopez, and other members of the Lopez family.

While all these preparations and discussion were going on, word reached Marcos that the Lopezes were ready to file suit. Marcos, Imelda, and Kokoy became frantic. Kokoy went to the Lopez family in Manila and assured them that payments under our "purchase agreement" would be made within 1 to 2 weeks. The Lopezes in Manila were delighted. Presy and I were furious. "Don't accept any payments," we told Geny. "All Marcos wants to do is legitimize the extortion agreement and stop you from filing the suit."

Within a few days, payments amounting to some 15 million pesos (equivalent to about two million dollars) were sent to the Lopezes. The funds were gratefully accepted. Since then, payments have continued in accordance with the stipulated terms of the "purchase agreement."

Imelda was now referring to these payments when she mentioned the "end of the financial difficulties of the Lopez family."

"I don't know much about the Lopez family finances," I said. "I guess they're okay. I haven't heard any complaints." I wanted to add, 'it must be painful for you to see *any* of the extorted money returning to the Lopezes. Your only consolation must be that this money is not given to the needy freedom fighters to help speed your downfall.' But of course, I didn't say it. Instead I said, "I imagine the preparation of the Lopez suit might have had something to do with your willingness to pay the Lopezes after six years."

"What suit?" she asked innocently.

"Oh! nothing" I said. "I thought you might have heard. I guess you haven't." However, we both understood.

At another point in our 45-minute "standing" conversation, Imelda said curiously, "you know, Steve, during my earlier visit to the States, I was invited by the Governor of Arizona to visit his state. When I arrived at the airport, I was shocked. I had never seen such tight security in my life. I asked the Governor what was happening and he told me 'Unfortunately, we heard that terrorists who want to overthrow your government have been training in our state. They may attempt to harm you during your visit. That's the reason for the unusually tight security. ' I wonder, Steve, do you know anything about that?" she asked very casually.

I started to laugh. I recalled all the headlines in her Manila newspapers alleging that I had been "training terrorists in the Arizona desert."

"If I didn't know anything about this, Mrs. Marcos, my answer would be, 'I don't know.' If I knew something about it, my answer would be, 'I don't know,' I said smiling. "Do you really want to know what my answer is?" I asked mischievously.

She fell for the trap. "Yes, I really would," she said eagerly.

"I don't know," I said, with a hearty laugh.

CHAPTER 17

Yes! We'll Give It a Try

As I took the elevator to the Tower's main lobby, I felt relieved. I hoped Imelda didn't feel slighted for my leaving her while she was still in the mood for talking. This was atypical of Imelda during the last eight years; in fact, it could have been another first.

I walked into the Waldorf coffee shop where Sonny had been waiting for six hours.

"Sorry, Sonny," I apologized. I was really quite embarrassed. "We sure didn't expect a six-hour session. I think we had a fruitful meeting. I'll brief you, but first, let me order a sandwich. I'm starving."

I briefed Sonny on the highlights, had a quick sandwich, and went out to get a cab for La Guardia. Sonny was pleased with the outcome of the meeting.

The temperature outside was about zero, and an icy wind was blowing at 30 to 40 miles an hour. There was a long waiting line for taxis, and when it got to be 8:30 p.m., it was obvious we wouldn't catch the last shuttle to Boston.

"Let's go inside and give Ninoy a call," I said. "I'll stay in New

York tonight. We can catch the first shuttle in the morning."

We called Ninoy and told him about the change in plans. He was anxious to hear the details of my meeting.

"I think you'll be generally pleased," I said, "but, please don't make me tell you on the phone; it'll take forever. I'll give you a full report in the morning."

"Okay," he said, agreeably, "see you tomorrow."

I gave Sonny more details on the discussion, and, before he left, we made a date for early the following morning. However, two hours later Sonny called to tell me that Fe Jimenez had just invited him to a meeting with Imelda for the following morning at 11 o'clock.

"In that case," I said, " I'll go to Boston alone tomorrow. Call us when your meeting is over. I hope you won't have to sit through the Nixon videotape, too," I teased.

I caught the 8 c'clock shuttle and was at Ninoy's house before 10. I gave him a detailed account of our discussion, and Ninoy was very pleased. He seemed a little surprised and very satisfied that I was able to discuss such "touchy subjects" quite openly without getting into a fist fight. What pleased Ninoy the most is when I said, "I am not sure whether the meeting will produce any results, but I can assure you of one thing without reservation: Imelda not only understood the determination of the revolutionaries, she also recognized their ability to destabilize the Marcos regime."

At the end of my briefing, Ninoy used his favorite rating method to grade the encounter with Imelda. "On a scale of ten," he said, "I give the meeting a nine point five." I knew he was satisfied. I had heard him use his favorite system on many occasions, but I had never heard anything rate higher than eight point five.

I asked Ninoy's opinion on the "link" with Imelda. "Why don't you agree to Zita Feliciano, if that makes Imelda comfortable," he said. "I don't feel that good about Paterno anyway, not that it makes much of a difference."

I called Presy in San Francisco for her views on Zita. "She's okay, but I have reservations about her ability to communicate the sensitive issues. However, I am sure she will do her best," Presy told me.

About 12 noon, I called Imelda's suite from Ninoy's house and asked for Colonel Zumel. I told him that I had already some suggestions for Mrs. Marcos regarding our direct communication link and would appreciate a call from her when she was free.

Ninoy had booked me a seat on the 7:30 p.m. flight to San Francisco. We spent the next two hours planning a course of action.

"We must give the peaceful process one last chance," Ninoy said with determination, "but brother, it's going to be tougher than hell. I really don't know if Marcos and Imelda will be really willing to normalize and step down, but I can tell you one thing: Our side may be as hard to convince as Marcos'."

"I know exactly what you mean," I agreed.

"I can't blame them," Ninoy continued. "They've endured many disappointments. They've tried every peaceful approach. It took years of soul searching before peaceful-loving Christians decided to resort to force. Now Marcos tells them, 'hold it; we'll do it peacefully.' They won't believe him, and I can't blame them. But just the same, we must give it one last chance. We have so much to gain and nothing really to lose except two or three months. What is your gut feeling, Steve?"

"I really have none," I said sincerely.

"Well, how do you think the young people will react to a moratorium?"

"They won't like it a bit," I answered with certainty. "It's our toughest problem. We must find a way to explain, but it's hard to do with our communication problem. How the hell do we reach all the independent groups? We must use couriers. You can't just pick up the phone and say, 'Eh! Sam, put down your gun. Imelda promised to give you freedom!' He'll laugh in your face."

"Do you really think Imelda is sincere?" Ninoy asked, needing more of a reassurance than an opinion. He had already decided to stick his neck out.

"I told you: I don't know. I can only assure you that she understands the real dangers. If logic prevails, they'll have no choice but to normalize. They don't want to be cut down. But the question is, Will logic prevail? I really have no idea."

"What our side must understand," Ninoy said, "is that if the Plan continues, Marcos will have no choice but to dig in and fight. We'll have another Iran or Nicaragua. We'll win in the end but how long will it take and at what cost will it come? But if Marcos also understands this–and if we give him the chance–he might, just might, make the right decision."

"A lot depends on you, Ninoy. You know your colleagues better than most people. As for the young ones, they respect you. I think, in general, they will follow your advice to hold off for a short time. After all, you won't ask them to surrender their arms, just to take their fingers off the trigger. If Marcos performs –whether from sincerity or necessity–look what you stand to gain. And if Marcos tries his old tricks again, I am sure you'll be the first one to join the rebels and help them squeeze the trigger. Remember, too, the moratorium works both ways. I'm sure the rebels will use the time well. They'll be better prepared to act, if it becomes necessary."

"Yes! We'll give it a try. It's worth it," Ninoy said decisively.

We spent the rest of the afternoon discussing specific plans of action. We were interrupted by Sonny's call. His meeting with Imelda lasted three hours.

"Yes! It was difficult at times. We almost had a confrontation."

"No! I didn't see the Nixon tape."

"Yes! She told me about the philodendron project."

"No! I didn't like a lot of what I heard."

"Yes! I think it was worthwhile."

Sonny gave Ninoy more details on the phone. It was nothing really new or earthshaking. Ninoy explained his decision to work for a brief moratorium and wait and see. Sonny agreed it was the right decision but also pointed out some of the dangers.

"I've decided to take the risks," Ninoy concluded.

We spent the rest of the afternoon finalizing our plans. It was about 6 p.m., and I was packing my suitcase when the phone rang. Ninoy answered. It was Colonel Zumel.

"Is Mr. Psinakis in, please? The First Lady would like to speak with him."

I talked with Imelda for about 20 minutes. She was very cordial and quite open. I was surprised and gratified. She knew I could be taping our conversation, and yet she didn't hesitate to discuss some of the sensitive points.

I told her I had talked to Presy, and she felt that Zita would be acceptable for our link.

"No. I think you were right, Steve. Zita is a good person, but sometimes she makes the one sound like a thousand. How about my assistant?" she asked.

I waited for his name but she didn't say.

"Who?" I asked.

"My deputy," she responded.

'She must have all kinds of deputies,' I thought.

"Who?" I asked again.

"Mel! Mel Mathay. Do you know him?"

"No, but I know of him. I really have no problem with anyone you want to assign. The idea is to have quick access to each other.

If you prefer Mel Mathay, it's okay with me." I wanted her to know I had no tricks in mind.

"Fine. That's settled for now."

Then I brought up the danger of a false alarm. I explained that some incident might give the impression that one side or the other was acting in bad faith.

"Before we start shooting at each other," I told her, "let's agree first to discuss the problem. It may be a false alarm, and there may be a reasonable explanation. If the war is to resume, let us at least make sure it is not a mere misunderstanding."

I explained again that no one controls the rebels, and it's possible that someone may act on his own. "Also, someone close to you could be shot for personal reasons–not by the rebels. Let's not jump to conclusions before we communicate."

Imelda found the suggestion reasonable. She then mentioned her meeting with Sonny. It had not gone too well, in her opinion. She characterized him as "too much of an academician" and "an idealist" with "abstract ideas on freedom."

I didn't want to start an argument on the phone, nor did I feel Sonny needed my defense. But when she also characterized him as "too much of a hardliner," I couldn't let it pass.

"Don't forget, Mrs. Marcos, he had one tragic death in his family," I said, referring to the mutilation of Sonny's brother by the military.

At that point, the subject changed and we chatted for five more minutes. We thanked each other for the "spirit of cooperation" and promised to exert our best efforts "to give the peaceful process a chance. She extended her best regards to Presy, and I wished her a happy trip.

I finished packing and left Ninoy's house for the airport. During the 6-hour flight to San Francisco, I did nothing but write notes on all the subjects discussed with Imelda. I had already decided to prepare a lengthy account of our dialogue. However, at that time,

I had no idea I would soon decide to publish this book. I was later glad I kept an accurate record while the conversation was still fresh in my mind.

The first call I received after arriving in San Francisco was from Alex Esclamado. He was anxious to hear the news. Alex had talked to Ninoy on the phone and knew we had changed our original plans to hand-deliver my letter. Ninoy had told him I had met with Imelda, but Ninoy did not want to explain on the phone much of what had transpired in the meeting.

I asked Alex to come over to my house and gave him a full account of the meeting. "Okay," he said, "I was dead set against the meeting but, I admit, I'm glad with the way it turned out. I think the meeting was very constructive and useful, and it may have some beneficial effects, but, brother, you'd better be prepared for some nasty reactions from our friends, particularly since you have to keep quiet."

"I don't mind that at all," I said, "if I keep quiet, it means we'll be getting some good results. If we don't see any positive results, then there won't be any further reason to keep quiet."

Alex is the kind of person who enjoys a good joke as much as anyone I know. When he likes a joke, he doesn't just find it funny; he finds it hilarious. I will never forget the day in December 1974 when I showed him a response I had received from a U.S. Senator to my appeal for help in the case of Geny Lopez and Serge Osmena.

On November 24, 1974, Geny and Serge had been on their hunger fast for 10 days. Marcos had placed them in isolation and no one knew what had happened to them. Their wives in Manila were frantic; they didn't even know if their husbands were still alive.

On November 24, Presy and I were on the East Coast commuting between Washington, D.C., and New York and trying desperately to attract the attention of our legislators and the major news media. On that date we sent a personal telegram to every one of the 100 Senators and 435 Congressmen, pleading for their assistance to "save the lives of two innocent prisoners who were on the tenth day of their hunger fast." To our surprise and great satisfaction, many of the Senators and Congressmen responded warmly to our telegram. Quite a few contacted the Philippine Embassy in Washington and some sent urgent cables directly to Marcos protesting the isolation of the two prisoners and criticizing the martial law regime for violating the human rights of the Filipino people.

One of the Senators who received our telegram was Quentin N. Burdick of North Dakota. Senator Burdick was the Chairman of the Senate Subcommittee on National Penitentiaries. Accustomed to receiving many inquiries on the status of prisoners in American jails, the Senator assumed that our reference to "Filipinos" referred to the nationality of prisoners in an American jail rather than to political prisoners in the Philippines. In response to our pleading telegram, the kind Senator initiated an inquiry into the status of Lopez and Osmena. Obviously the inquiry failed to located the two prisoners in any of the U.S. prisons. Obligingly, Senator Burdick informed me of his problem and asked me for "further identifying information."

A few weeks later, when our agony over the Lopez-Osmena hunger strike was over, I related to Alex Esclamado some of our experiences in Washington when Presy and I were trying to rouse support among Congressional leaders. I remembered the Burdick incident, and, after giving Alex a brief background, I handed him the Senator's letter. Before Alex finished the first paragraph, he burst into uncontrollable laughter that lasted for 15 minutes. Tears started to flow from his eyes while he was holding his stomach to soothe the pain from his stomach cramps. I, too, found the letter amusing, considering the circumstances at the time it was written, but I found Alex's reaction to it even more entertaining and had joined him in his unforgettable laughter. The November 27, 1974, letter of the conscientious and considerate Senator is shown below:

JAMES O. EASTLAND, MISS., CHAIRMAN
JOHN L. MC CLELLAN, ARK.
SAM J. ERVIN, JR., N.C.
PHILIP A. HART, MICH.
EDWARD M. KENNEDY, MASS.
BIRCH BAYH, IND.
QUENTIN N. BURDICK, N. DAK.
ROBERT C. BYRD, W. VA.
JOHN V. TUNNEY, CALIF.
ROMAN L. HRUSKA, NEBR.
HIRAM L. FONG, HAWAII
HUGH SCOTT, PA.
STROM THURMOND, S.C.
MARLOW W. COOK, KY.
CHARLES MC C. MATHIAS, JR., MD.
EDWARD J. GURNEY, FLA.

PETER M. STOCKETT,
CHIEF COUNSEL AND STAFF DIRECTOR

SUBCOMMITTEE:
QUENTIN N. BURDICK, N. DAK., CHAIRMAN
PHILIP A. HART, MICH.
BIRCH BAYH, IND.
MARLOW W. COOK, KY.
CHARLES MC C. MATHIAS, JR., MD.
JAMES G. MEEKER, STAFF DIRECTOR

United States Senate
COMMITTEE ON THE JUDICIARY
SUBCOMMITTEE ON NATIONAL PENITENTIARIES
(PURSUANT TO SEC. 14, S. RES. 56, 93D CONGRESS)
WASHINGTON, D.C. 20510

November 27, 1974

Mr. Steve Psinakis
13 Aroyo Drive
Kentfield, California

Dear Mr. Psinakis:

This will acknowledge receipt of your telegram concerning two individuals on a hunger strike. I have checked with Director Norman A. Carlson of the U. S. Bureau of Prisons, and while there are a number of prisoners in the federal system with the surname Lopez, there are none with the surname Osmena, and as far as he can determine there are no prisoners who are currently on a hunger strike in excess of seven days.

I have been assured that Bureau of Prison policies provide that every reasonable step be taken to preserve the lives of prisoners. If you can send further identifying information, I will again attempt to look into this matter.

With kind regards, I am

Sincerely,

Quentin N. Burdick

QNB/jmj

Like every leading opponent of the Marcos dictatorship, Alex Esclamado has suffered the consequences of Marcos' brutal retaliation. In addition to the usual forms of harassment and intimidation, Alex became a victim of "economic strangulation." Having failed to entice Esclamado with "attractive offers" to change his newspaper's editorial policy from anti-Marcos to pro-Marcos, Marcos attempted to have the paper closed down by coercing its advertisers to cancel their contracts with the *Philippine News.*

Alex managed to obtain considerable "hard evidence" proving the illegal Marcos activities, some of which were committed within the United States. The evidence was submitted to the appropriate U.S. authorities as well as to Congressional leaders and to the press. The well-documented case attracted considerable attention in the news and from several Congressional leaders who demanded a formal investigation by the Department of Justice. The Jack Anderson column of October, 1975, was devoted to the *Philippine News* case. It read:

San Francisco Chronicle

Wed., Oct. 1, 1975

Merry-Go-Round

The Marcos Affair

Jack Anderson

IN WASHINGTON, both Congress and the Justice Department are investigating our charges of last July that Philippine President Ferdinand Marcos offered a witness a $50,000 bribe not to testify on Capitol Hill about corruption and tyranny in the Philippines.

In Manila, Marcos reacted in a different way. He brougnt criminal charges against the witness, former press censor Primitivo Mijares, and is now using the criminal complaint as a ruse to seek his extradition.

★ ★ ★

MARCOS has also retaliated against a San Francisco newspaper, the weekly Philippine News, which played up our bribe story. He brought pressure through his Secretary of Tourism, Jose Aspiras, on U.S. travel agencies to withdraw their ads from the paper.

The Marcos regime has the power, of course, to deny Philippine visas, commercial papers and other documents to clients of the travel agencies. As a result, four travel agencies have closed their accounts with the Philippine News.

A spokesman for the Philippine Embassy in Washington told us that the embassy has no knowledge of any advertising boycott against the Philippine News.

On the contrary, we have obtained the actual letter that was sent to two of the travel agencies. It confirms the extortion in the baldest terms. We have also established that the pressure came directly from Marcos' personal aide, Dr. Guillermo De Vega. The letter was written by Hotel Filipinas president Jose Cobarrubias.

In a cable to the Philippine Embassy, Cobarrubias has taken full responsibility for the extortion letter.

We have an affidavit that we have verified, however, that the real pressure came from Marcos' Malacanang palace. His personal aide in Manila and Philippine consul Trinidad Alconcel in San Francisco put the heat on the travel agencies, according to our sworn evidence.

★ ★ ★

THE TWO AGENCIES, Phil-Am and Gem, regularly send officials to Manila. Both Phil-Am's Emile Heredia and Gem's Joseph Libunao encountered pressure in Manila. Libunao sent a cryptic cable to his San Francisco office declaring: "Requested by Aspiras to cooperate with Malacanang to help with the scandal . . . Will explain details."

Spokesmen for the travel firms were shocked that we had obtained the extortion letter. They confirmed that they had canceled their ads but refused to comment on their reasons. Explained Heredia: "I have a lot of employees. I do not want to get involved."

Publisher Alex Esclamado told us he had broken with Marcos over his totalitarian tactics but "never thought he'd get away with reaching into the U.S. to bully our advertisers."

The Congressional leaders requesting a formal investigation by the U.S. Department of Justice included, among others, Senator Alan Cranston of California, Congressman Donald Fraser of Minnesota, and Congressman Philip Burton of San Francisco. Senator Cranston wrote directly to the then U.S. Attorney General, Edward H. Levi, calling the incident "a serious infringement upon the rights of American citizens," which, in Cranston's opinion, "constitute extortion in violation of federal criminal law." The actual Cranston letter to Levi requesting an investigation is shown below:

ALAN CRANSTON
CALIFORNIA

United States Senate
WASHINGTON, D.C. 20510

October 2, 1975

The Honorable Edward H. Levi
Attorney General
Department of Justice
Constitution Ave. between 9th & 10th
Washington, D.C. 20530

Dear Mr. Attorney General:

In his column of October 1 in the Washington Post, Jack Anderson has described pressures brought against certain travel agencies who do business in the Philippines and who also advertise in an American weekly newspaper to force these agencies to withdraw their business from the newspaper in retaliation for editorial criticism of the government of Philippine President Ferdinand Marcos.

This incident, as described, is a serious infringement upon the rights of American citizens and Philippine resident aliens who lawfully enjoy the protections of our Constitution and Bill of Rights. The pressures brought against the advertisers of the Philippine News of San Francisco in my opinion constitute extortion in violation of federal criminal law.

I request that the Department of Justice investigate this incident to determine whether federal laws have been violated by any persons in the incident described by Mr. Anderson. In particular, I request the Department to determine whether the Extortion and Threats provisions of the Federal Criminal Code, 18 U.S.C. 875 (Interstate Communications), 18 U.S.C. 876 (Mailing threatening communications) and 18 U.S.C. 877 (Mailing threatening communications from a foreign country), may have been violated.

The fact that the Philippine News serves an audience of newly-arrived Philippine nationals does not strip the Philippine News, its readers or its advertisers of protections guaranteed them by the United States Constitution and our laws. If foreign agents can so easily stifle political criticism among newly-arrived immigrants, much information and editorial criticism on issues of interest to all Americans will be cut off. People who have sought a new life here should be free to live unmolested by their former government. I hope that the Department of Justice will take the lead in vindicating the rights of a free press and free speech.

I look forward to hearing from you soon.

Sincerely,

Alan Cranston

An investigation was, in fact, ordered and conducted by the FBI. The two special agents of the San Francisco FBI Bureau assigned to head the investigation were the same two agents assigned several months earlier to investigate the Mijares case: Agents Mike Henry and Daniels McDaniel. Despite the strong evidence in both cases, the FBI "failed to produce sufficient evidence to prosecute either case." Alex Esclamado and I followed the developments during the two investigations and protested what we considered an obvious coverup by the "Kissinger-run State Department." Our protests, notwithstanding the support we generated in Congress, were futile. Both cases are now considered closed by the Justice Department.

CHAPTER 18

The First Signs Were Encouraging

Imelda left for Manila on December 20, the day after our meeting. Her encounters with Ninoy, Sonny, and me were not unduly exploited by the government-controlled media. The press did report Imelda's meetings in New York but avoided mentioning specifics or any of our names.

One of the Manila dailies, however, published a story under the banner headline "Rebels Assure First Lady–NO MORE BOMBINGS." The story reported that Mrs. Marcos "appealed to opposition leaders in the United States to help develop the country and people rather than destroy and kill innocent Filipinos." A second story appearing on January 2, 1981, quoted Imelda having "expressed great satisfaction that she was able to get the assurance of the Filipino opposition leaders in the United States for a 'moratorium' on terroristic activities after she had appealed to them to stop hurting innocent Filipinos and help instead in the development of the country."

On our part, Ninoy, Sonny, and I held to our agreement more faithfully. Our general response to the many inquiring reporters, was to acknowledge our meeting with Mrs. Marcos, but to give no comment.

The reaction of Filipinos both in the Philippines and in the United States was, as most of us expected, initially negative—with few exceptions.

"Ah! Imelda used her charm to get what she wanted from Ninoy, Sonny, and Steve," was the often-heard comment.

"Yes, Imelda got her moratorium. That's all she wanted and these fools believed her usual line," was another popular response.

Presy became furious. I don't remember ever seeing her so outraged. "How can these people believe Imelda could charm you and fool you? After all they have done to us and we never gave in? They almost killed you, but we never changed our course. How can they believe, after all that has happened, that you can still be fooled by that despicable woman?"

"Don't get excited," I said quietly, trying to calm her down. "It's not like you to lose your temper. I'm usually the one who does, and you are always more reasonable."

"Well, I am also human. I don't always show it, but I have the same feelings as everyone. All these people do is criticize. When Marcos tries to smear you and pin the bombings on you, these crazy people believe him and criticize you for engaging in terrorism. Now that Imelda says you gave her a moratorium, they believe that too and criticize you for stopping the bombings. What kind of fools are they, anyway? How would you be able to order bombs to explode in the Philippines and how would you be able to order anyone to stop the bombings?"

Presy's anger was uncontrollable. I really had never seen her that outraged before.

"I don't think you should get angry with people who don't know what is happening," I said. "They're entitled to believe what they want."

"No! It's not that. What makes me so mad is that so many of

my countrymen sit still and do nothing for their suffering people in the Philippines because they are too damn scared; they won't even *speak* out against the injustice, torture, and murder of innocent Filipinos.

"You can't blame people for being scared. You know what the Marcoses can do to them. You know what they have been doing." I tried to appease her—unsuccessfully.

"That's fine if they're scared and can't risk anything of their own. But when these same people have the nerve to criticize us after all we've gone through, I can't help but feel outraged. Do they know what it's like to wonder everyday whether my husband will come home alive? Do they know what it's like to feel the cold barrel of a gun on your temple?"

I was now seeing a side of Presy I had never seen before. Over the past five years, we had been threatened many times—sometimes through letters, sometimes through telephone calls at all hours of the day and night, sometimes by goons in passing cars pointing a gun at us. In every instance, Presy had reacted calmly and philosophically.

"We know what we're in for," she had said many times, "we're opposing ruthless criminals who have tortured and killed countless people. They can get rid of us quite easily. If that is God's will, it will happen; if not, it won't. We won't live in fear. Somebody has to stand up to these criminals; otherwise the world will be ruled by gangsters."

That had been Presy's typical reaction in every case when a threat was made on our lives. The only exception, which perhaps was the cause for her present outburst, was the "chilling" threat of October 15, 1979. Most of the previous threats were never reported to the authorities. We felt that anonymous calls, unsigned letters, or even the flashing of a pistol from a passing car were not threats worth reporting. We had no evidence to substantiate them. There were, however, two or three occasions where we obtained some evidence. Although the evidence would probably not stand up in court, it was nevertheless convincing. These two or three cases, we felt, should be reported to the local police, the FBI, and the Department of State. But even then our authorities were unable, or perhaps unwilling, to take any action.

There was the incident of February 3, 1976, when Presy's brother, Geny, was taken from his jail cell in Manila by Secretary Johnny Ponce Enrile. He called us in San Francisco at 3 a.m. to convey a threat on behalf of Marcos. When Presy picked up the receiver—still half asleep—and heard her brother, who was supposed to be in prison, she was shocked. She thought she was dreaming. She assumed Geny had been freed. But her dream soon turned into a nightmare. After saying a simple, "Hello, Presy," Geny asked to talk to me. Presy woke me up and handed me the receiver. "It's Geny," she said, still in shock. "He wants to talk to you. I don't know where they've got him but something is wrong. I can feel it."

I tried to shake myself awake before I picked up the receiver. Although nervous and stuttering, the voice on the other end of the line was unmistakably Geny's. He said that he was calling from his house where he had been brought on Secretary Enrile's instructions. Geny explained that Enrile had come to see him in jail "to convey the President's deep concern about the information they had received from their intelligence sources." He went on to say that Marcos had obtained evidence that I had "hired professional killers to murder members of the first family," and if that's the way I wanted to play the game, "the President wanted me to tell you that two can play this game as well as one." This was Marcos' way of communicating his threat through Presy's incarcerated brother.

Marcos had to convey the threat clearly enough for me to understand. At the same time, he had to word it in such a way that he would have some grounds for denial if I had managed to record the conversation. Enrile could not have instructed Geny to just say: "Look, Steve, Marcos and Enrile said they will kill you if you don't stop your exposés about their corruption and about their human rights violations." Such a message, if recorded, would not have left Marcos any way of denying the threat. On the other hand, since Marcos knew that I had not hired anyone to assassinate members of his family, the message of "two can play this game" was as clear a threat as could have been made over the telephone.

Presy and I still speculated, however, as to why Marcos had taken such a risk simply to transmit one more of his ineffective threats. We concluded that he had taken this risk because he must have felt we had ignored all of his previous threats, perhaps because we had not believed they were serious and that they had been ordered personally by him. "What better way to convince us that Marcos himself is behind the threat," Presy explained, "than to have his personal prisoner, my own brother, Geny, whose every move is completely under Marcos' control, communicate it to us."

We did report this incident to the U.S. authorities. Marcos, of course, denied the threat, but he could not deny that the telephone call had taken place because he feared we had taped it. In his official denial to the press, Marcos looked very foolish trying to explain how one of his prime "personal prisoners," Geny Lopez, could have made an overseas telephone call without Marcos' explicit instructions. The official denial, published by some newspapers, was branded by a State Department official as "the clearest admission of Marcos' guilt."

Another incident occurred in June of 1978 when a Marcos associate, an American from Fond-du-Lac, Wisconsin, named Norman Kirst, was taped while talking on the telephone to a certain Joe Naud of Chicago. Naud was the agent and close friend of the well-known American psychic, Olof Johnson, also an associate of Marcos. During this taped conversation, Kirst informed Naud that two Philippines "liquidator-generals" had arrived in San Francisco. These "liquidator-generals" were allegedly sent to contract with the Mafia to murder me and Kirst's former "partner," an American named Robert Curtis.

Norman Kirst, Robert Curtis, and Olof Johnson were friends and business associates. They were also friends and business associates of Marcos and had been his personal guests at Malacanang Palace several times. Olof Johnson, in particular, had become relatively close to the Marcos couple, who are known to be very superstitious and quite fond of psychics and psychic phenomena. Johnson had stayed at the palace as Marcos' guest for several days at a time on at least three different occasions.

It was Olof Johnson who introduced Norman Kirst to the Marcoses as an alleged "financial wizard" with vast connections in the international financial community. Both Kirst and Johnson later introduced Robert Curtis to Marcos as a "mining expert" specializing in the technology of gold and other precious metals. The three American "experts" were gradually taken into Marcos' confidence and later became "equal-share partners" with Marcos in his 11-man secret combine known as the "Leber" group. The Leber group, headed by Marcos himself and directed by his top intelligence officer, General Fabian Ver, had undertaken the bizarre project of locating and retrieving the legendary Japanese treasure–known as "Yamashita's treasure"–which General Yamashita had reportedly buried in the Philippines just before Japan surrendered to the Allies.

The project was fraught with illegality and deviousness. The treasure, believed to be mostly gold bars plundered by the Japanese from the Asian countries they occupied during World War II, was to be located with the help of secret maps that had been found in General Yamashita's headquarters after the Japanese surrendered. Olof Johnson was to help pinpoint the buried

The five key "partners" of the "treasure hunt" group in Marcos' office at the Presidential palace. Right to left: Marcos, Kirst, Johnson, Curtis, and General Ver. March 9, 1975.

treasure through the use of his psychic powers. The retrieved gold was to be melted, reprocessed and "stamped" so that it would appear as if it were gold mined in the Philippines. That's where Curtis' alleged expertise came in. The newly stamped "Philippine" gold was to be sold in England and Switzerland through some unscrupulous schemes contrived by Norman Kirst. Kirst's contacts with the international financial community were to have been tapped for this stage of the operation.

The treasure hunt project moved along quite smoothly for about a year. The evidence documenting the activities of the Leber group is extensive. It includes more than 100 hours of authenticated, taped conversations between several members of the 11-member combine, photographs of the participants with Marcos and Ver, as well as photographs of the participants on several excavation sites, progress reports on the operations, contractual agreements, and many other types of evidentiary documents.

According to Robert Curtis, while the project was progressing satisfactorily, "the extreme secrecy of the operation and the conduct of the Philippine security agents assigned to monitor the movements of the three Americans," led Curtis to believe that Marcos never intended to share the treasure with his "partners," especially with his three American partners.

"It gradually became clear to me that Marcos would never risk disclosure of his illegal and unscrupulous schemes. I realized that he would have all three of us eliminated when our services were no longer needed," Curtis said during one of my many interviews with him. Fearing for his life, Curtis broke off with Marcos, left the Philippines, and exposed the situation to the American press.

The bizarre Curtis revelations attracted the attention of both the U.S. press and the U.S. Congress and caused considerable damage to the already-deteriorating image of Marcos and his martial law regime. The Washington syndicated columnist, Jack

Ferdinand Marcos (in cap) entertaining his "partner" Curtis during a fishing trip on board the Presidential yacht. March 11, 1975.

Anderson, and the publisher of the *Las Vegas Sun*, Brian Greenspun, investigated the treasure hunt story and reported their findings in great detail over a period of several weeks. At that time, I had also undertaken a 3-month investigation and had prepared a 300-page report that was being serialized by the *Philippine News* and the *Philippine Times.*

While Robert Curtis had broken off with Marcos and was revealing his knowledge and participation in the secret and illegal treasure hunt operations, Norman Kirst had remained "loyal to Marcos" because he feared for his life. Kirst was understandably upset and concerned about the Curtis disclosures, since they not only implicated Marcos and General Ver, but also Kirst.

During the taped telephone conversation between Kirst and Naud, Kirst explained the dangers the Curtis revelations were creating for Marcos and for everyone else involved in the "top secret operation." Kirst informed Naud that two "liquidator-generals" had just arrived in San Francisco presumably to plot Curtis' and my assassination.

The taped phone conversations–a total of four, two on June 24 and two on June 25, 1978–all were discussions related to the treasure hunt project and to the murder contracts.

Discussing the reports that appeared in the U.S. press, Kirst tells Naud: "this is the hottest thing that's ever hit the country over there (the Philippines). And it's the most sensitive because it is a C-7 security classification. This will put you on the blacklist. Anybody who has anything to do with this. Olof [Johnson] does not seem to understand this."

Commenting on the on-going publicity of the treasure hunt, Kirst says: "It is not to be publicized under any condition . . . Even though the fire is raging, the more gasoline you pour into it, the higher it gets and the more damage it can do."

During the conversation, Naud had expressed his concern about Olof Johnson's life and had explained that, under the circumstances, the best way to assure Olof's safety was to reveal the truth about his involvement to the U.S. government and to the American press. Naud had arranged a press conference for Johnson and, during the same taped phone conversation, he told Kirst: "Olof is concerned about his safety, and the more publicity this gets, the less chance there is of anybody doing anything to him. Would you like to be on the news conference?"

"Oh, hell, no! Oh, God, no!" Kirst answered excitedly, "that's the last thing I'd want to do. I'd rather jump off the moon without a parachute."

Advising Naud that Johnson should lie during the planned news conference, Kirst says: "As long as [during the press conference] he [Olof] doesn't talk about his experiences over there [in the Philippines]. He should just state that this whole thing was Curtis' invention."

"Olof is not going to tell a lie for anything," countered Naud. "Olof is going to tell what he knows the truth is."

The information about the arrival in San Francisco of the "liquidator-generals" was discussed several times during the lengthy phone conversations. At one point, Kirst explained: "I was in San Francisco [last week] and my confidant formerly worked with the [Philippine] government, and they recognized these two liquidator-generals in San Francisco, but the liquidator-generals did not recognize my confidant. They are known liquidators and the parties who told me this became so alarmed that they moved [out of San Francisco]."

At another point Kirst tells Naud: "You see, for your information, and this is an absolute truth, I'm getting all this information from a very solid source. What they do is they work with the M [Mafia] in touchy situations away from their home base. The M here [in Chicago] will probably take care of something in another part of the United States. You know, they mix them up. The M from the San Francisco area, where two more generals who were reported by my source, who are liquidators, might be there [in Chicago] for something in the Midwest. That is, to hire someone in the 'Frisco area to come to the Midwest."

Kirst confirmed his concern for his own safety during the next exchange:

Naud: If what you feel is right, that there are people here maybe to do something, I think the only protection anybody here could have is to get enough publicity so that they would be afraid to do anything. Do you feel that your life is in danger, because you are also incriminated in those papers?

Kirst: I feel that it could be; yes.

Naud: That's why I am saying–hiding from it, I don't think it's to the benefit of anybody. I wouldn't want not to do anything about it and read that so-and-so was dead one morning.

All of the above statements attributed to Kirst and Naud are taken from the tape of their conversation that is still in my possession. I made a copy of this tape and personally brought it to the San Francisco FBI bureau. I reported the incident to FBI agents Bob Cratty and Ray Guertin who promised to investigate this matter by, firstly, "contacting and interviewing Norman Kirst." The response of FBI agents Cratty and Guertin to my frequent inquiries on their progress over a period of three years indicated that the FBI was not willing to investigate a case that might prove embarrassing to Marcos.

Initially, I was told that when the FBI in Fond-du-Lac, Wisconsin, attempted to contact Kirst, they found his house boarded up. Kirst's neighbors allegedly informed the FBI that the Kirst family had gone overseas for an extended vacation. Later, I was told that Kirst had reportedly returned to the United States but could not be located by the FBI. At another point, Cratty told me that Kirst had not been interviewed but had sent the FBI a written statement. According to Cratty, Kirst's statement alleged that all those stories about Marcos' secret group to retrieve the buried Japanese treasure were concoctions of Robert Curtis. When I asked Cratty whether he had confronted Kirst with all the evidence and authenticated documents in Kirst's own handwriting, Cratty told me they hadn't yet been able to talk to Kirst.

That's how this particular FBI "investigation" ended. When I had first met the FBI agents and handed them the tape, I had the impression they did not welcome an investigation of alleged illegal activities of Marcos and his agents. In fact, at one point, Cratty tried to intimidate me and perhaps discourage me from pursuing the case, implying I may have violated some U.S. laws by taping the Kirst conversation without Kirst's knowledge and consent. I countered by expressing my disbelief that they seemed more concerned with the possible violation of taping the conversation than with its contents, which revealed that foreign killers had allegedly arrived in the United States to murder American citizens. All this happened when Henry Kissinger was still the Secretary of State.

A friend of mine once cautioned: "You are exposing some pretty powerful people. Aren't you afraid that the FBI or Kissinger, for instance, might sue you for libel for insinuating that they participated in a cover up—or even do something worse?"

"No at all," I responded, "I am only stating the facts as I know them. In my opinion, the facts not only insinuate, but confirm, that the FBI and/or Kissinger helped cover up Marcos' illegal activities. Nobody can sue me for stating the facts, and nobody can sue me for my own opinion that these facts signal a cover up. I am not concerned about being sued. In fact, as I have often stated, I would welcome a suit from Marcos or anyone else, including Kissinger. Now, as for the FBI, that's a different matter. They are certainly in a position to cause me harm. We'll have to wait and see."

Presy had taken all the harrassment and threats in stride. It was I who felt outraged at times with the inability—or unwillingness—of our authorities to take any action against Marcos and his agents operating in the United States. However, an incident occurred on October 15, 1979, and it affected Presy more than any other. On that date, on the way to our restaurant in downtown San Francisco at about 5:20 in the morning—it was still dark—a car pulled up alongside mine and its passenger suddenly took out a gun and placed the cold barrel right on my temple. "You son of a bitch" a middle-aged man said to me, "you don't seem to believe we mean business; this is your last warning; if you don't wise up, next time we'll let you have it."

I froze. I didn't move or say a word. After a few seconds' pause, the car moved straight in front of me and disappeared in the darkness. I was surprised I had the presence of mind to note the make of the car and its license number. It was a 1978 or 1979 Cadillac Seville with California license number 433 DGH.

I had decided to keep this incident from Presy, but I did mention it to Alex Esclamado. Understandably, he became very upset and insisted I report the incident to the FBI. "You never know," Alex had said, "Although in all probability the car did not belong to the goon who pulled the gun, it's possible it was stolen and the thief may be caught. That would really be a break. You have to report it, if for no other reason than to get it on record."

I thought Alex had a valid point, so, later that same day, I filed a report with the San Francisco FBI Director, William Newmann. To this date, I have not had the courtesy of a response from the FBI.

Presy learned about the incident when Alex and I decided to file my report. She had managed, as usual, to control her emotions, but she remained depressed for several days. I can't explain why, but this particular threat, more than any others in the past, had convinced Presy of how easy it really is to have someone murdered. When I had later asked her why this threat affected her much more than any others, Presy broke down in tears.

"I am not sure," she had said sobbing, "maybe it's because I feel more shame than fear. Here you are, a non-Filipino, and you are risking more to help my people than most of my countrymen."

We had, of course, discussed our involvement in the Philippines many times, and we had always agreed that "a struggle for truth, justice, and freedom had no national or geographic boundaries." Our deep involvement in the Philippine situation was more a case of fate and circumstance than a choice. The truth is—and we always admitted this to ourselves—that without Geny's 1974 hunger strike, we probably would not have been drawn into the struggle for the liberation of the Filipino people.

When Presy finally calmed down from her reaction to my meeting with Imelda, she apologized. "I am sorry," she said as tears still trickled down her cheeks. "I guess things had piled up. Just because I can usually control my emotions doesn't mean I don't feel anxiety and constant fear for you and the children. I can understand, however, why most people don't get involved. I don't mean they don't care. There are so many other factors to consider. What really angers me are the people who always assume the worst and do nothing but criticize."

I embraced her and knew she felt my deep love and admiration. "Don't let these few people affect you so. They are the exceptions," I said, comforting her.

While Presy had been outraged with the initial response to our meetings with Imelda, the A6LM guerrillas in Manila became more furious than Presy when they read the headline about our alleged promise of "No More Bombings." They assumed it was just a lie from the Marcos-controlled press. Their immediate reaction was "we'll see." Ninoy and I were afraid of this and had warned Imelda to be careful with her press statements until we had the chance to explain to the opposition and, somehow, to the rebel groups what really transpired in New York.

Within hours after the Manila headline of "no more bombings," the guerrillas of the A6LM issued a threatening letter addressed to the Prime Minister of Japan who was scheduled to arrive in Manila for a state visit in a few days. The letter read in part:

> We appeal to you to cancel your scheduled visit as a recognition that our struggle for the liberation of our country is honorable and justified.
>
> Your government, your country's multinationals, especially Marubeni, and your compatriot tourists, are some of the biggest sources of economic support to the illegitimate Marcos regime.
>
> Should you go to Manila, it is quite possible that the extreme security measures which the Marcos regime will take . . . may succeed in guaranteeing your own personal safety . . . but your disregard of our appeal will place in jeopardy the safety of every Japanese multinational and every Japanese tourist who may stay in our country after you have gone.

The news media in Japan reported the A6LM threat and a friend of Ninoy's in Tokyo called to tell him the news. I, too, became anxious. "Imelda should have been more careful with her press," I said.

"Never mind that now," Ninoy said. "Let's try to avert a catastrophe. We must plead with the A6LM guerrillas to hold their horses for a few days until we can explain the situation. We must give peace a chance. Let's start passing the word around but *fast.* Let's also send a secret emissary to Manila to contact some of the A6LM people."

"I am with you chief," I said jokingly. We talked a little more and agreed on some plans.

"Also you better call Zumel," Ninoy said, "and tell him to explain the situation to Imelda."

"Check," I said and hung up.

After my meeting with Imelda, Ninoy had told me that Colonel Zumel was, in fact, one of the top intelligence officers and a very sharp fellow. I was very pleased. Whatever Imelda could not grasp from our conversation, I thought, would not escape a sharp intelligence officer. Ironically, Zumel's brother is one of the top communist NPA leaders fighting the regime in the countryside.

It was now 7:30 p.m., San Francisco time, Christmas day. I picked up the receiver and dialed 0.

"Merry Christmas, sir," the operator greeted me.

"Merry Christmas to you," I said. "I'd like to place a person-to-person overseas call to Manila to Colonel Carlos Zumel. You can try either 583-369 or 406-555."

"I hope we can get through, sir," the operator said as she was trying the number, "The traffic has been heavy all day."

The phone rang on the first try, and a man answered. When the operator asked for Colonel Zumel, the man asked us to hold for a minute. After a pause, a man's voice greeted us with a hello.

"Is this Colonel Carlos Zumel?" the operator inquired.

"Yes."

"Thank you. Go ahead, sir," the operator said as she left the line.

"Hello, Colonel Zumel. Good afternoon," I said. It was the afternoon of December 26 in Manila. "This is Steve Psinakis. How are you?"

"Yes, sir, fine."

"First of all, Merry Christmas to you."

"Merry Christmas to you, too, sir."

"Thank you. I wanted to call you immediately to convey a very important message to Mrs. Marcos."

"Yes." Zumel responded.

"We just had a call from Japan. We were told the TV and newspapers there are reporting an alleged threatening call or threatening letter they have received from the April 6th Liberation Movement."

"Yes, sir."

"A warning to the Prime Minister of Japan not to go there because there would be retaliation and so forth. I just talked to Senator Aquino. We're both quite concerned and immediately wanted to call and advise Mrs. Marcos." I explained we were trying to obtain more information and determine whether it was a hoax or an act of the A6LM operatives. He confimed that he had learned the news earlier that morning.

"Have you had a chance to discuss this matter with Mrs. Marcos?" I asked.

"No, sir. In fact, it's only today that this item has come up in the papers and my first impulse was to find out if it was an accurate report."

I explained that our agreement with Imelda in New York stood and that we didn't want to "upset the apple cart" through a misunderstanding. I told him we'd do what we could to prevent any "incidents" during Suzuki's visit and we agreed to keep each other informed of any developments. Zumel was very courteous and seemed pleased with my call. He told me he would inform Imelda immediately and stay in touch. We wished each other happy holidays and hung up.

This was the first time I had had a real conversation with Zumel. Ninoy was right. Zumel sounded pretty sharp.

We spent the next few days trying to communicate with people in Manila. We found it very difficult to touch base. We contacted only a few groups, but the word was somehow being passed around. "Hold your horses," was the message. "There is a good reason for a brief ceasefire. Can't explain details. Have faith and give us the benefit of the doubt until we find a way to explain."

The word came back. Most of the guerrillas, like the general public, were unhappy about our meetings with Imelda and believed we had been taken. However, all of the rebel leaders who sent word to the States were reasonable and were reluctantly willing to wait for details.

In the meantime, Ninoy had talked several times with Deputy Defense Minister Mike Barbero. Ninoy was negotiating with Barbero to dispatch Charlie Avila to the Philippines as an emissary to the various rebel groups. Ninoy explained that "communications were very difficult and that the secret emissary's contacts with the rebels were rather limited. Charlie's contacts were much more widespread."

But there was a problem with Charlie. First of all, he was too well known, and, secondly, he was included in one of Marcos' lists of "terrorists" and subject to arrest. Ninoy was asking Marcos, through Barbero, to guarantee Charlie's safety and, at the same time, to allow him freedom of movement without surveillance. Marcos was to guarantee Charlie's safety by informing Cardinal Sin and the U.S. Embassy. The cost of Charlie's overseas ticket and local traveling expenses were to be paid by the Philippine government. "What I am asking is difficult," Ninoy told me. "How can Marcos guarantee Charlie's safety and yet agree to let him loose without security escort? Anyway, we'll see. Maybe they'll come up with some better solution."

On Saturday, January 3, Presy, Charlie, and I, together with two mutual friends, Tommy and Joanne, were driving back from Lake Tahoe where we had gone five days earlier to spend the New Year's holiday. On the way back to San Francisco late in the afternoon, we ran into a terrible storm. At about 7 p.m., we stopped at a roadside restaurant for something to eat, and I gave Ninoy a call. I found him very excited. "Where are you?" he asked. "I've been trying to reach you everywhere."

"We're on the way to San Francisco."

"Okay, okay. Barbero called, and Marcos agreed to our conditions for Charlie. I want him on the first plane to Manila—tonight if possible."

"That's good news," I said, optimistically. "It looks like they understand what's happening and are really concerned. They're sure being cooperative."

"Yes, precisely," Ninoy responded. "As long as they seem to want to cooperate for a peaceful solution, I want to prove our sincerity to them. We have to try to hold to the ceasefire. If there's going to be war again, let them fire the first shot, *not* the guerrillas."

"That's right," I agreed. "Charlie is the right man. He has many contacts and knows his way around. He should be able to meet with many groups and give them your advice."

"Can he leave tonight?" Ninoy pressed.

"No way," I said. "We're at least two hours from San Francisco. The night flight for Manila leaves at 9 or 10 p.m. We can't make it. Besides there is lots to do before he leaves. Maybe tomorrow night."

"What do you mean *maybe,* Greek? He *has* to be on that plane tomorrow. Tomorrow is the fourth; he'll get there the sixth. That's cutting it close. Suzuki is arriving in Manila on the eighth. If the rebels have something planned for his arrival and Charlie doesn't reach them on time, there goes our peaceful chance, and, come to think of it, there goes Charlie too," Ninoy said anxiously.

"Okay, chief," I answered, "we'll do our best. I'll have Charlie call you tomorrow to brief you and get your instructions."

When I told the news to Charlie, Presy and the two friends who were riding to San Francisco with us, they were jubilant. "I guess you did get through to Imelda," Charlie said. "That's great news. I didn't expect Marcos to accept Ninoy's conditions. They're sort of contradictory. How can he guarantee my safety without providing military security? He's taking a hell of a chance. If something happens to me, Marcos is in hot water."

"If that happens," Tommy smilingly told Charlie, "it means you won't be around to see what happens to Marcos." We all laughed, but at the same time we were aware of the danger.

There was a lot to do. As it turned out, Charlie didn't make it the next day. We booked him on the January 5th PAL flight to Manila.

Ninoy informed Minister Barbero of Charlie's arrival plans, and Barbero promised personally to meet him at the Manila airport.

"We better book you in first class, buddy," I told Charlie. "You'll need some rest on the way. You haven't had much sleep in the last 48 hours. Anyway, Marcos is paying for your ticket. You might as well go first class, man."

"No," said Charlie, "that's not my style. What are you trying to do? Ruin my reputation? Book me on economy." So that's what I did.

Monday night we took Charlie to the airport and, with some apprehensions, we walked him to the gate and wished him good luck as he stepped onto the PAL plane.

Lupita Concio, Ninoy's sister, had come with us to the airport and on the way back, we stopped at her place for coffee. Soon after we arrived at Lupita's, the phone rang. We heard Lupita yell, "what happened? Did the plane break down?"

It was Charlie on the phone. Barbero had called Ninoy right around boarding time and informed him that, during a second meeting of the Security Council in Manila, it was decided the risks for Marcos were too great.

"Avila is too well known," Barbero had told Ninoy. "Somebody could kill him, maybe some communist, just to humiliate the President. The risk is too high for the President to personally guarantee his safety. We'll have to find some other solution. The President is ready to go all the way to help. Let's try to think of a more practical solution."

"Okay, Mike," Ninoy had answered. "The point is reasonable. I'll get back to you later. Let me go now. I'll have to try to catch Charlie at the airport. It's boarding time now."

Ninoy had paged me at the airport, but I had left. He asked frantically for the PAL Manager, Jimmy Agcaoili. He caught him just in time. The plane had closed its doors and was about to leave the gate when Agcaoili called the pilot on the radio. They opened the gate and asked Charlie to step out.

We were all disappointed but also relieved. The more we thought about it, the more we appreciated the risks. If Charlie were hurt, it was not only Marcos who'd be in trouble. The chance for peace would be gone and so would Charlie.

We talked things over with Ninoy and neither of us could come up with any equitable solutions. The previous week, during Ninoy's initial negotiation for contacts between our group in the United States and the rebel leaders in the Philippines, Barbero had offered to send anyone Ninoy wanted to the United States, "except those under detention—or those on the top of the wanted list."

Ninoy had countered to Barbero: "We can't talk to second-line operatives, and we can't ask for top leaders other than those you already know. Naturally, those you know are either in jail or on the top of the wanted list. Mike you don't expect us to give you names and ask for leaders from the underground who are not known to you yet."

Barbero had understood Ninoy's reasoning and had agreed. But now, in view of the new impasse with Charlie, I thought we might resort to Ninoy's original approach.

"Ninoy, suppose I call Zumel and ask them to reconsider sending us the known rebel leaders even though they are in jail or on the wanted list. Anyway, you proved your sincerity by putting Charlie on the plane to Manila."

"Well, you can try, but I don't see how they can agree. It's a hell of a request."

"Let me try anyway. We have nothing to lose, and we have no other ideas for now. Let's see what happens. If they won't agree —and I also admit it's hard—they may propose something else. One thing is certain," I said, "there is no question that their attitude so far has been cooperative. You can see they're trying hard to accommodate us. Whatever objections they have raised so far have been reasonable."

"That's right," said Ninoy, "let's give it a try."

The next day, December 6, I called Zumel, but he was in a meeting with Imelda. I left my name. At 4:45 a.m. the next morning, December 7, my phone rang and woke me up. We exchanged greetings, and after apologizing for calling at that hour, Zumel said:

"It must be something urgent."

"That is correct, and I'm very glad you called, Colonel. The time doesn't matter; I told them to have you call me whenever you got back."

"Eh, yes, the two notes were on my table when I returned and so I called you right away."

"I appreciate your call. Happy New Year, Colonel."

"Same to you, sir. How was your holiday?"

"Well, we were up in the mountains to go skiing with the children, but, unfortunately, we had no snow at all." I laughed and so did Zumel.

We had a long conversation, and Zumel was extremely courteous. I told him that we had sent a secret emissary to Manila to contact some of the rebel leaders and asked them to please refrain from any planned action during the Suzuki visit. The emissary had also informed the rebels he had contacted that Mrs. Marcos had promised real and speedy reforms and that Senator

Aquino was asking them to delay any further action until they had the chance to determine whether Mr. Marcos was serious about moving toward normalization. The emissary had explained Aquino's plea to give the peaceful process a chance.

I also told Zumel that the emissary had returned the previous day and reported on his mission. He told us that the rebels were generally agreeable, but had said, "we want to see some sincere indications which are meaningful to us."

Then I explained what happened with Charlie. Zumel, of course, had already heard. I expressed our agreement with their apprehension about Charlie's visit, but I also stressed the urgency for some face-to-face discussions between Ninoy and as many of the leaders in Manila as possible. I told Zumel that since we could not disclose names of rebel leaders unknown to them, we were necessarily limited to those leaders familiar to the regime and consequently either under orders for arrest or already arrested. I asked him to consider sending "Jerry Esguerra and the son and granddaughter of Senator Tanada–Renato Tanada and Karen Tanada. These three people are, as you well know, wanted and in hiding; of course, they're underground," I said. "The fourth person we'd like to talk to would be Manny Cruz who is under arrest–and he is a man belonging to a different group than the three previous people. And the fifth person, and last one, we'd like to talk to–who is *not* an activist and *not* arrested or in hiding–is Father Antonio Olaguer." I went on to explain that Father Olaguer does not represent any activists, because, as far as we know, he is not involved, but he is the brother of Eddie Olaguer and could be trusted to communicate Ninoy's message to his brother.

I told him we realized the difficulty of our request but that Senator Aquino proved his sincerity by being ready to send Charlie to Manila. The impasse with Charlie came from their side. If we simply wanted to free those four people and bring them to the States, we would not have volunteered to send Charlie to Manila. I then explained that even if they assumed the worst, that we were insincere and just wanted to get these four people out—Father Olaguer was no problem—even then, the government had nothing to lose. "At the worst, if we deceive you, and we just keep them out here, you'd have gotten rid of four activists who are nothing but trouble to you anyway."

Zumel's few remarks during my presentation gave me the impression that he knew our proposal would be difficult to accept. I asked for his personal reaction to my suggestion.

"Well . . . hmmm, actually . . . I, . . . I . . . I will not be in the decision process, but I'll make sure that this is conveyed right away so that a decision can be made and we can communicate right back with you, Mr. Psinakis."

Zumel ended very politely. "We certainly appreciate what you're doing, what you have committed to do to help out in solving this problem, so that all our efforts and the understanding that you have had with the First Lady would be carried out, and, as I said, I am very sorry to get you up at this time, but I was very sure it would be something very urgent. I took the liberty of getting in touch with you even at this time."

I also responded to the Colonel with courtesy. "I am glad that you did," I said. "I know we seem to be on opposite sides, I suppose, but I think, deep down, all of us are on the same side: the side of the Filipino people and of peace. There must be a way to find out that sincerity in a situation like this is the key to success, and we must first give sincerity a chance before we give peace a chance."

Zumel promised that either he or Imelda would get back to me as soon as our proposal was discussed and a decision was reached. We parted warmly as he told me that he would present the case to Imelda as convincingly as I would have wanted him to.

Both of my lengthy phone conversations with Zumel left me with the impression that, firstly, he was a very intelligent man and an experienced negotiator, and, secondly, as far as he personally was concerned, he was speaking with sincerity and had made a realistic appraisal of the situation.

I briefed Ninoy on my call with Zumel, and we both agreed that the chances of Marcos accepting our proposal were indeed small, but all we could do was wait and see.

The following day, January 8, Zumel called at about 5:30 p.m. As expected, he confirmed the difficulties of our proposal. He explained that although he saw no problem at all with Father Olaguer, "Mr. Manny Cruz is inside [jail] right now. The three others are right now, I understand, in hiding; they are being sought by the authorities . . . it is because these three are subject to an arrest order and if they are allowed to leave through the normal departure points, there would be some legal questions . . . the problem is mostly the legal implications of the case."

I could see the point, but I also felt there was a more covert reason he wouldn't discuss. I told him it would be to everyone's interest to be open because only then could we define the problem. I said, "usually 90 percent of the solution of a problem is knowing that there is a problem and understanding what the problem is."

I thought Marcos might be concerned that these four members of the opposition would leave the Philippines, never to return. I explained these people *didn't* want to leave the battlefield even if we asked them to. All we wanted was to *talk* with them. But, I told Zumel that if Marcos was worried about their return, "we'd be willing to offer an exchange of sorts. We want to be sincere. I'd be willing myself to just come there and be in your hands until they come back," I said. "The point here is only to be able to communicate freely."

We talked for more than thirty minutes. Zumel asked us to

reconsider sending someone less controversial than Charlie, someone whose safety could be guaranteed by Marcos personally, and yet who would also be allowed freedom of movement. If we insisted on Charlie, he asked that we agree on some arrangement for government security to prevent any "mishap" that might be catastrophic.

I promised to convey his message to Ninoy and Charlie and explore alternative solutions. I then asked him to please reconsider our proposal of sending the five people or to think of some way to assure Charlie's protection without preventing him from holding confidential meetings with some of his contacts.

At one point I indicated that the "legal technicality" could be solved by Marcos if he really wanted to. "I would think, Colonel," I said, "that, considering the stakes for the whole country, such legal technicalities could be solved if Mr. Marcos had his mind set on it."

The long conversation ended very cordially, and I had the clear impression that Zumel, at least, was trying to find an acceptable middle ground. Five days passed without any word, and it became obvious that Manila was having as much difficulty coming up with a solution as we were here in the States.

In the meantime, we received word from one rebel group that Teodoro "Doroy" Valencia, a political columnist in one of Marcos' newspapers in Manila, had written a "provocative" article. Doroy Valencia is viewed as the unofficial spokesman and apologist for Marcos. Whatever he writes in his daily column is assumed to reflect Marcos' views. He is an obnoxious individual and a cowardly "commentator" who enjoys attacking, humiliating, and ridiculing anyone who, in his opinion, may be critical of Imelda, Marcos, or the martial law regime–I say cowardly because he knows his vicious and hysterical attacks cannot be answered in the mass media, all of which are completely controlled by the regime.

While I had earlier agreed with some of Imelda's nasty characterizations of Tibo Mijares, I felt Doroy Valencia, who ironically assumed most of Mijares' duties as Marcos' top propagandist, was much worse than Mijares in every respect. On January 5th, Doroy wrote a column belittling the "terrorists" in the United States, claiming that they "have suddenly quieted down" because "they have lost their support." He went on to say that "all along they [the U.S. rebels] have been bragging that they are actively collecting money to bomb the Philippines or arm rebels in the Philippines. They have stopped bragging."

The communication from the rebel group in Manila was very disturbing.

"How can we hold to a moratorium when Marcos, through Valencia, is provoking us and challenging us to prove that we have *not* quieted down because we lost our support, but because *you* people asked us to give him a chance to prove his sincerity. Is this the kind of sincerity we are supposed to see? We'll have to blow up that son of a bitch and his newspaper to teach him a lesson."

The rebel group was furious. "We cannot let emotion and someone like Doroy ruin our chance for peace," Ninoy told me. "We'll have to cool down that rebel group. Meanwhile, you should mention this to Zumel. Maybe Imelda can have someone talk to Doroy."

The next day I placed a call to Zumel. He was out. At 7:40 p.m. the following day, January 15, Zumel called me back. He apologized for his five-day silence and told me that he had been in bed with the flu. However, I later surmised from his comments that his silence resulted from the inability to reach an acceptable solution to our proposal. He explained that our proposal to let Manny Cruz and the three other guerrillas leave the Philippines presented difficult problems that could not be resolved at this time.

"We would rather have the first option," Zumel said. "Maybe you could send somebody who is not as controversial as Charlie Avila, somebody maybe like Captain Tony Daza, but if you feel the presence of the security men here would hamper his movements in order to perform the mission which he's coming here to perform, well, we can do away with the security."

I pretended I didn't hear Zumel mention the name of Captain Tony Daza. I didn't think he was the right person for this particular assignment, but also I didn't want to discuss the reasons why. Captain Daza is the brother of former Congressman Raul Daza. Marcos has implicated Captain Daza in the bombings, and he is included on the list of some "30 terrorists" in the United States who are under arrest orders.

I was pleased with Zumel's confirmation that they were now willing to guarantee the safety of an emissary without providing security. Our long conversation was again cordial, and Zumel agreed that Charlie Avila could now go to the Philippines under our terms and that Father Olaguer would be sent to the United States (at the Philippine government's expense) to confer with Ninoy and others.

Zumel said he would have to get the final okay "right away" and get back to me "right away." He explained that "they [the Security Council] are in conference right now. If I cannot get it right away, I would not like to get you up again at a very ungodly hour. So, I'll call you early tomorrow morning, your time. How is that?" he asked.

"That would be fine, Colonel,"

"Fine, then. I'll get back to you soon."

"Okay. Now, I have two more items to mention to you, please," I said.

Colonel Zumel asked me to continue.

"Number one," I said, "we were very, very distressed yesterday. We have a report here that this senile old man, Doroy

Valencia, wrote a column on January 5th, and I'd like you to refer to that column. I would greatly appreciate it if Mrs. Marcos would talk to that idiot and tell him to stop making statements that are inflammatory and that are daring our side to prove that we can blow things up." I went on to explain the report we had received from one of the rebel groups and the dangers such provocative articles presented. He agreed with the seriousness of the situation and laughed heartily when I referred to Valencia as a "senile old idiot."

"I don't read his columns. I don't subscribe to that paper," Zumel said and started to laugh again. "Oh boy! I really have not read that column, but I can understand very well the reaction of your people in the field."

"Well, of course," I responded. "Here we are struggling to do something useful and save lives and help the country, and you have an idiot like that who is doing nothing but inflaming the situation and daring people to act. As you know," I continued, "many people assume that this character reflects the views of Mr. and Mrs. Marcos."

Toward the end of the conversation, Zumel confirmed that the next day (January 17th, Manila time) Marcos was expected to announce the lifting of martial law as "the First Lady had promised you in New York." He spoke of "the President's and the First Lady's sincerity," and confirmed that the lifting of martial law was only the first step toward full normalization. I expressed my hope that during the announcement of the lifting of martial law, Mr. Marcos would also announce some steps indicative of his sincerity toward the revolutionaries.

We ended our conversation on a high note, feeling that we had found a mutually acceptable solution to the main problem of communicating directly with the guerrillas. I was very pleased and called Ninoy to report the good news. He was surprised, but very satisfied, that his conditions for Charlie's trip had been accepted. Charlie was also delighted.

"I am very pleased," Ninoy told me on the phone after I finished reporting on my conversation with Zumel. "The signs so far are indeed encouraging."

I also told Ninoy about the conversation on Doroy Valencia, and he had a good laugh. "Let's watch his columns the next few days and see," Ninoy said.

We were happy to note that after my call to Zumel, Doroy's hysterical attacks on the guerrillas, Ninoy, and the "rebels" in the United States had stopped. "It looks like Imelda got to Doroy," I told Ninoy. "Imagine how that senile old idiot must feel to be censored by his favorite rebels in the States," I said, as we both laughed.

With the announcement of the lifting of martial law on January 17th, Marcos also announced the release of 341 prisoners. I wondered whether the list of prisoners included any of the real guerrillas from the revolutionary groups. It did—only a few—but it did. 'There's another encouraging sign,' I thought.

CHAPTER 19

The Hardliners Prevailed

The lifting of martial law was announced by Marcos on January 17, 1981, with a great deal of pomp and fanfare. The general public received the news skeptically. All of the opposition groups in the Philippines and in the United States condemned the decision as "a cosmetic gesture" and "a cruel deception."

The commentary in the U.S. media was generally critical. All the news reports noted that, despite the lifting of martial law, Marcos had retained almost all of his former dictatorial powers. Some American commentators, however, felt that, although the lifting of martial law was a "small step," it was nevertheless "a step in the right direction." Stephen Cohen's article published in the *Washington Post* is representative of most. Cohen wrote: "Lifting martial law was considered by many observers to be more public relations than substance, designed to impress the new Reagan administration—as well as the Pope." (The Pope's visit was forthcoming at that time.)

I smiled as I read the comments of the American correspondents who, almost unanimously, had logically concluded that

Marcos lifted martial law to "impress the Reagan administration."

'If they only knew,' I thought to myself, 'that Reagan had told Imelda *not* to lift martial law and if they also knew about our December discussions with Imelda, their reports would have been different.' Presy and I discussed this matter at length.

"It is not important what the foreign correspondents assume is the reason behind Marcos' lifting of martial law," I told Presy the day after Marcos made the announcement. "What *is* very important is that it is a meaningful step, as Imelda promised, rather than another 'cosmetic change' or 'cruel deception.' As a matter of fact, if the step is sincere, it would be better if no one else knew what prompted Marcos to take it. If the foreign press detects Marcos' fear of the guerrillas, it would embarrass him and force him to reverse his position to prove he is not afraid of them."

"Well, do you really think the Marcoses can possibly change all of a sudden and become sincere?" Presy teased me.

"Oh, come on! Don't give me a hard time, too," I told Presy irritably. "I've been answering this question since my meeting with Imelda. We know people like Imelda and Marcos don't change. If the lifting is meaningful, it's not because they wanted to do it or because they are sincere. It's because they had to. Interestingly enough, not a single serious newspaper attributed Marcos' step to sincerity. They all looked for some other motive. The most natural conclusion was the new Reagan administration and the visit of the Pope. We are not the only ones who are wary of the Marcoses. Every foreign correspondent who follows the Philippine scene knows what kind of people the Marcoses really are."

Presy then moved our conversation on to some of the humorous aspects of my dialogue with Imelda in New York. We laughed as I recounted in greater detail Imelda's "poor barrio experiment" and her Meralco general who ordered the leaky boiler tube not to explode to avoid embarrassing Marcos. But we laughed the most when I explained Imelda's ipil-ipil dendro-thermal project. At one point, Presy said, "Steve, I am sure Imelda wasn't lying when she told you she had called Henry Ford and asked him to replace the gasoline engine with her ipil-ipil wood-burning gismo. I wondered how Ford responded."

At another point, I told Presy, "I'm glad about one thing. Imelda will teach the OPEC countries a needed lesson. They've been choking the world with their unreasonable oil price increases. Now Imelda, with her ipil-ipil fuel, is going to run the Arabs out of the oil business."

Presy and I had a few good laughs that evening, but, at the end, the subject reverted to the serious implications of the lifting of martial law. "I marvel sometimes," Presy said skeptically, "how we can maintain our sense of humor at times like these. I'm glad we do. Otherwise, we would go insane. You know, this is more of a Filipino trait than Greek. It's a good trait. You Greeks are too emotional. You can lose your sense of humor during difficult times, and, with it, you can also lose your mind."

"You're absolutely right about that," I agreed. "I've been trying to copy the Filipinos in this regard."

"When all is said and done," Presy asked in a tone that was now quite sober, "what do you think are the chances of Marcos moving toward real normalization with a view to turning power over to a legitimate and freely-elected government?"

"You're like Ninoy now," I answered. "You're looking more for a reassurance than for an answer to your question. I don't know; I think the chances are really slim. However, I know that Imelda—and I'm sure Marcos, too—is scared and sees the danger of a bloody revolution and of their own miserable end if they pursue the same course. Consequently, I have to believe, or at least hope, there is a chance, no matter how slim, that Marcos will move toward normalization *voluntarily*. Ninoy is right. Peace must be given one more chance."

"I pray that my people can be set free without more bloodshed, but I guess we'll have to wait and see," Presy concluded.

We didn't have to wait long to determine that the lifting of martial law was, in fact, a lifting in name only, not in substance—a "cosmetic change" and another attempt at a "cruel deception." As the conditions of the lifting became known, it became clear Marcos would continue to wield the same absolute dictatorial powers as he had under the provisions of martial rule. All the decrees issued by Marcos prior to the lifting of martial law are still in force, granting Marcos arbitrary power in all political, economic, and social issues of the country.

In addition to the many known "Presidential Decrees" and the "National Security Code" defining the unlimited dictatorial powers, a new decree surfaced for the first time in early January 1981, although it was dated September 12, 1980. It is believed the decree was issued shortly before the announcement of the lifting of martial law but that it was backdated to September.

This document, Presidential Decree 1737, is now known as the Public Order Act, and, among its many provisions, it stipulates:

> Whenever in the judgment of the President/Prime Minister there exist a grave emergency or a threat or imminence thereof, he may issue such orders as he may deem necessary to meet the emergency including but not limited to preventive detention, prohibiting the wearing of certain uniforms and emblems, restraining or restricting the movement and other activities of persons or entities with a view to preventing them from acting in a manner prejudicial to the national security or the maintenance of public order, directing the closure of subversive publications or other media of mass communications, banning or regulating the holding of entertainment or exhibitions detrimental to the national interest, con-

trolling admission to educational institutions whose operations are found prejudicial to the national security, or authorizing the taking of measures to prevent any damage to the viability of the economic system."

Note: Decree is shown on the following page.

The powers granted to Marcos by this Public Order Act exceed the powers specified in the decrees issued during the previous eight years. While, for instance the President always had the power to issue Arrest, Search, and Seizure Orders (ASSO) for "subversives," now he can also issue orders for "preventive detention." This means that a person can be arrested at any time without having committed any crimes or even being suspected of having committed a crime. He can be arrested simply if "in the judgment of the President," he is capable of committing a crime sometime in the future.

As such decrees started to surface about the time of the lifting of martial law, it became very clear that, as Alex Esclamado put it, "this step is anything but a sincere step toward democracy. It is pure deception."

Meanwhile, the call Colonel Zumel had promised to make "right away" to confirm Charlie Avila's visit to the Philippines and Father Olaguer's trip to the United States never came. It was evident that whatever transpired in the meeting of the Security Council, which was being held during my January 15th conversation with Zumel, had cancelled the agreement I had reached with Zumel.

Three days later, on January 18th, we received reports from "highly placed" reliable sources that "the palace and the key generals have now been divided into two camps; the hardliners and the moderates." Our intelligence sources reported that "the hardliners had prevailed." A few days later, an emissary was dispatched to the United States from Manila to tell us that several generals, headed by the chief of intelligence, General Fabian Ver,

MALACAÑANG
MANILA

PRESIDENTIAL DECREE NO. 1737

AN ACT PROVIDING FOR THE PRESERVATION OF PUBLIC ORDER AND THE PROTECTION OF INDIVIDUAL RIGHTS AND LIBERTIES DURING PERIODS OF EMERGENCY AND EXERCISE OF EXTRAORDINARY EXECUTIVE POWERS

WHEREAS, it is recognized that the State exists for the individual and that it is the responsibility of government to protect his rights and liberties;

NOW, THEREFORE, I, FERDINAND E. MARCOS, President of the Philippines, by virtue of the powers vested in me by the Constitution, do hereby order and decree:

SEC. 2. Whenever in the judgment of the President/Prime Minister there exist a grave emergency or a threat or imminence thereof, he may issue such orders as he may deem necessary to meet the emergency including but not limited to preventive detention, prohibiting the wearing of certain uniforms and emblems, restraining or restricting the movement and other activities of persons or entities with a view to preventing them from acting in a manner prejudicial to the national security or the maintenance of public order, directing the closure of subversive publications or other media of mass communications, banning or regulating the holding of entertainment or exhibitions detrimental to the national interest, controlling admission to educational institutions whose operations are found prejudicial to the national security, or authorizing the taking of measures to prevent any damage to the viability of the economic system. The violation of orders, issued by the President/Prime Minister pursuant to this Decree, unless the acts are punishable with higher penalties under the Anti-Subversion Act, the Revised Penal Code or other existing laws, shall be punishable by imprisonment for not less than thirty (30) days but not exceeding one (1) year.

SEC. 4. This Act shall take effect immediately.

Done in the City of Manila, this 12 day of September in the year of Our Lord, nineteen hundred and eighty.

President of the Philippines

had taken the position of "why deal with a bunch of amateurs?" Ver reportedly said, "we can wipe them out anytime. We have already most of them in jail, and we will catch the few remaining terrorists soon. Everything is under control. With Carter out and Reagan in the White House, we have nothing to be concerned about."

In January, 1981, Marcos announced another "important step toward normalization." He called for "Presidential" elections in May of 1981 and challenged any of his opponents to run against him, including Senator Aquino. The Manila papers headlined Marcos' "invitation" to Aquino in an attempt to convince the people that Marcos would allow Ninoy to run against him in an honest election. "I AM WILLING TO TAKE ON AQUINO" was the headline of the January 31st *Daily Express.*

While this impression was being created by the Philippine news media, which remain totally government controlled despite the lifting of martial law, Marcos sent two emissaries to Ninoy with a very clear and definite message: "Don't come to the Philippines, or I'll have you arrested immediately." One of the two emissaries was the "Grand Old Man" himself, Senator Lorenzo M. Tanada.

Tanada arrived in San Francisco February 1, just a few days after the Manila papers announced Marcos' challenge. I met the Senator at the airport and joined him on his connecting flight to Boston to meet with Aquino. Tanada told me that the day before his departure from Manila, Marcos invited him to the palace. During their one-hour meeting, Marcos had asked Tanada "to explain to Ninoy" why he shouldn't come to the Philippines at this time and why "he would be arrested with all these cases pending against him."

"It appears that Marcos decided to conduct another farcical election," Ninoy told Tanada upon hearing the news. " I guess he really cannot dismount his tiger, even if he wants to. This election looks like one more of the deceptive maneuvers that have characterized the past eight years of martial rule."

Senator Lorenzo M. Tanada visiting Senator Benigno "Ninoy" Aquino, Jr., at the latter's Harvard University office, February 3, 1981.

During the Marcos-Tanada meeting, the subject of the arrest orders for Renato and Karen Tanada was brought up. "Tani," Marcos had said, "I am a father like yourself. I can understand your concern for your son and your granddaughter. I want to help. I want to give them amnesty. All they have to do is surface and surrender, and I will give them amnesty and set them immediately free."

"Mr. President," responded the Grand Old Man, "first of all, it's not only my son and granddaughter who are involved. It is also my grandson."

"Oh! Is that so? I didn't know," Marcos responded.

"Yes, Mr. President. Secondly, your offer of surrender and amnesty is the second one I've received. The same offer was communicated to me several days ago through an emissary of the First Lady. I transmitted the offer to my children because I have no right to decide for them. They have turned down the offer to surrender and receive amnesty. They prefer to be arrested by the military. Surrender, they said, would be demoralizing to their fellow freedom fighters."

"I admire your son, but what are we going to do, Tani?" asked Marcos.

"The only fair solution I see is to grant amnesty to everyone, not only to a few. Also, the amnesty should be given voluntarily by you without requesting the hunted to surrender and beg for amnesty."

"The military will not easily agree to give amnesty to the hard core communists and other hard core terrorists who have been arrested or are being pursued."

"In that case," the Senator said, "I don't see any acceptable solution."

"Please study this problem, Tani, and give me your suggestions when you return."

Before the one-hour meeting ended, Marcos also told Senator

Tanada to ask the "holdouts" in the States for their grievances. "Please ask them to put their grievances in writing and bring them to me when you return," Marcos told Tanada, "and in the case of the Psinakises, please also find out what motivates them."

The Senator left for Manila on February 19. Before his departure, we handed him the following letter for Marcos:

February 3, 1981

Mr. Ferdinand E. Marcos
Malacanang Palace
Manila, Philippines

Dear Mr. Marcos,

The Honorable Senator Lorenzo M. Tanada informed us that during his meeting with you on January 30, 1981, you asked him to obtain our written response to your two specific questions:

1. What motivates us?
2. What are our grievances?

We are pleased to respond to your questions:

1. We are motivated by our absolute commitment to truth, justice, and freedom as well as by our commitment to oppose oppression, violence and terrorism wherever it occurs.

2. We are aggrieved by your untruths, injustices and suppression of freedoms of the Filipino people as well as by the illegal continuation of your "Conjugal Dictatorship" which is maintained in power through oppression, violence and terrorism.

Sincerely,

Presy L. Psinakis—Steve E. Psinakis

Pope John Paul II arrived in Manila as scheduled on February 17, 1981. The reception arranged by the Marcoses was like a carnival. The Conjugal Dictators attempted to use the papal visit for their own political propaganda, but the Holy Father's speeches on human rights and on the suffering of the poor focused attention on the prevailing conditions under the Marcos one-man rule.

During his first speech and with Marcos seated next to him, the Pontiff condemned the suspension of civil rights and violations of human rights under martial law. The *New York Times* report on the Pope's speech read in part as follows:

THE NEW YORK TIMES, WEDNESDAY, FEBRUARY 18, 1981

POPE, WITH MARCOS BESIDE HIM, DELIVERS HUMAN RIGHTS TALK

ALSO PRAISES RECENT MOVES

Cautions Philippine President That Nothing Can Justify Violation of the Individual's Dignity

By HENRY KAMM
Special to The New York Times

MANILA, Feb. 17 — Pope John Paul II delivered a homily on human rights today in Malacanang, the presidential palace, while President Ferdinand E. Marcos, his host, sat beside him.

"Even in exceptional situations that may at times arise, one can never justify any violation of the fundamental dignity of the human person or of the basic rights that safeguard this dignity," the Pope declared as Mr. Marcos sat stolidly on one of the thronelike gilt chairs on the stage. "Legitimate concern for the security of a nation, as demanded by the common good, could lead to the temptation of subjugating to the state the human being and his or her dignity and rights.

"Any apparent conflict between the exigencies of security and the citizens' basic rights must be resolved according to the fundamental principle — upheld always by the church — that social organization exists only for the service of man and for the protection of his dignity and that it cannot claim to serve the common good when human rights are not safeguarded."

President Marcos, discarding his prepared remarks, apologized for what he called "petty and small" church-state differences. "Forgive us, holy father," he said. "Now that you are here, we resolve we shall wipe out all conflicts and set up a society that is harmonious to attain the ends of God."

On February 20th, the Pope delivered his most explosive speech before a large crowd of sugar cane workers. Excerpts of the report filed by the UPI correspondent in Manila read as follows:

S.F. EXAMINER ☆☆C Fri., Feb. 20, 1981

Pope to workers: fight exploiters

ILOILO, Philippines (UPI) — His face sunburned from a day under the scorching tropical sun, Pope John Paul II delivered the most politically explosive speech of his Asian tour today, telling impoverished sugar cane workers they should unionize to resist exploitation by their employers.

The pontiff spent the fifth hectic day of his 20,500-mile Asian odyssey in island hopping from violence-torn Davao to Iloilo and Bacolod, where he spoke forcefully for the rights of sugar cane workers before a crowd of 250,000 worshipers sweating under a fierce sun.

Shadowing the pontiff as he stopped at three island cities in the southern Philippines was first lady Imelda Marcos, wife of President Ferdinand Marcos, who rented a private jet to keep up with the pope.

Vatican aides made little effort to hide the fact they were annoyed by Mrs. Marcos turning up to greet the pope wherever he went, regarding it as an attempt to capitalize politically from the papal visit.

Wearing a pink butterfly dress and carrying a pink lace-trimmed parasol, she followed the papal party along with Christina Ford, a close friend and former wife of auto magnate Henry Ford.

Today's speech on the effort by sugar plantation workers to unionize is a politically explosive subject in the Philippines.

At least nine Catholic lay workers have been executed for trying to help sugar workers, who earn as little as $3 a day, to organize unions.

Declaring it was "not admissible" that the profits of the land go only into the pockets of the rich, the pope told a cheering crowd in Bacolod that "the worker is entitled to wages that give him a just share in the wealth he helps to produce.

"Working conditions should be geared not to the ever-increasing economic profit of the enterprise but to the inviolable dignity of man as an individual ...

"Injustice reigns when within the same society some groups hold most of the wealth and power while large strata of the population cannot decently provide for the livelihoods of their families even through long hours of back-breaking labor in factories in the fields."

The reaction of the Marcoses to the factual and uncensored reporting by the U.S. news media on the Pope's visit is reflected in the commentaries of their unofficial spokesman, columnist Teodoro "Doroy" Valencia. Doroy's hysterical daily columns, published during and after the Pontiff's visit, exemplify the kind of paranoid and vicious attack he launches against anyone and anything critical of his "masters"–Ferdinand and Imelda.

The attacks against the prestigious U.S. news media also illustrate how the Marcoses, their spokesmen, and their controlled press seed distortion in the minds of the Filipino people. A few of Doroy's daily columns on the Papal visit are shown on the next four pages.

PHILIPPINE DAILY EXPRESS Wednesday, February 25, 1981

OVER A CUP OF COFFEE

□TEODORO F. VALENCIA

NOTES: The papal visit saw the most vicious and malicious reporting by the American press calculated to smear the Philippine government and the President. Fortunately, the Pope was not reading them... The Pope was humble but the President equalled his humility to assure a spirited and warm welcome for the Holy Father..

*** * ***

"When in Rome do as the Romans do" is a saying we all know by heart. It was shocking that when the Romans go East, they don't do as we do. The speechwriters of the Holy Father made it sound as if the Holy Father did not understand the Oriental custom of giving credit to the wife of a

host. The Pope was profuse in thanking President Marcos for everything but forgot to mention Mrs. Marcos. In truth, if only one is to be thanked for the success of the visit, it should be Mrs. Marcos, not the President. Mrs. Marcos used to visit the Rizal Park construction of the altar even at 3 a.m., to make sure everything was as the Catholic hierarchy wanted it to be. She herded the faithful. She made certain the welcome was all right in all the papal destinations. The Catholic hierarchy only took all the credit.

* * *

PHILIPPINE DAILY EXPRESS Friday, February 27, 1981

OVER A CUP OF COFFEE

TEODORO F. VALENCIA

Time and *Newsweek* magazines went to town on the papal visit in their March 2, 1981 issues. These American magazines utilized the papal visit to renew and improve their campaigns to downgrade the administration of President Marcos. This was obvious from the pictures – the American press "boys" whom they depend to fight President Marcos were given special treatment. Reading these magazines, I was moved to wonder if they were talking about the same papal visit I saw. The Filipino people saw most of what happened because everything was on television. They guessed what happened beyond the camera range. We don't have to be told about what we saw, heard and knew about even more than these foreigners.

* * *

Newsweek was specially vicious when it said that President Marcos insisted on greeting the Pope as a fellow head of state. If so, the Pope graciously acceded by trooping the line and speaking from the same platform. The American weekly said that the First Lady was "expressly uninvited" but managed to welcome the Pope everywhere. I wonder who told that to the *Newsweek* people. Obviously, *Newsweek* is not aware of Oriental customs and traditions and would have wanted to impose the American system on us. The Philippines is our country. Nobody needs to invite the First Lady to an affair involving a guest. The Church does not have any business deciding how a foreign visitor is to be received here. Acting Minister Greg Cendana says that those who wrote distorted stories were anti-Filipino. Some of those referred to are Filipino colonials.

* * *

PHILIPPINE DAILY EXPRESS Tuesday, February 24, 1981

OVER A CUP OF COFFEE

☐TEODORO F. VALENCIA

The Pope kept saying that his mission was "religious and spiritual" not that of a statesman or a politician. The Western press kept insisting he came as an inspector-general to scold President Marcos and find fault with human rights observance in the Philippines. As if the Holy Father took over from President Jimmy Carter. What do they think of the Philippines? Everybody's colony? Is the Western press not aware that Filipinos who live in the Philippines are not the same breed of colonials as some of those who live in the United States?

* * *

NOTES: Nowhere in the speeches of the Holy Father, except that one in the Morong Refugee Center, was the First Lady alluded to. Obviously, the local clergy had a hand in those speeches. . . If the Holy Father did not allude to the First Lady, it was thoroughly un-Asian. In Asia, we always allude to the wife when he allude to the husband. . . If the Holy Father made obvious that his visit was pastoral and spiritual, the Philippine Government welcome made it also obvious that he is the head of the Vatican state. Troop in the line at the MIA made that clear from the start of his 6-day stay.

* * *

PHILIPPINE DAILY EXPRESS Sunday, February 28, 1981

OVER A CUP OF COFFEE

☐TEODORO F. VALENCIA

Filipinos complain about the way the American press has been downgrading the Philippine government to force its will on our people. This is not new. They have been doing this since the end of World War II. Only the viciousness of the attacks accelerated in proportion to the progress we made despite the American press. Until we surrender and do as we are told, this campaign of villification will continue. We fought on the wrong side of World War II. Look at the Japanese – they have prospered with American help by merely pretending to follow American cues.

* * *

The American press used the Pope as a springboard for the most concentrated viciousness we have experienced in many years. If the idea is to get the Pope to dictate to us what government we must have and who will govern, it failed. Our people have not forgotten the Revolution of 1896 and what caused it.

* * *

The *New York Daily News* quoted an unnamed New York City Catholic source as saying that there was a rift between Pope John Paul II and

Mrs. Imelda Marcos – Mrs. Marcos wanted the Pope to say Mass in Malacañang but the Pope refused. This is pure gossip. Nobody would have dared tell the Pope to do what he did not want to do.

***

In addition to Doroy's columns, Marcos' *Philippine Daily Express* ran an editorial on the alleged "bias" of the American news media. In the editorial shown below, the "two most widely circulated news magazines" are *Time* and *Newsweek*.

PHILIPPINES SUNDAY EXPRESS February 22, 1981

Editorial

Typical Western bias

THERE seems to be no end to what a publication will do to sell copies. In the name of interpretive reporting, the two most-widely circulated newsmagazines – both American owned – zeroed on the papal visit to the Philippines.

One spoke of the "cosmetics" that were being applied to make, it said, the Pope unaware of the extent of poverty in the metropolis. The other magnified a difference of opinion and approach into a story that said the Philippines was now a house divided, rendered asunder by a rift between the government and the church.

Both succeeded only in showing the bias and prejudice that their reporters and editors harbor towards the country and its leaders. Both succeeded only in doing a disservice to the Pope, placing him in the role of a political nit-picker, and even a tool of the anti-government (or anti-Marcos, if you will) elements.

When the Pope makes a general statement about the church's teaching on human rights, it is seized immediately by the foreign media as a lecture to the country. The Pope knows better than that, and he only knows too well, as he has often said, that his job as leader of the Catholic faithful would be eroded if he meddled in temporary affairs and worse, if he presumed to interfere in the internal affairs of a sovereign nation.

And yet some vicious elements of the foreign media have chosen to ignore the realities; they have instead fed on their own wishful thoughts, projecting as fact what they wish were the facts.

Touching up the Tondo area, in preparation for the visit, is called a "sanitizing" job; a discussion on how some facets of the visit should be handled has resulted in a "rift"; it is now being made to appear that the leaders of both the government and church are not talking to each other, and indeed, are going their separate ways.

It would not be so bad if these two magazines were circulated only in the Philippines; they would be exposed for what they are. What is sad is that these magazines and the bias and prejudice they spout are being foisted upon a people whose understanding and knowledge about the country is therefore distorted. This is their loss, not ours.

CHAPTER 20

You Tell Reagan . . .

The events that transpired during the last week of February 1981 and the first two weeks of March confirmed the reports we had received from our own "intelligence source." In addition to the deceptive political maneuvers–the lifting of martial law and the calling of another staged election for "President"–the military had resumed the persecution of the revolutionaries with renewed vigor and cruelty. The hunt for the guerrillas intensified; new arrests were confirmed, torture of those arrested continued; two rebels from the Tondo area were brutally murdered; the farcical trials of the "subversives," which had been postponed, now resumed; even the senile Marcos columnist, Doroy Valencia, resumed his hysterical attacks on Ninoy Aquino, the Filipnio "terrorists," and the "U.S. rebels."

On March 19, 1981, Presy was contacted by a Philippine nun who told her she had just arrived from Manila. The nun claimed that she was asked by "a mutual friend" to bring us a letter and meet with us to explain the latest developments in Manila. Presy was cautious. "Do you think she may be planted by Marcos or even by the FBI?" Presy asked me.

"I don't know," I answered, "it's quite possible. We'll have to meet with her and play it by ear. If she is not a plant and if she has something important to tell us, I am sure she'll be able to give us some convincing credentials." We met with Sister "X". She was, in fact, an emissary of one of the revolutionary leaders and had no difficulty in establishing genuine credentials.

"I am sorry to be the bearer of sad news," the Sister told us. "Your meetings with Imelda were a waste of time. We now have proof that the hardline generals are calling the shots. We don't know if Marcos or Imelda had any other plans in mind, but, even if we assume they did, it makes no difference."

"I am afraid we received similar reports last month," I said. "If it makes you feel any better, you're not the first bearer of these disturbing reports. However, we'd like to hear the latest news."

The nun went on to explain in more detail and with more concrete information the "intelligence" reports we had been receiving since late February.

"There should be more accurate information in this letter of our friend," the Sister told me as she handed me a thick envelope. "What disturbs most of us back home—and also puzzles us—is the attitude of the Reagan administration. Marcos and Imelda keep bragging about their alleged friendship with Reagan and the support they are now getting from the U.S. government. Is this correct or is it just the usual Marcos propaganda? Can Reagan be so blind or misinformed about the inevitable course of events in my country?"

"That's a difficult question to answer with any certainty, Sister," I replied. "We'll need a little more time to evaluate Reagan policies. But, frankly speaking, the initial signs are that Reagan and Haig will pursue a foreign policy similar to that of

Nixon and Kissinger. From the way Reagan received the Korean dictator, Chun, and from what we've heard so far on Nicaragua and El Salvador, it appears that Reagan will, like Nixon, support any tin-horn dictator who plays up to the United States and claims to be anti-communist. This means he will probably support Marcos."

"God help us," said Sister "X" as if she were praying, "how can Reagan fail to see that the surest way to strengthen the communists is by trying to prop up the Marcos dictatorship."

"I don't understand, either, Sister," Presy concurred.

"Doesn't Reagan understand that the traditional friendship of our people toward America is turning into hatred because America is viewed by the people as the collaborator and supporter of our oppressor? The Philippines will surely become another Iran. What do the Reagan advisers tell him about the situation in the Philippines?" Sister "X" asked angrily.

"You are asking difficult questions, Sister," I said with a smile. "I don't know why Reagan doesn't see the obvious, nor do I know what his advisers tell him. But I can assure you that practically every American political commentator has said pretty much the same thing you're saying. Every prestigious U.S. paper has editorialized the same view. Why Reagan doesn't understand it is beyond me."

"You know, Steve, the whole world seems to be in a state of confusion. America is no exception. Look at what's happening in Afghanistan and El Salvador. In Afghanistan, the rebels are fighting an oppressive communist regime while in El Salvador the rebels are fighting an oppressive right wing regime. The peoples of both countries are fighting for freedom from oppression. Yet, the Soviets condemn the Afghan rebels as terrorists and praise the Salvadorans as freedom fighters. Why? Because in one case they are fighting a Soviet-backed regime and in the other, a U.S.-

backed regime. Is the U.S. different? I don' think so. The United States condemns the Salvadoran rebels as terrorists and praises the Afghan rebels as freedom fighters. It seems that the criteria is not the wish and the right of the people to free themselves from oppression of the left or of the right. The criteria seems to be only the interests of the Soviet Union and America. Is America any better than Russia?" she asked rather philosophically.

"No matter how disappointed you may be with America, it is not fair to equate the two countries. However, I will agree with you that there are cases where our government arrives at the wrong decision. Don't forget; American presidents are ordinary human beings, not gods. They make mistakes like all normal people; the same applies to the President's advisers. When that happens, the American people express freely their disagreement. They are free to criticize the President and can take several steps—through their representatives; through the press, etc—to affect the President's decisions and change policies which, in the opinion of the general public, are wrong. There is an example, for instance, why you should not equate Russia with the United States."

"Of course, we understand that; but the point I am making is that the primary, if not the only, consideration in formulating U.S. foreign policy seems to be its own interests. The interests of the other countries affected do not enter the picture. It is in this regard I equate the United States and Russia. The Afghanistan and El Salvador situations are clear examples of this. Oppression is oppression whether it comes from the extreme left or the extreme right. When the United States supports oppressive regimes when it suits her and opposes them when it doesn't suit her, then the United States is no better than Russia," the nun said rather logically and convincingly.

"I have to agree with you on this point," I said. "I personally believe that the U.S. policy towards the Philippines, and other such oppressive regimes, is wrong. I have criticized it and will continue to do so until it is changed. I believe, and have said so many times, that our policy of supporting regimes like Marcos', is not only immoral, unjust, and against the interests of the Philippines but also against the long-term interests of the United States. . . ."

"Precisely," the nun cut in, "we are struggling for our fundamental human rights. We will fight Marcos as vigorously as we will fight the atheist communists. We are Christians. The United States will support us when we fight oppression from communists but will oppose us when we fight oppression from Marcos. That's definitely hypocritical and unjust. Our views on America are changing fast. Our former admiration and respect is turning into hatred. It is becoming clearer every day that our suffering is not caused only by Marcos but also by the U.S. government which persists in supporting Marcos by supplying him with vast amounts of military and economic aid and helping him prolong his ruthless, corrupt, and illegal regime. How is it really possible that Reagan doesn't see this?" she asked again with exasperation.

"I really can't answer you, Sister," I responded. "All I can do, and I have been doing this even with Carter, is try to project the truth and the facts, not only to the administration, but also to the Congress and the press."

"Well, you tell Reagan that Marcos is nearing his end. We will soon free ourselves, but it looks like we'll have to do it with the blood of many innocent people. You tell Reagan that when our brothers and sisters, our fathers and mothers, our sons and daughters are killed by American bullets and are tortured by experts trained in the United States, you tell Reagan not to look surprised when we turn our hatred against America." The passion of her words both surprised and impressed me. I always perceived nuns to be gentle, dispassionate, and soft-spoken people but there was nothing dispassionate or soft-spoken about Sister "X" as she delivered her warning to Reagan.

"I don't think I can tell Reagan myself, Sister. The last person he'd want to see is me," I said, "but I promise to include your message in the book I have almost finished."

We talked with Sister "X" for several hours about the latest events in the Philippines and about our mutual acquaintances. We were happy to learn that some of our friends who had gone underground and had not communicated with us for a while were safe. We thanked the Sister for contacting us and bringing us the letter, and, before we parted, we made arrangements to meet again three weeks later prior to her return to Manila.

When we returned home, Presy worked for more than seven hours to decode the lengthy letter the nun brought us. The letter contained more detailed information on the same general subjects we discussed with the Sister. It explained the effects of the new hardline position of the military and confirmed the guerrillas' preparations for action. "The battle-line has now been drawn," the letter stated. "We were disappointed with the failure of your negotiations with Imelda even though we expected that they would be useless. I personally," wrote the author of the letter, "being a man of peace and wearing a 'habit,' am very pleased that Ninoy, Sonny, and you talked with Imelda—particularly Ninoy. God knows we have exhausted every possible approach to a peaceful solution. Sadly, many criticized Ninoy for meeting with Imelda, but most of us who are dedicated to peace and who value human life more than anything, praise and admire Ninoy for making a last effort to save the Filipino blood that now must be spilled to free our people from our home-grown tyrant."

I was reading the letter over Presy's shoulder as she was decoding it and when she finished, she handed it to me and said: "You know, prior to the New York meetings with Imelda, I had already resigned myself to the fact that my country would be freed only through violence and bloodshed. Those meetings, however, gave me a new hope that there was a chance for a peaceful solution. Now that hope is gone, and I have to go through the same sad realization all over again. Maybe it would have been better if those meetings had never taken place."

"No. I don't share this view," I said. "I share the view you've just read in the letter. If there was a chance for peace, no matter how small, it had to be explored. Before decent Christians decide to resort to violence, they must first exhaust all chances for a peaceful solution."

While I said this to Presy, I also understood her feelings and, to some extent, I shared her view. It was depressing to realize once again that the last effort for peace had failed.

The following day we learned that the Manila newspapers headlined news stories about the forthcoming trials of the "subversives" and the "terrorists." New names had been added to the list of those charged, including another Jesuit priest, Father Blanco. We picked up the *New York Times* and found the following brief news item:

THE NEW YORK TIMES, FRIDAY, MARCH 20, 1981

Jesuit Priest Charged With Plotting to Oust Regime in Philippines

Special to The New York Times

MANILA, March 19 — The Rev. Jose Blanco, a militant Jesuit, has been charged with seeking to destabilize the regime of President Ferdinand E. Marcos by means of violent acts, including a series of bombings last year.

Judge Ernani Cruz Pano said today that Father Blanco was the second Jesuit to be named in the case. The other was the Rev. Romeo Intengan. Ninety-six people have been accused in the alleged destabilization conspiracy, which the Government charges was led by the opposition politicians Jovito Salonga, Raul Manglapus and Benigno A. Aquino Jr. The three politicians are in the United States, as are 20 other people named by the authorities.

Father Intengan and some 50 others accused in the case are in hiding in the Philippines. Father Blanco has not been arrested and is still at the Jesuit headquarters in Manila. "He is here right now saying mass for the order," the Rev. James B. Reuter said.

Seventeen suspects have been jailed since October, most of them young people in their 20's and 30's who are alleged to have belonged to a group called the April 6 Liberation Movement.

The Government has accused them of planting bombs in public buildings between August and October 1980, causing the death of an American and injuries to 70 other people.

Doris Nuval Baffrey, one of two women accused, was said to have planted the bombs that interrupted a convention here last year of the American Society of Travel Agents.

Handcuffed to one another, 12 of the youths were brought to Judge Pano's court this morning for a preliminary investigation of charges originally filed against them by military prosecutors. The transfer to the civilian court was a result of the lifting of martial law last January.

Defense lawyers asked the court to release the defendants, saying the youths had not been served proper judicial warrants and the preliminary investigation was still being done. The judge placed the request under advisement.

Father Intengan and Father Blanco are supporters of social action by the Roman Catholic Church. They have worked with young people to improve the lives of laborers, squatters and poor farmers.

During the previous eight years, Marcos had carefully avoided any actions to antagonize the Catholic church and had played down the growing conflict between his regime and the progressive sector of the church. Now, the banner headlines on the accusations and charges against the two well-known Jesuits was another indication that the hardline generals were calling the shots. I thought of our friend, Father Toti Olaguer. "Any day now," I told Presy, "we'll read that Father Toti has also been picked up."

I completed the manuscript of this book on March 22, 1981. That same day, I received a call from Manila and was told that the first large demonstration in eight years was held the previous day. During the demonstration, the opposition vowed to overthrow the Marcos dictatorship. 'What a coincidence,' I thought. When I read the *San Francisco Examiner,* I found the following brief news story:

S.F. Sunday Examiner & Chronicle Mar. 22, 1981

Foes vow to topple Marcos

MANILA, Philippines — Opposition leaders returned for the first time yesterday to a square where terrorist bombs killed 12 of their followers a decade ago and vowed before a

> crowd of more than 5,000 to topple President Ferdinand Marcos from power. "We have come here together for the first time to bring down the Marcos dictatorship," said former Senator Gerardo Roxas, one of about 100 people wounded in the 1971 bombing. Marcos has ruled the Philippines for more than 15 years. The leaders of the United Democratic Opposition urged the more than 5,000 people packed in Manila's Plaza Miranda to reject proposed constitutional amendments which they said would perpetuate Marcos in power as a "dictator." The amendments are to be voted on in a nationwide referendum on April 7, and would enable Marcos to pick his own prime minister.

The following morning, March 23, 1981, I handed the last chapter of the manuscript to my publisher.

Epilogue

The Philippine crisis remains. No one is really certain whether the latest decision of the Marcoses to continue on their course of deception and repression was entirely their own choice or whether it was forced on them by their hardline generals. In either case, the result will be the same. This course will lead to confrontation, bloodshed, and destruction.

The responsibility for the consequences rests completely with Mr. Marcos. Even if he now prefers to relinquish power voluntarily and peacefully, but is prevented from doing so by his generals, the responsibility is still his. It is he who created the "Frankenstein"—the corrupt military elite—which he used to perpetuate the "Conjugal Dictatorship" for eight years. Now he must confront his Frankenstein or he must answer to the people who suffered the injustices of his own creation. Marcos' choices are limited and are all fraught with grave dangers.

On the other hand, the revolutionaries have taken the only available course for the liberation of their country from tyranny: Force. As long as Marcos is in power, the revolutionaries will be branded as "terrorists." When they succeed in overthrowing the "Conjugal Dictatorship," they will be acknowledged as the heroes and the liberators of their country.

How long the Marcos-Romualdez families will manage to stay in power is difficult to predict. It could be six months, one year, two years, or, perhaps even longer. But there is no question that the oppressive Marcos rule will come to an end.

There is, however, an uncertainty about the policy that the Reagan administration will adopt toward the Marcos regime. Will it endorse and support the "Conjugal Dictatorship" and encourage Mr. and Mrs. Marcos to continue on their present course? Or will it keep a safe distance from the present regime while it urges the dictators to return the country to its traditional democratic ways?

The answer to this question will determine whether the Filipino people will maintain their friendship toward America or whether their hatred for their Filipino oppressors will be similarly directed against the United States.

The prospects of seeing another Iran in the Philippines are indeed great. The warnings have been given countless times, not only by Filipinos like Sister "X," but also by scores of knowledgeable American commentators. The developments of the past few months have shown beyond doubt that the Filipino people, like human beings everywhere, will fight for their human rights no matter how great the cost or the sacrifice of their sons and daughters.

Appendix

"MANILA, PHILIPPINES. A coordinated bombing attack was carried out today against government offices and businesses around Manila . . . . The bombs did not contain shrapnel, as it appeared that they were intended to cause damage, not injuries . . . . The group taking responsibility for the explosions . . . calls itself the April 6 Liberation Movement . . . . 'We have decided to use force as the ultimate weapon against a repressive regime which has refused to listen to reason' a statement issued by the Movement said."

The New York Times, August 23, 1980

"Says Eduardo Olaguer, 44, a newspaper executive and Harvard Business School graduate, currently on trial (by the Marcos military tribunals) for leading the Light-a-Fire terrorist group: 'When all peaceful means to battle an illegitimate, corrupt and repressive regime are to no avail—and we tried for seven years—we are forced to use force' . . . . Philippine Defense Minister Juan Ponce Enrile admits that the new breed of middle-class guerrillas cannot all be dismissed out of hand. He said of Olaguer: 'This is not the kind of man I would like to contend with as an adversary.' The new guerrillas may be less professional as terrorists than they are as doctors, lawyers, or businessmen—but they have clearly been able to prove that they are a force to be reckoned with."

Newsweek, November 3, 1980

CONCLUSIONS of Amnesty International published in its official 1976 annual report after Amnesty's fact-finding mission to the Philippines in November and December of 1975:

"1. THE MISSION FOUND CONVINCING EVIDENCE THAT THE EMPLOYMENT OF TORTURE WAS WIDESPREAD . . . "
(Conclusion and Recommendation No. 1, Page 11)

"2. THE CONCLUSION IS UNAVOIDABLE THAT TORTURE OF PRISONERS WAS PART OF A GENERAL APPROACH TO THE TREATMENT OF SUSPECTS. THIS HAD THE EFFECT OF INTIMIDATING ALL THOSE ARRESTED ON SUSPICION OF HAVING COMMITTED POLITICAL OFFENCES."
(Conclusion and Recommendation No. 2, Page 11)

"3. NONE OF THE PRISONERS INTERVIEWED HAD BEEN CONVICTED, ALTHOUGH TRIAL PROCEEDINGS HAVE BEGUN FOR SOME OF THEM . . . "
(Conclusion and Recommendation No. 3, Page 11)

"4. . . . THE MISSION FOUND THAT ALL KNOWN CASES HAD BEEN TAINTED BY RELIANCE ON SO-CALLED EVIDENCE EXTRACTED FROM A NUMBER OF PRISONERS BY TORTURE. THE CONCLUSION IS UNAVOIDABLE THAT IN THOSE CASES THE SO-CALLED EVIDENCE WAS LITERALLY TORTURED INTO EXISTENCE."
(Conclusion and Recommendation No. 4, Page 12)

"AS OF THE TIME OF THE AMNESTY INTERNATIONAL MISSION, THE PHILIPPINES HAS BEEN TRANSFORMED FROM A COUNTRY WITH A REMARKABLE CONSTITUTIONAL TRADITION TO A SYSTEM WHERE STAR CHAMBER METHODS HAVE BEEN USED ON A WIDE SCALE TO LITERALLY TORTURE EVIDENCE INTO EXISTENCE . . . " (Page 55)

"RIGHTS GROUP ASSAILS PHILIPPINES REGIME. The International Commission of Jurists, in a study to be published in Geneva, asserts that the Government of President Ferdinand E. Marcos of the Philippines is continuing its martial law rule "to perpetuate the personal power of the President and his collaborators and to increase the power of the military to control Philippine society."

The report based on the findings of three missions of inquiry dispatched by the commission to the Philippines since May 1975, also alleges a broad range of violations of democracy and human rights and widespread detentions without charge or trial and torture. . . .

The report charged that Mr. Marcos using military authority, has denied or inhibited a wide range of basic constitutional rights to Filipinos. It cites:

The Right to elect their government.

Habeas corpus.

Press freedom.

Freedom of speech and information through arrests of opponents and denial of access to media to those at liberty.

The right of labor to strike.

The right to travel abroad or return from abroad."

The New York Times, July 31, 1977

"RELIGIOUS LEADERS SAY MANILA REGIME TORTURES PRISONERS. MANILA, the Philippines, April 29 (AP)—In a 100-page pamphlet distributed through the Roman Catholic Church in the Philippines, the Association of Major Religious Superiors has accused the Government of torturing and killing political detainees. . . .

Citing what it described as case histories, the pamphlet reported that the military had beaten prisoners, administered electrical shocks, burned victims with lighted cigarettes, forced detainees to sit naked on ice blocks and sexually abuse males and females.

The pamphlet alleged that the treatment led to the death of some and that some persons had not been heard from after their arrests. . . . "

The New York Times, April 30, 1975

"RED CROSS REPORT ON PHILIPPINES TORTURE. MANILA. (AP)–Investigators of the International Committee of the Red Cross have uncovered evidence that supports allegations of torture in Philippine martial law detention centers, Red Cross sources said yesterday.
The investigators toured most Philippine detention centers between June 5 and their departure last Wednesday, the sources said. . . .
Sources said the Red Cross observers found there was evidence to support allegations in a secret Amnesty International report–based on interviews with detainees last November and December–of widespread torture of prisoners in Philippine detention centers. . . ."

San Francisco Chronicle, July 26, 1976

"U.S. REPORT HITS MARCOS ON RIGHTS. Washington–The State Department, in a report prepared for Congress, has criticized the Philippine government of President Ferdinand Marcos for the use of torture and "severe intrusions on individual rights. . . ."
While saying the government's use of torture against political enemies of the Marcos administration appears to have "declined in frequency," the report accused the government of continuing to use torture employing "such methods as water treatment, electric shock, long isolation and physical beating."

San Francisco Chronicle, February 6, 1978

"MARCOS DENIES U.S. REPORT ON RIGHTS VIOLATIONS. MANILA, Jan. 7 (AP)–President Ferdinand E. Marcos today branded as a "provocation" a State Department report that human rights had been violated by his martial-law regime in the Philippines. President Marcos also said treaties with the United States could be terminated if they were no longer in his country's best interests. . . ."
In a televised address from the University of the Philippines, President Marcos denied allegations that political prisoners were tortured. "We have no political prisoners as defined in the accepted international law term," he said. "As of today, (we) have ordered the release of those prisoners against whom there are no charges filed."

The New York Times, January 8, 1977

"ARMY ARRESTS 200 IN MANILA PROTEST. MANILA–Philippine Army units detained more than 200 striking workers yesterday as part of one of the biggest security crackdowns since President Ferdinand Marcos declared martial law three years ago, knowledgeable sources reported. . . . The Marcos regime has evidently made the arrests to counteract a growing wave of political opposition and labor unrest, which has included a sudden rash of strikes, largely illegal under martial law."

San Francisco Chronicle, January 31, 1976

"CRACKDOWN ON CLERICS. MANILA–The government has expelled an American priest and arrested a second American clergyman for allegedly engaging in subversive activities, informed sources said yesterday. The martial law regime of President Ferdinand Marcos deported the Rev. Edward Gerlock, 36, Binghamton, N.Y. Father Gerlock had been active in social action work in Davao, in southeastern Mindanao. Government troops later seized the Rev. Albert Booms, from Harbor Beach, Mich., a missionary of the Pontifical Institute for Foreign Missions. Father Booms was parish priest of Tondo, a village near the Manila waterfront slums. It was expected that he would be deported."

S.F. Sunday Examiner, November 21, 1976

"MANILA SHUTS DOWN TWO CATHOLIC PAPERS. MANILA – Armed police yesterday closed the offices of two Philippines Roman Catholic publications here in what appears to be a continuing campaign against alleged church activists.

One paper is the Signs of the Times, a weekly that has carried strident criticism of the 4-year-old martial law government of President Ferdinand Marcos. The other is the Communicator, a monthly publication generally considered more moderate in its criticism.

The closures had been predicted by many churchmen following the shutting down of two Catholic radio stations and the deporting of two U.S. priests."

San Francisco Chronicle, December 6, 1976

"MARCOS ON FREEDOM. MANILA (AP)–Philippine President Ferdinand E. Marcos yesterday defended the curtailment of "small freedoms" so that large ones can be protected and the small ones eventually restored. Marcos made the comments, evidently his answer to criticism in Washington of alleged human rights violations under his martial law regime, to a largely American audience on Memorial Day."

San Francisco Chronicle, May 31, 1977

Los Angeles Times, July 19, 1978

"A PRESIDENT WHO'S ABOVE CRITICISM. MANILA. (AP)–The government has ordered newspapers and magazines not to criticize President Ferdinand E. Marcos and his wife, Imelda, the head of the government's Print Media Council said yesterday.
Retired Brigadier General Hans M. Menzi, who also publishes the newspaper, *The Bulletin Today,* said the ban was a guideline issued as part of the watchdog activities of the council. Marcos created the council by martial-law decree as a regulating body and empowered it to issue permits to publish."

San Francisco Chronicle, June 29, 1976

"THE TEN RICHEST WOMEN IN THE WORLD.—Elizabeth of England, Imelda Marcos, Juliana of the Netherlands, The Begum, Duchess of Alba, Dina Merrill, Christina Onassis, Barbara Hutton, Doris Duke and Madeleine Dassault.

There is nothing plain or unassuming about Imelda Marcos, wife of the Philippines president who spends prodigious sums of money and is rumored to be the richest woman in the world bar none. . . . In the first five years of Ferdinand's administration, the Marcoses amassed more capital than all of his predecessors combined, became multimillionaires in their own right.

Meldy is a charter member of the Jet Set, a long-time bosom buddy of Christina Ford's, always favored couture by Dior and international shopping sprees at such outposts as Bergdorf's and I. Magnin's. Today, vital, vibrant, perhaps the most influential beauty in all of Asia, Imelda Marcos thinks nothing of flying her chums halfway around the globe when she's in a party mood. Entertaining is always on an extravagant scale, whether at Malacanang Palace in Manila, her official residence with its priceless statuary; or aboard 777, the presidential yacht; or at her sumptuous beach house, a resort in itself, snuggled in Talago Cove on a piece of land that splits the sea between China and the Philippines.

And when Meldy travels—to Washington, Osaka, Grosse Point, Persepolis—it's always with an enormous entourage. Lots of dear dear friends for diversion. Lots of bodyguards to protect her from the enemy. . . ."

Cosmopolitan, December 1975

"NEW YEAR SWINGERS PARTY IN MANILA. MANILA (UPI)–The first couple of the Philippines played host to the jet set at a sunset-to-sunrise New Year's party that began in a jet set floating casino, moved to the Malacanang presidential palace and ended on a yacht as the sun rose over Manila Bay.

The 400 guests of President and Mrs. Ferdinand Marcos included Count Mario D'Urso, Princess Maria Gabriella of Savoy, Italian movie producer Franco Rosellini, Bolivian tin king Atenor Patino and a smattering of models, starlets and businessmen.

The show belonged to Mrs. Marcos, a diplomatic trouble-shooter, oil buyer, roving negotiator, governor of Manila and jet-set hostess. Her husband, the man who put the Philippines under martial law three years ago, stood on the sidelines during most of the bash. In his New Year's message, he called on Filipinos to live austerely "without ostentation, without show."

The "beautiful people" began the New Year's Eve festivities by inaugurating the $4 million casino ship Philippine Tourist, lying like a floating garland on Manila Bay.

Mrs. Marcos, bedecked with diamonds and star sapphires, rolled the first dice on the new crap table. "I am lucky in love," she said after failing to win anything at the table.

At the presidential palace, Actress Gina Lollobrigida swept past three lavishly decorated, ceiling-high Christmas trees onto the terrace. The dancing started and Marcos gallantly swept to the floor with La Lolla. The champagne, poured over iced grapes, flowed. And flowed and flowed. There was no sense of time, no countdown. The stroke of 12 passed unnoticed until the distant sound of firecrackers heralded the moment."

San Francisco Chronicle, January 2, 1976

"THE IMPERIAL STYLE OF PRESIDENT MARCOS HAS MADE A SCANDAL. NAIROBI–The turn taken by the visit of Mr. and Mrs. Marcos to Kenya has caused some snickers and not a few resentments among the delegates to the fourth session of UNCTAD.

The imperial style adopted by the presidential couple was dubbed "scandalous" by a delegate from Western Europe. Some Africans worried about the "discredit" that was thus cast on their demands in a most inopportune setting.

Preceded by about thirty security agents and by Philippine journalists, Mr. and Mrs. Marcos arrived at Nairobi on 5 May, heading a retinue of one hundred thirty two persons, aboard two DC-8's.

The presidential couple of the Philippines, which maintains itself in power thanks to Martial Law proclaimed about four years ago and is believed to have accumulated a fortune during the eleven years of presidency, was received by President Kenyatta on Friday morning. But on two counts, Mr. and Mrs. Marcos were not able to get what they wanted: President Marcos did not get a state visit which he evidently wanted, and his wife, who is also governor of Manila, was refused in her request that children be made to throw flowers at her feet upon her arrival."

Le Monde, 10 May, 1976

"PHILIPPINE FIRST LADY SINGING AND OLD SONG"

"DEFENDING MARTIAL LAW 'WITH HEART'. NEW YORK. She is like so many dictators' wives, sitting in a roomful of orchids defending her husband's rule. But Imelda Marcos is queen of them all, perhaps the most skilled since Eva Peron.

In the wake of the bombing of an American travel agents convention last Sunday in Manila—where 18 were injured and her husband, Philippine President Ferdinand Marcos narrowly escaped himself—she is using her fabled persuasive talents to counter a picture of explosive unrest by insisting "what a happy little country we are."

Marcos'eight years of martial law is misunderstood, she suggested in an interview with *The Washington Star*. It is "martial law with heart," she said, coining a new phrase....

In a speech designed to pacify anxious American corporations with Philippine investments, she blamed the recent bombings on international rather than domestic terrorism.

Her husband, she continued, has created stability; the economy is thriving—inflation down, population growth down, exports up. If "certain sectors" are spreading alarm then "Americans must stop them before it is too late...." "My role as first lady is to be a star and a slave—I call it S and S—and to set some standards to motivate and inspire the people."

She was not disarmed by flattery about how her charm has swayed world leaders—men as diverse as Mao Tse-tung, Fidel Castro, Maummar Kadafi, Johnson and Nixon and her latest conquest, Mexico's Jose Lopez-Portillo.... "If our New Society plan stands for anything it is for human rights ... if there is anyone to be tortured among the political prisoners it would have been Aquino because he has been most vicious. Yet we have treated him with great humanity. He should be a perfect example of what the Philippines is not...." she said, calling him "a damn liar...."

Martial law has a bad reputation, she admitted, "because it was a bad thing in some cases. Yet martial law with a heart has brought about a little more discipline when we needed more discipline....

"But if you go to our little country, you'll find it is a happy little country. It is one of the nicest little countries in the world...."

The Washington Star, October 26, 1980

"S.F. EXEC. ACCUSED IN PHILIPPINE PLOT. MANILA–Philippine military authorities declassified secret documents linking San Francisco executive Steve Psinakis in the supposed plot (to topple the Philippine government, murder top officials and set-off bombs in Manila) and said they have seized huge quantities of explosives and documents on urban terrorism marked "CIA." Brig. General Prospero Olivas claimed that the confiscated explosives were shipped to the Philippines by Psinakis, a son-in-law of the late Filipino industrial tycoon Eugenio Lopez, a political foe of President Ferdinand Marcos. The general said it was Psinakis who helped Manila newspaper publisher Eugenio Lopez, Jr., a son of the elder Lopez, to escape from martial law detention. The younger Lopez was detained for three years on charges of plotting to assassinate Marcos but escaped in 1977 and sought asylum in the United States."

United Press International, December 31, 1979

"MANILA ASKS EXTRADITION OF 4. Manila, Philippines–The Foreign Ministry has asked the United States to return to the Philippines a San Francisco man and three Filipinos accused of conspiring to overthrow the Manila government. . . . The San Franciscan was identified as Steve Psinakis."

San Francisco Examiner, April 29, 1980

THE WALL STREET JOURNAL, THURSDAY, JANUARY 29, 1981

Mr. Marcos and the Future of the Philippines

By BENIGNO AQUINO

On Jan. 17 Philippine President Marcos ended the eight-year martial rule. But what should have been a day for national rejoicing passed barely noticed in spite of broad play in the Marcos-controlled media.

To the average Filipino, this latest Marcos maneuver means very little. President Marcos remains ensconced in his palace with all his authoritarian powers intact and even strengthened by "safeguards" decreed a few days before the lifting. Life in the country continues to be a drudgery to a few and a struggle to many. Tweedledum has been replaced by Tweedledee.

Hailed by his controlled press as "the first man in history to deliberately and voluntarily lift martial law," Mr. Marcos fooled no one because he moved more with caution than with conviction. For example, a few days before the lifting, Mr. Marcos decreed a new security code and a public order code. These laws permit the police to make preventive arrests, meaning that a citizen may be arrested for crimes which the state believes he might commit in the future. These decrees are even worse than the martial law orders that sanctioned mass detentions.

The infamous Amendment 6 to the Marcos-dictated constitution remains undisturbed. This amendment, "approved" by the people in a mock referendum in 1976, institutionalized Marcos's one-man rule for life; it permits him to legislate even after a regular national assembly is constituted in 1984.

To add to all these powers, Mr. Marcos decreed that the print media council, the instrument for suppressing press freedom, be retained. And the ban on the right to strike in vital industries remains.

To a man, the united opposition in the Philippines denounced the lifting as "mere paper lifting" because only two visible symbols of martial rule were phased out: the military tribunals and the army detention centers. Everything else remains: no free press, no free speech, no peaceful assembly, no strike for labor, no independent legislative body.

The Filipino opposition groups in the United States said that the mere lifting of martial rule without dismantling the institution of dictatorship is a "cruel deception."

Since Jan. 17 many Filipinos have been trying to divine the motives behind Mr. Marcos's maneuver. Some believe he is out to impress the Reagan administration, to mollify American opinion and pave the way for the smoother flow of U.S. economic and military aid. Others say he wanted to remove possible irritants in the face of a forthcoming visit of Pope John Paul II. More cynical observers say he was forced to buy time to ride out the present economic crisis.

By this maneuver, Mr. Marcos hopes to mollify the urban guerrillas who have been threatening to bring his government to its knees by discouraging foreign tourists and investors with a well-planned destabilization program.

The World Bank has just released a 392-page report raising serious questions as to whether its funds are "making a dent on poverty in the Philippines." The report documents a sharp decline in real Filipino wages since the 1960s. Purchasing power, the report says, has dropped in both urban and rural areas, in all regions and in practically all occupations. Thus, the World Bank acknowledges that, after eight years of martial rule, the Philippines is a great "political risk" to potential international creditors and investors.

With external debt passing $12 billion and projected to hit $20 billion by the end of 1983, Mr. Marcos faces an imminent economic collapse which calls for either a political accommodation with his opposition to harness the national potential or for more repressive measures to contain growing unrest.

Faced by a grim economic reality, the opposition has two options: to accelerate the downfall of the Marcos regime by violent guerrilla action, or to negotiate for the dismantling of the martial law regime now that Mr. Marcos has signaled willingness to take the first short steps on the long road back to freedom and political normality.

Violent confrontation carries with it the seeds of a national catastrophe such as recently witnessed in Nicaragua and El Salvador. Mr. Marcos has full control of all forces of repression and should he decide to dig in, he could condemn the Philippines to a similar catastrophe. No sane Filipino favors this option; it could only represent a final act of desperation.

The second option calls for a negotiated gradual reduction of Mr. Marcos's absolute powers and a programmed return to democracy. This requires an understanding and an acceptance by opposing camps that the consequences of violent confrontation could only condemn both the victors and the vanquished to defeat.

Mr. Marcos must believe that there are now Filipinos who are ready and willing to lay down their lives in the struggle for freedom. The urban guerrilla actions in Manila late last year are just samples of worse things to come. With an unabated and worsening economic crisis, stepped up rural and urban insurgencies would insure an early collapse of the repressive regime.

President Kennedy once advised that "we should never negotiate out of fear." On the contrary, the Filipinos, both the pro- and anti-Marcos elements *should* negotiate out of fear: fear of each other's potential, and fear of a violent and a bloody upheaval that threatens to engulf the entire nation if sanity and good will do not prevail.

The choices are: freedom for the Filipino or a protracted bloody struggle; national survival in the face of a rapidly escalating economic crisis or national disaster.

Mr. Aquino is a former senator and opposition party leader in the Philippines who was incarcerated for eight years after martial law was declared. He currently is a Fellow at Harvard University's Council for International Relations.

Giving peace a chance

Although some opposition figures remain sceptical, Aquino is looking to Marcos to make meaningful concessions

By Richard Nations

Washington: With the history of betrayal and deceit which the Philippine opposition claims tarnishes President Ferdinand Marcos' record of political negotiations, the very question of whether to talk with Marcos is one of the most divisive issues among dissident Filipinos both in the United States and at home. But former senator Benigno Aquino says that lifting martial law in Manila would mean the question can continue to be ignored only at the risk of missing "a historic opportunity" to force the pace towards genuine elections.

Other leaders here fear that negotiations now would merely play into Marcos' hands at a moment when his regime most needs this sort of exercise, both to mark a clean start with the incoming Reagan administration here and to prepare a human rights bouquet to present the Pope when he visits the Philippines early next month.

The current phase of negotiations between the opposition and Marcos began in earnest when First Lady Mrs Imelda Marcos talked to Aquino – and separately to three other Filipino exiles associated with the Movement for a Free Philippines (one of the principal Filipino exile groups in the US) – in New York shortly before Christmas.

Rumours that recent political violence in Manila would soon escalate to a full blown assassination campaign against Marcos' associates worried the president, informed sources say. During their four-and-a-half-hour meeting, Mrs Marcos asked Aquino to use his influence to obtain a moratorium on bombings and other threats attributed to the April 6 Liberation Movement, particularly during last week's official visit to the Philippines by Japanese Prime Minister Zenko Suzuki. In return, Mrs Marcos gave assurances that the president was sincere in his intention to lift martial law.

After meeting Mrs Marcos, Aquino organised an informal gathering in Boston of many of the opposition leaders in the US, where, he says, he gained a general agreement to abjure violence for the time being and pursue "the peaceful political path.

"We have two options. One is to take the route of violence and revolution, in which case we stop all talks. The other option is political accommodation," Aquino told the gathering, which included representatives of the April 6 movement. "From the very start I have been against violence. If I have temporarily accommodated some of the more radical elements it is only to push Marcos towards peaceful negotiations. But if Marcos is now willing to negotiate, that is the best thing that can happen to us . . . The opposition must now make a fundamental choice."

Over the past two months Aquino has been in close touch with the Marcos regime through Deputy Defence Minister Carmelo Barbero. On January 11 Barbero telephoned Aquino at his Harvard University flat to inform him of Marcos' intention to lift martial law on January 17 by:

- dismantling all military tribunals;
- abolishing arrest, search and seizure orders;
- restoring the writ of habeas corpus, except in two military regions;
- offering newspapers, radio and television stations closed in 1972 back to their owners;
- permitting student assemblies, and
- recognising the right to peaceful assembly.

Aquino says this is a small step, but if Marcos does take it on January 17 when he lifts martial law it will be enough for him to attempt to carry to Marcos the political dialogue which he has been having with other members of the regime for nearly a month.

Marcos revealed the details of a plan to lift martial law to Richard Holbrooke, US Assistant Secretary of State for East Asia and the Pacific, who visited the Marcos family in the Philippines in late December. State Department officials say that the lack of any mechanism to secure a transition of power in Manila has been a preoccupation of American policy.

Holbrooke flew directly from Manila to Boston, where Aquino is staying while on a fellowship at Harvard University. Holbrooke says he went to Boston to attend the wedding of a friend and that his meeting with Aquino was purely coincidental, but, though careful not to appear to be mediating between the regime and its opponents, he told Aquino that he thought talks with Marcos could be helpful.

Aquino credits Holbrooke with considerable influence in his own decision to seek talks with Marcos now: "I think his recommendations and his analysis of the situation contributed immensely in clearing the air, because he feels that the president is really trying his very best now to lift martial law, and I thought that was a very important piece of information." Other Philippine opposition leaders in the US object to Holbrooke's "meddling."

Carl Rowan/

Philippines resemblance to Iran

The release of 52 Americans by their Iranian captors may have caused millions of Americans to forget the larger damage to U.S. strategic interests that was involved in the revolution of religious leaders and the fall of the shah. But someone ought to be looking even beyond questions such as "Who lost Iran?" and "Why didn't our intelligence people see this coming?" We must face this question: "Can this kind of political calamity befall the United States again soon, and if so where?"

My answer is: "Yes, soon, in the Philippines."

This ought not shock Americans — not if they take a look at the ways in which the situation in the Philippines parallels that of Iran:

Both Iran and the Philippines were made important links in the U.S. chain of defense against aggressive communism — with American military bases in the Philippines probably more important to the United States than the intelligence facilities and other military operations that we had in Iran. As in Iran at the time of the shah, most U.S. leaders feel they must pretend not to see political oppression and human rights violations in the Philippines because "we need those bases."

The shah ruled ruthlessly, thus building up a vast network of people who hated him. President Ferdinand Marcos has ruled the Philippines through martial law, jailing or exiling his foes, with more than a few dying mysteriously — and he has created hordes of enemies.

Marcos and wife Imelda, like the shah and his family, have avoided final censure by the United States and other Western democracies by hobnobbing and jet-setting with the power elite who frequently are entertained lavishly on monies Marcos' foes claim was stolen from the people.

Marcos, perhaps even more than the shah, has pursued policies that have enriched only a small upper-crust band of his sympathizers. The shah could make legitimate claim to putting land in the hands of peasants, partially liberating women, lifting the level of literacy and building Iran up as a petroleum and military power. Marcos has left the masses incredibly poor and helpless.

We face the classic dilemma about how to deal with a tyrant who is "a friend." Note that Jimmy Carter, our most outspoken "human rights" president, did not denounce Marcos and draw a curtain between him and the United States. I don't expect Ronald Reagan to declare the Philippine dictator a pariah.

What, then, does the United States do to avoid hastening a Philippines eruption that could leave us with no bases and new and hostile groups running that country? We should take special pains not to cozy up to Marcos or his wife in a way that guarantees that the Filipinos' hatred of them rubs off on the leaders of this country. That means, most obviously, that President Reagan ought not rush off to Manila or invite Marcos here on an official or state visit.

Deep trouble has been brewing in the Philippines for a long time. This is one column that I don't want to refer to two years, or 10, from now and say, "I told you so!"

MARCH 18-24, 1981 Philippine News

GUEST EDITORIAL

After Marcos, what?

Editorial of Los Angeles
Herald-Examiner, Feb. 26, 1981

THE ELOQUENT Philippine opposition leader, Benigno Aquino, Jr. visited Los Angeles this past week with some thoughtful observations that suggest a second look by the United States at its policy towards the Philippines would be a smart and timely move.

The charismatic Aquino, a former Philippine senator who spent nearly eight years in jail as a political prisoner of his former classmate, President Ferdinand Marcos, began with the observation that people will tolerate the suspension of their political rights only if they perceive it somehow makes them economically better off. But, he added, when the economy shatters and there is no longer an excuse for denying simple freedoms, discontent sprouts and grows into revolution.

The United States, of course, hardly needs to be reminded of that after learning such costly lessons from Iran. But it does need to understand Aquino's basic message: The United States must realize it runs a risk of provoking the same type of anti-American turmoil in the Philippines by propping up an unpopular and dictatorial regime.

Our own self-interests are very much at stake here. A change of power in the Philippines is inevitable, if not imminent. Should the United States valiantly fight for the status quo and end up on the loser's side, not only would we forego the good will of the Filipino people and the historic friendship between the two countries, we would also lose our largest military installations outside the contiguous United States - the strategically indispensable Clark Air Field and Subic Naval Base.

Indicators abound, according to Aquino, that the country is nearing a breaking point now under President Marcos. Though Marcos lifted martial law last month after eight long years, political freedom has not truly returned: Marcos still retains his far-reaching emergency powers and thereby his political grip on the nation.

At the same time, national discontent is on the rise as the country continues its alarming economic deterioration. 75 percent of the country's 49 million people are subsisting below poverty level, according to the World Bank; their calorie intake is the second lowest in the world, next only to Bangladesh; fully 40 percent of Filipino babies die before they reach the age of 2.

And the powerful mobilizing forces of religion are emerging there, as they did in Iran. Certain leaders in the Roman Catholic Church have taken to the streets in protest, espousing revolt in the name of religion, and their cries are finding a ready following among many of the country's 41 million-plus Roman Catholics - 85 to 90 percent of the total population.

In light of these developments, the United States must formulate some type of policy response. We're not suggesting that this policy should seek to oust President Marcos, a man who, for better or worse, has been a good and faithful friend of American interests. But it may prove wise in the long run for the United States to refuse to prolong in any way the excesses of the Marcos regime. That could be done through a hands-off policy or by insisting that the upcoming elections are truly *free* and *honest*.

Fortunately, there's still enough good will towards the United States among most Filipinos to assuage American fears of Iranian-style retribution and castigation when the reins of power, as they eventually must, finally pass from Marcos' hands.

But there's no guarantee that this good will will last. American policy, for so many years geared to one man's vision of Philippine destiny, now must be reshaped for the inevitable day when the needs of the rest of the Filipino people take precedence.

WEEK OF MARCH 18-24, 1981 Philippine News

Are U.S. interests in R.P. hurt by links to Marcos?

By STEPHEN B. COHEN
Washington Post

WASHINGTON - On his second day in the Philippines, Pope John Paul II visited the slums of Manila. Afterward a student rose to speak to the Pope about his people's need for political freedom and economic justice. As the student knelt to kiss the papal ring, the Pope lifted him up to embrace him and the crowd cheered.

Before mass audiences and face to face with President Ferdinand Marcos, the Pope, who arrived in the Philippines on Feb. 17, one month to the day after Marcos declared an end to eight years of martial law, called for "greater respect for human rights." His strong appeal and the response he evoked raise a serious question: How much was really changed by Marcos' declaration? The answer is important to the United States because of our military bases there, and because of the Philippines' role as a pro-Western country in Southeast Asia.

Despite the end of martial law, Marcos' exceptional powers are virtually intact. He can still legislate by personal fiat. He can detain, without trial, anyone he regards as subversive. His family and friends, who took ownership of all significant newspapers and radio and television stations when martial law began, continue to control the mass media.

Lifting martial law was considered by many observers to be more public relations than substance, designed to impress the new Reagan Administration as well as the Pope. Many Filipinos still consider the government corrupt, incompetent and frequently repressive.

How bad is official corruption? Filipinos from all walks of life say that it is more pervasive than ever before in their history, and that the worst corruption involves Marcos, his wife, Imelda, and their families and close associates. One popular Philippine riddle goes: "How do you do the Marcos dance?" The answer: "One step forward, two kickbacks."

It is widely believed - and in political terms perception is reality - that the Marcoses demand a cut of major investment projects as the price of governmental approval, and that the amounts accumulated by them run into the hundreds of millions of dollars. Even defenders of Marcos' record freely concede, as one said, that "he can be faulted for one thing: failing to stop corruption."

Filipino businessmen who are not part of the inner circle are expressing strong opposition to Marcos, at least in private, as they find themselves victimized by official favoritism and extortion. Using his power to legislate by fiat, Marcos exempts certain firms from taxes applied to all others. One Marcos ally in the filter-cigarette business, for example, is relieved from customs duties that his competitors must pay. A second, who manufactures television sets, can import Japanese component parts without paying the usual taxes.

Another Marcos tactic is to force the sale of successful businesses at a bargain price to his close associates. Filipino businessmen fear doing too well lest, as one told me, "they notice your success and decide to make you an offer you can't refuse."

The more desperate members of the business community have resorted to violence. Several, including one Harvard Business School graduate, were arrested last year for joining a so-called "Light a Fire Group," which allegedly conspired to set fire to properties belonging to Imelda Marcos. Others have begun to finance the communist insurgency, in the belief that it will never be strong enough to seize power, but may cause enough trouble to force a change of regime.

The Catholic Church, as well, has become increasingly open in its criticism of Marcos. Last year a Catholic conference in the southern Philippines began with a morality play about the pharaoh's abuse of Hebrew slaves in ancient Egypt. The Egyptian pharaoh who was shown beating the slaves bore an unmistakable resemblance to Marcos, and the Hebrews were dressed as Filipino peasants. The political message was clear: "Let my people go."

Over 80 percent of Filipinos are Catholic and the church is the most important nongovernmental institution in the Philippines, with an extensive network of schools and hospitals. A large majority of the priests are staunchly anti-Marcos, and a significant minority now argue that violence is justified and required to achieve change.

The church hierarchy - about 50 bishops - periodically criticizes specific practices of the Marcos regime, including corruption, election fraud and the imprisonment and torture of political dissidents. The archibishop of Manila, one of two Philippine cardinals, has warned of civil violence if Marcos does not end authoritarian rule and permit fair elections.

Among all segments of the population, anti-Marcos sentiment has grown as the economy has deteriorated. Per-capita income has fallen about 15 to 20 percent since Marcos declared martial law. Inflation ran 20 to 25 percent in 1979 and 1980, and wages have not risen to make up for the increased cost of living. Roughly three-quarters of Filipino households have an income at or below the poverty threshold. The Philippine government estimates that 60 percent of all children are malnourished........

Whether or not Marcos survives the next five years, American interests will be affected by the evolution of Philippine attutudes toward us, the long-run prospect is for increasing nationalism, assertion of Philippine self-worth and anti-Americanism.

Filipinos admire the United States and most things American. There is a wide difference, however, in how older and younger Filipinos view the United States. Among the older generation, there is strong pro-American sentiment, a product of the joint struggle against Japanese occupation of the Philippines in the 1940s, the granting of independence after the war and American aid over the years since. The younger generation (over 50 percent of the population) knows less of World War II and the immediate postwar years. Its formative political experience has been government under Marcos, and younger Filipinos increasingly resent the United States for supporting his regime.

The crucial issue for US foreign policy is how to protect American interests in the Philippines - not just for the moment, but for the longer terms as well.

A centrist Filipino journalist remarked, "There is a perception that the US is selling the Filipino people down the river, that the US is willfilly supporting Marcos. You need' to be less supportive."

The primary cause of this perception was an agreement in 1979 that doubled the amount of military aid provided to the Philippines in return for the US use of bases there.

The objective of increasing aid was to secure US access to the bases. Instead, the new agreement has increased the risks by associating the United States with a regime that so many Filipinos find repugnant. One opposition leader recently commented that US support for Marcos could lead to "widespread and open hostility (that could) render these bases eventually untenable."

Moreover, while the term of the previous base agreement ran until 1991, the new one provides for review of its provisions by January 1984. At some earlier date the process of review and renegotiation will begin, thereby increasing once again the US identification with Marcos.

How will the Reagan Administration conduct relations with the Philippines? There are already signs that it will read - or choose to read - the end of martial law as genuine progress, justifying warmer relations with the Marcos regime. President Reagan met with Imelda Marcos in New York for an hour last December, one of the few exceptions he made to his own rule against seeing foreign leaders before his inauguration. And a meeting between Marcos and Reagan (something that Marcos assiduously sought but never obtained from Carter, Ford or Nixon) is being considered.

Instead of seeking warmer relations, the United States would do well to consider distancing itself from the Marcos regime. While there is essential business that we must conduct, the relationship could be more cool, correct and formal than it is today. In concrete terms, how might we conduct a diplomacy of distancing?

We could abstain from unnecessary public acts that indicate our support for the regime. There could be a ban on high-level official visits to Manila, such as the 1977 trip by then-Vice President Walter Mondale. Our ambassador could be instructed to avoid public appearances with the Marcoses that are trumpeted in the Philippine press and taken as a sign of our approval. And we could refrain from inviting Marcos to Washington.

Furthermore, we could adopt a position for the 1984 review of the new base agreement designed to disassociate us from the worst practices of the regime. As a sign of concern over widespread military abuses, for example, we might propose shifting part of the base-compensation package from military to economic assistance.

A prudent foreign policy, therefore, would recognize the growing opposition to Marcos, the approaching end of his rule and the unfavorable trends in Filipino attitudes toward the United States. It would therefore be designed to lessen our identification with Marcos and his government.

Stephen Cohen, who made two extended visits to the Philippines as deputy assistant secretary of state for human rights in the Carter Administration, now teaches at the Georgetown University Law Center.

Philippine News (AE) WEEK OF MARCH 10-16, 1979

The Philippine revolution is on!

THE REVOLUTION by the moderate democratic forces in the Philippines has started. Marcos has "shut the door to every peaceful means for the return of democracy" and the Filipino people have accepted the challenge; they have started their struggle for the liberation of the Philippines through the only available means: FORCE.

In the first commentary of this columnist after the April 7 farcical and fraudulent election last year, I commented on the reasons for which Marcos called the election and I discussed the reasons for which Marcos was forced to resort to mass fraud and declare his defeated KBL candidates as the "victors."

It was pointed out at that time that the reaction of the Filipino people to the one and only dramatic appearance of Ninoy Aquino and the unprecedented support for the LABAN Party displayed on the eve of the election through the "noise demonstration," made it absolutely clear to the Marcoses and his collaborators that they would have suffered a humiliating defeat. Marcos pressed the panic button. He disallowed any further appearances of Aquino, clamped down on the opposition, conducted the most fraudulent election in the history of the Philippines and arrested the few brave oppositionists, including the 80-year-old respected statesman Senator Lorenzo Tanada, who attempted to protest against the falsified election results.

The conclusion of this columnist at that time was that Marcos "shut the door to every peaceful means for the return of democracy" and that he would have to be virtually dragged out of Malacanang "feet first."

The development since the April "elections" indicate that the same conclusion was reached by most of the moderate opposition leaders as well as by the younger activist groups who, until that time, hoped that Marcos would yield peacefully to the cry of the nation for the restoration of their civil and human rights.

Now "THE REVOLUTION IS ON."

The activities of the democratic revolutionary forces are not yet reported in the international press and are certainly not reported factually in the Marcos-controlled press in the Philippines. The international press has not yet realized the significance of certain recent incidents and Marcos is understandably attempting to suppress the news of any serious revolutionary movement by the Filipino people. But "THE REVOLUTION IS ON."

Most of the known respected opposition leaders have joined hands in unity and many of the unknown young dedicated activists have quietly organized and slowly but surely have started their revolutionary struggle for the liberation of the country.

Surprisingly the Philippine press reported recently several fires in Manila, including an attempt to burn down Imelda's gigantic Rustan's store, and attributed the fires to sabotage by dissidents whose aim is to destroy the Philippine economy. These fires were in fact the work of the democratic revolutionary forces and they were only but one of several such activities which have been taking place recently. There have been reports (and many more rumors) of kidnappings, fires, sabotages and other similar activities attributed by the Marcos press to "accidents," or to the NPAs, or to the Moslem separatists and, most frequently, to terrorists and gangsters. The fact is that few people know at this time which of these activities are due to the lawless elements and other existing extremist groups and which activities are due to the organized patriotic forces fighting for the overthrow of the Conjugal Dictatorship.

'THE SHOE IS ON THE OTHER FOOT'

The democratic revolutionary forces are already openly taking credit for some of their activities, i.e., the fire that destroyed the COMELEC building; the firest that burned down the PUYAT factory; the fires which were started, but did not damage severely, two of the symbols of Imelda's corruption and extravagance - the RUSTAN'S store and her multi-million-dollar luxurious hotel, the PLAZA.

During the past seven years, Marcos and his dreaded torture specialists under the guidance of Secretary Enrile and the personal leadership of General Fabian Ver, have terrorized the Filipino people. Thousands of helpless Filipinos bear the scars of tortures inflicted on them in the Marcos torture chambers; many have died in agony; and the whole nation lived in fear.

The trained torturers like Col. Abadilla and Col. Aure have been given promotions for their "loyal services to the New Society"; the Marcos propagandists like "Doroy" Valencia have been brainwashing the people with lies and glorifying their IDOLS; many of the relatives and close friends of the Marcos-Romualdez families have been enriching themselves at the expense of not only the rich but primarily at the expense of the poor; many of the so-called "apolitical" businessmen, have been raking it in under martial law but keeping quiet about the Marcos-Romualdez injustices while globe-trotting in style, spending the millions of the people's blood money.

Time has not come for PUBLIC JUSTICE. The shoe is going on the other foot. Fear is being switched from the oppressed to the oppressors.

Those who acquired properties through corruption are wondering when their buildings will perish by fires.

Those who amassed vast wealth under the "flourishing economy" of the New Society are wondering when they may be kidnapped and asked to hand over their illegally gotten millions.

The propagandists who for seven years paraded like kings - Doroy is the best example - are wondering when and how the people will get even.

The torturers who were promoted over and over again for their "loyal services" of torturing and murdering innocent helpless people are now wondering when they will become the victims of bullets from a freedom-fighter.

The Generals who have been propping up the Conjugal Dictatorship are wondering when they may be lynched in the streets like the Generals in Iran or face the firing squad after a quick trial by the free courts.

The time for the "fence-sitters" is running out.

YES!!! The shoe is on the other foot. I don't know how long it will be before the democratic forces will emerge victorious but whether they will succeed in liberating their country, is NOT all Greek to me.

Marcos Aide Fearful of New Group of Foes

By William Chapman
Washington Post Foreign Service

MANILA, Oct. 24 — An organization of church-oriented activists believed responsible for bombings in Manila poses a more serious threat to the Philippines than armed communist guerrillas long active in the countryside, Defense Minister Juan Ponce Enrile said today.

It is "the more potent and dangerous group" because of its access to money, high leadership talent, and a religious orientation attractive to many Filipinos, Enrile said in an interview.

At the same time, the defense minister confirmed that official estimates show the number of regulars in the Communist Party's armed force has increased substantially in two years and now stands at 5,400, about half of them armed.

Enrile, defense minister since 1970, is one of the most influential figures in President Ferdinand Marcos' martial-law government and virtually the sole source, other than the president, of official information on the several anti-Marcos organizations trying to undermine the government.

He is currently in charge of tracking down persons responsible for six bombing attacks that have injured more than 60 and killed one.

Enrile said the bombings are the work of a violence-prone faction of an older Christian activist organization that embraces both Roman Catholic and Protestant church members and includes, besides students and workers, a number of doctors, lawyers and engineers.

"This is the more potent and dangerous group," he said, "because they have the capacity to generate more funding. The quality of leadership is higher and their ideas are more acceptable to our people."

"There is a moral quality to their movement," he added. "Our people are basically very religious and religious people have a strong influence on the people."

So far, he said, only a "small core" of the movement has been identified by authorities. "It is not large yet but it has the potential for becoming a large force if we do not stop them," Enrile said.

His comments were the clearest exposition so far of the seriousness with which the government views the bombings and the potential for more serious trouble from a spreading movement.

During the interview, Enrile occasionally thumbed through a thick report marked "secret," which he described as a new analysis of the organization believed responsible.

The organization is loosely known as Social Democrats and sprang up several years ago as an attempt to apply Christian thought to social issues in the Philippines. Of its four factions, Enrile said, one is pro-violence and another does not reject violence as a solution. Out of the violent factions, he said, have grown such splinter groups as the Light a Fire movement, responsible for a series of Manila fires last year, and the April 6 Liberation Movement, which has claimed responsibility for several of the bombings here since Aug. 22.

"Their tendency is to create a lot of [organizational] names to give an aura of broadness and of bigness," Enrile said.

Although an indigenous movement, it is directed, Enrile asserted, by members of the American-based Movement for a Free Philippines. He cited that movement's leader, Raul Manglapus, and a California businessman, Steve Psinakis, and said long-time Marcos foe Benigno Aquino Jr., now at Harvard, is involved "maybe."

Both Aquino and Manglapus have denied any connections with the bombings in Manila.

Enrile's estimate that the Communist Party's armed wing, the New People's Army, has 5,400 regulars represents a sharp revision of the rural guerrillas' strength.

For years, the number was officially estimated at about 3,000 and in the eyes of officials had not grown in manpower. The New People's Army operates mainly in northern and central Luzon, north of Manila, and on the rugged eastern island of Samar. It attempts to grow by radicalizing poor farmers and has achieved success in areas where abuses by the Philippine military are especially severe.

Enrile acknowledged the New People's Army has enjoyed "a sizable increase in the past two years, despite martial law," and has found access to better communications and more military equipment. However, only about 2,800 of the regulars are armed, he said.

Despite the New People's Army's growth since 1978, Enrile said he does not regard the armed bands as a serious threat now, observing that their numbers are apparently smaller than before martial law when the guerrillas operated close to Manila.

"It is annoying but it does not cause any major instability — not for a long, long time, anyway," Enrile said.

Philippine News (A-E) WEEK OF AUGUST 11-17, 1979

Who are the real terrorists in the Philippines ?

ABOUT TWO years ago I raised this question in connection with the events surrounding the trial of Napoleon Lechoco in Washington. It will be recalled that Lechoco was being tried for having held Ambassador Romualdez (Imelda's uncle) at gunpoint, in order to force Marcos to allow his son, Napoleon Lechoco, Jr., to join his family in the U.S.

The basic question put to the jury during the trial was simple. *Who was really the terrorist*? Was it Lechoco who resorted to violence to free his son or was it Marcos who was holding an innocent minor "hostage" in the Philippines? The jury didn't take long to reach its unanimous decision. The jury, in effect, declared Marcos the terrorist by setting Lechoco free on the basis that the inhuman act of Marcos drove Lechoco "temporarily insane" forcing him to resort to violence to free his son. Two of the jurors had tears in their eyes as the jury announced the acquittal of Lechoco.

The Lechoco incident may have been forgotten by many but has not been forgotten by those who are now resorting to "violence" in the Philippines, not just to free their own sons, but to free a whole nation held hostage by the worst group of terrorists the Philippines has ever known; the Marcos gang of terrorists.

The question of "who are the real terrorists" is being raised again because the revolutionary activities of the "moderate democratic forces" in the Philippines, which were first reported in this column, are slowly but surely escalating and Marcos has been finally forced to acknowledge them. In a speech delivered last week, Marcos attacked the "subversives" who are attempting to take advantage of the economic problems of the country to "discredit the (Marcos) Government". Referring to the revolutionary activities of the "subversives", Marcos said "when they engage in *terrorism*, this usually is the mark of desperation."

Were those who fought in Nicaragua to free their country from the tyrannical rule of Somoza "subversives" and "terrorists" as Somoza claimed before his cowardly departure from Nicaragua or were they the heroes of the Nicaraguan people? Were the millions of Iranians who stood up to their tyrant and the tens of thousands who were murdered by the Shah's military" subversives" and "terrorists" as the Shah used to call them before his cowardly departure from Iran or were they the heroes of the Iranian people?

Were the thousands of Greek students who line-up in front of the tanks of the Greek dictator Papadopoulos, some of them literally being run over by the tanks, "subversives" and "terrorists" as Papadopoulos used to refer to them before he was overthrown, arrested, convicted and now serving two life sentences in a Greek jail with his collaborators, or were they the heroes who either risked or actually lost their lives to free their country from a repressive dictatorship?

Were those who fought oppression since the ancient times and gave up their lives for freedom and justice, "subversives" and "terrorists" as the dictators of their times used to call them or are they the heroes recorded in the history books of their respective countries?

The answers to the above questions are as obvious as the answer to the title question of this column; "Who are the real terrorists in the Philippines?" Are they those who, having suffered under seven years of oppression and having exhausted all peaceful means of regaining their lost freedoms and rights, are now fighting to free their country, or is it Marcos and his gang who continue to hold on to their illegal positions of power through the force of the gun?

Yes! The answer is obvious. Marcos and the scums surrounding him are clearly the real terrorists. Those who are finally resorting to violence, fighting against all odds to free the Philippines, are the true Filipino patriots and the heroes who will soon be embraced by the people when the cowardly terrorists in Malacanang flee the Philippines, like Somoza and the Shah, or are arrested and jailed like Papadopoulos or are killed like many of the terrorists who refuse to free their hostages until they are attacked and killed.

"The Revolution Is On" and the patriots who are fighting for the freedom of their country deserve the admiration and support of every freedom-loving person in the world. Marcos is correct when he says that "terrorism is the mark of desperation". He should know! He is the terrorist and he is desperate and whether or not his end will be the end of a terrorist is NOT all Greek to me.

PHILIPPINES

A stronger strongman

Marcos asks the country to approve constitutional changes that will make his position more secure

By Sheilah Ocampo

Manila: As one of the Philippines' most brilliant legal minds, President Ferdinand Marcos has buttressed his authoritarian rule since 1972 by relying on constitutional fiat. On April 7, Filipinos will be asked in a plebiscite to endorse another constitutional variation which will effectively secure Marcos' position of power — this time as newly and duly elected president. And, if he should step down from power in future, he and his subordinates will be covered by an immunity against any legal action against them.

Martial law, which Marcos declared in September 1972, was a constitutional manoeuvre, as were the transitory provisions tagged on to the 1973 Constitution which legitimised his rule by decree for an indefinite period. Amendments to the Constitution in 1976 were intended to place him in an unassailable position as a powerful prime minister after lifting martial law, which he did on January 17. Now, the 63-year-old Marcos is asking the country to ratify a totally new Constitution, with a "Philippine-style" presidential system, to replace the 1973 charter, with its British-style parliamentary system, which itself had succeeded the 1935 Constitution with its American-style presidential system.

In a lengthy nationwide *pulong-pulong* (dialogue) last week, Marcos told his audience on radio and TV that he stood before his "master [the people]." He wanted to know if the people wanted him to continue with his mission . . . "and that's all that I would like to happen in the presidential elections [scheduled for July]."

Marcos said that the new presidential system conformed with national culture and experience. He also said that he would have less power by giving up the prime ministership — he has technically held the posts of both president and prime minister since the Interim Batasang Pambansa (National Assembly — IBP) was convened in June 1978. As newly-elected president, he will have a six-year term.

He said all the powers vested in the prime minister will have been transferred to the presidency by virtue of the constitutional amendments recently approved, at his urging, by an IBP stocked by an overwhelming majority of his supporters. One constitutional provision states that "all powers vested in the president of the Philippines under the 1935 Constitution and the laws of the land which are not herein provided for or conferred upon any official shall be deemed and are hereby vested in the president unless the Batasang Pambansa provides otherwise."

Marcos is obviously confident that he will win the presidential election. It is not even certain who will stand against him. He will also remain commander-in-chief of the armed forces, his main power base.

He even gives himself the power to legislate by "formulating the guidelines of the national policy," which is basically a legislative function. Under the 1976 constitutional amendments, which will still remain in force, he can continue to rule by decrees whenever in his judgment "there exists a grave emergency or a threat of imminence thereof, or whenever the IBP or the regular assembly fails or is unable to act adequately . . ." This change can be effected by transferring such power from the prime minister to the president.

Under the new Constitution, he can also contract and guarantee foreign and domestic loans, exercise powers to name the prime minister (who is then elected by the IBP); the 14 members of a new body called the executive committee, which will assist him in his duties, and high-ranking officials of the armed forces. He can also order the preventive detention of anybody suspected of subversion, as provided for under the new public order decree. He will also control all the ministries. In other words, Marcos will continue to exercise considerable power.

Marcos, as head of the Kilusang Bagong Lipunan (New Society Movement—KBL), which has a huge majority in the IBP, managed also to secure from the IBP a constitutional guarantee of immunity from law suits during, and even after, his tenure for "official acts" carried out by him "and by others pursuant to his specific orders."

Originally, the immunity clause discussed by the IBP would have applied only during his tenure. However, during a KBL caucus, Marcos reminded IBP members that the subject of immunity both during and after his tenure had been long agreed. "If we cannot agree on this, we may as well part ways now," Marcos was quoted as saying. His KBL supporters got the message.

The immunity provision triggered a mild stir even among pro-establishment people. Former senator Arturo Tolentino, a well-known community leader who occasionally takes an independent position, described this act as "immoral and scandalous." Marcos' insistence on the inclusion of his subordinates in the immunity is thought to have been intended to placate the military, which has been singled out by human rights supporters for its record under martial law.

However, Defence Minister Juan Ponce Enrile said that this was not the case. "It says official acts — these official acts must be done in accordance with lawful orders of the president," Enrile said. Marcos lost no time in relaying the news to the military. On February 27, he told a group of Philippine Military Academy alumni: "I would have re-established the crisis government all over again if the IBP had not included the subordinates."

The proposed new executive committee is intended to exercise the powers of the presidency in case of the president's "permanent disability, death, removal from office or resignation," until the IBP has called an election for a new president. In effect, the executive committee will serve to solve the crucial political problem of Marcos' succession.

The concept was primarily inspired by Marcos himself, Assemblyman Emmanuel Pelaez told the REVIEW. The idea was apparently drawn from the existing cabinet standing committee, headed by Finance Minister Cesar Virata. Half of the executive committee's membership will come from the IBP, while the rest will comprise military officers, members of the loyal opposition and the private business sector.

The debate over the constitutional changes and the coming plebiscite has begun in Manila's social circles. Elsewhere, except in politically-active places like Cebu City in the central Philippines' Visayan region, there has apparently been little motivation to participate in either the plebiscite or the election.

Some opposition politicians say they will campaign for a "no" vote in the plebiscite wherever they can find a group willing to listen. But a boycott has not been advocated yet because it carries a minimum punishment of six months' imprisonment. The atmosphere of cynicism is pervasive. "Who cares about the amendments in a bastardised Constitution?" asked one political observer. It is generally thought that Marcos' political machinery will ensure an overwhelming "yes" vote.

Fielding a credible candidate has been a problem for the United Democratic Opposition (Unido), the umbrella organisation of seven fragmented political opposition groups. The opposition's best bet, former senator Benigno Aquino, still living in the United States, is effectively barred from running against Marcos because of the proposed new constitutional age requirement. He is 48, and a presidential candidate must be at least 50.

On top of that, Aquino, who is still engaged in academic matters at Harvard University, will have to face a string of criminal and subversion charges if he decides to return to the country: apart from his convictions for murder, subversion and illegal possession of firearms, he has been officially accused of involvement in the bombing campaign in Manila last year.

With the new developments, there is increasing danger that the country's politics will be polarised — a trend which will be welcomed by radical elements, such as the Marxist New People's Army (NPA). By keeping the door closed against the possibility of a coalition with the moderate opposition, Marcos could be playing into the hands of underground revolutionaries, who can claim that they are the only credible opposition. And, in the improbable event of an opposition candidate winning the presidency, the IBP, which is dominated by Marcos' KBL, can veto the president-elect by a two-thirds majority. This could cause a constitutional crisis.

As the opposition agonises over who, if anyone, should run in the election, one opposition group, the Mindanao Alliance, has been gaining some prominence. Its main political figures have gained several election successes against the KBL in the IBP and local government polls in 1978 and 1980. The group has also attracted some interest among American diplomats in Manila.

During the visit to Manila this month of John Negroponte, United States Deputy Assistant Secretary of State for East Asia and the Pacific, Mindanao Alliance leaders were among a few selected personalities chosen to meet the visiting state department official. However the US Government, because of its deep involvement in the Philippines, remains a target of criticism by Marcos' opponents, who feel that the administration of President Ronald Reagan will simply close its eyes to alleged massive corruption under Marcos' regime.

However, Marcos objects to being called an "American puppet" by his critics. During the TV dialogue he said: "I deny that I am . . . I've been one of the most consistent critics of American policy . . . discreetly, not in a combative manner." He claimed that if the US military bases' agreement had not been concluded in 1979, "we would be in the same situation as Fidel Castro of Cuba."

FAR EASTERN ECONOMIC REVIEW • MARCH 20, 1981

Philippine News WEEK OF MARCH 20 - 26, 1976

WHAT IS A MAN?

WHEN I STARTED my column two months ago, I promised to devote some space to "philosophical" and/or personal discussions. Today's column could be considered philosophical and personal.

The front page news story on "Another Lopez Illegally Detained" reports on the most recent Marcos coercion on my imprisoned brother-in-law, Geny Lopez and his wife Chita, wherein Marcos is using their 22-year old son Gabby, as a "hostage".

My expose' of the events surrounding the current Marcos blackmail will undoubtedly result in renewed retaliation against Geny, Chita and their son Gabby. It is even possible that Marcos might fabricate some new imaginary charges against Gabby Lopez to hold him in jail, in an attempt to conceal the fact that Gabby's illegal detention since January 26 is for the purpose of blackmailing his parents and possibly even my wife and me.

The same type of scheme has been used by Marcos with my brother-in-law. It is widely known in Manila that Marcos was willing to release Geny after his hunger strike and after his father had turned over the Lopez properties to the Marcoses. However, when we exposed the true reason for Geny's imprisonment, which was to hold him as a "hostage" in order to blackmail Eugenio Lopez, Sr.,

Marcos retaliated by releasing fabricated reports on assassination plots and by continuing to hold Geny in jail.

It is now history that before "Old Man Lopez" died, he not only failed to secure the release of his innocent son by giving in to all the blackmails of the Marcoses, but even his last wish to see his three sons by his death bed, was denied by Marcos.

When my father-in-law passed away last July, my wife and I asked permission to attend our father's funeral in Manila; the Marcoses refused to grant us the requested assurance that we would not be arrested.

There was a good reason for Marcos' denial to grant us our request. Imelda was planning to attend the funeral herself and pay "her respects" to old man Lopez. She wanted to put a show of her "benevolence" by attending the funeral and offering personal "condolences" to every member of the Lopez family present at the funeral.

Imelda knew that, had my wife and I been allowed to attend the funeral, we would not have permitted Imelda's audacity and mockery to go unnoticed. We may not have degraded ourselves by spitting on her face in public, but we certainly would not have given her our hand when she went around greeting and offering condolences to every member of the Lopez family.

The Marcoses keep hoping that our (my wife's and my) pain and sorrow for the tortures they are inflicting on our loved ones, or their threats on our lives, will weaken us and force us to "surrender". How wrong could the "all powerful" Marcoses be! Their inhuman and degenerate acts contribute only to their own weakness and bring them closer everyday to their own destruction.

My wife and I are naturally now concerned about the new injustices which will be inflicted on Gabby and his parents. God only knows our anguish when we are reminded that our actions are partly responsible for the continued imprisonment of our brother and now even our nephew. Yet, when our choice is either the freedom of our few loved ones or the freedom of a whole nation, the decision is painful but clear. The only balm to our painful decision is the knowledge that Gabby is a strong and principled youngster who, like his father and mother, would be willing to suffer for the principles of truth and justice to his fellow man.

When I was 14 years old, my father gave me the most precious gift of my life: it was a simple poem by Kipling entitled "If". Eight years ago, on Gabby's 14th birthday, I presented him with the same gift. We discussed the meaning of the poem which Gabby understood very well even though he was then only a boy of 14; now, he is a young man of 22. The framed poem still hangs on the wall near his bed. It may be worthwhile to remind him of Kipling's words during this testing period of his life.

If

By RUDYARD KIPLING

If you can keep your head when all about you
Are losing theirs and blaming it on you,
If you can trust yourself when all men doubt you,
But make allowance for their doubting too;
If you can wait and not be tired by waiting,
Or being lied about, don't deal in lies,
Or being hated, don't give way to hating,
And yet don't look too good, nor talk too wise:

If you can dream--and not make dreams your master;
If you can think--and not make thoughts your aim;
If you can meet with Triumph and Disaster
And treat those two impostors just the same;
If you can bear to hear the truth you've spoken
Twisted by knaves to make a trap for fools,
Or watch the things you gave your life to, broken,
And stoop and build 'em up with worn-out tools:

If you can make one heap of all your winnings
And risk it on one turn of pitch-and-toss,
And lose, and start again at your beginnings
And never breathe a word about your loss;
If you can force your heart and nerve and sinew
To serve your turn long after they are gone,
And so hold on when there is nothing in you
Except the Will which says to them: "Hold on!"

If you can talk with crowds and keep your virtue,
Or walk with Kings--nor lose the common touch,
If neither foes nor loving friends can hurt you,
If all men count with you, but none too much;
If you can fill the unforgiving minute
With sixty seconds' worth of distance run,
Yours is the Earth and everything that's in it,
And--which is more--you'll be a Man, my son!

* * *

What additional injustices will now be inflicted on Gabby and his father is not yet know, but whether they both know the meaning of "What is a Man" is NOT all Greek to me.

About the Author

A native of Athens, Greece, Mr. Psinakis came to America in 1949 on a college scholarship. After studying at the University of Pittsburgh, he graduated in 1955 with an engineering degree, specializing in electric power plant design. Mr. Psinakis acquired American citizenship in 1959 and soon thereafter accepted a managerial position in the Philippines with the Manila Electric Company (MERALCO), the country's largest electric power company.

During his ten-year residency in the Philippines, the author participated in the business community of the Philippines and gained exposure to high-level political circles. In addition to his associations with several Philippine Congressmen, Senators, and Cabinet members, Psinakis became personally acquainted with President Ferdinand Marcos and his wife, Imelda.

In 1969, he married a Filipina, Ms. Presy Lopez, the daughter of business typcoon Eugenio Lopez and moved to his native country, Greece, where he stayed until President Marcos declared martial law in late 1972. He then returned to the United States with his family and lived with his self-exiled father-in-law in San Francisco. Soon after his arrival in the United States, the author and his wife became deeply involved with the political developments in the Philippines and joined the "Movement for a Free Philippines" (MFP). MFP is an international organization with headquarters in Washington, D.C., dedicated to the restoration of democracy to the Philippines. The author is currently an officer in the MFP.

Mr. Psinakis then turned to journalism and to lobbying in Washington for the MFP. He started writing a political column, "It's NOT all Greek to me," in the San Francisco-based *Philippine News.* His column gained wide readership and was later syndicated in other Filipino-American newspapers. His lobbying activities in Washington brought him in contact with many members of Congress and officials of the U.S. government.

The activities of Mr. Psinakis since 1974 have made him feared and hated by Ferdinand and Imelda Marcos. He was instrumental in planning and executing the dramatic escape of Marcos' two prominent political prisoners, Eugenio Lopez, Jr., (Psinakis' brother-in-law) and Sergio Osmena, III, an event which caused considerable embarrassment to the Marcos regime.

The author's activities include contacts with opposition leaders in the Philippines, not only political leaders but also underground guerrillas. Since 1979, President Marcos has accused Psinakis of engaging in "terrorism" and has formally charged him before the Philippine military tribunals.

Mr. and Mrs. Psinakis and their three younger children currently live in San Francisco.